D0099303

THE PRICE OF
PROSPERITY

ALSO BY TODD G. BUCHHOLZ

THE PRICE OF PROSPERITY

Why Rich Nations Fail and How to Renew Them

TODD G. BUCHHOLZ

HARPER

An Imprint of HarperCollins*Publishers*

THE PRICE OF PROSPERITY. Copyright © 2016 by Todd G. Buchholz. All rights re-
served. Printed in the United States of America. No part of this book may be used
or reproduced in any manner whatsoever without written permission except in the
case of brief quotations embodied in critical articles and reviews. For information,
address HarperCollins Publishers, 195 Broadway New York, NY 10007.

HarperCollins books may be purchased for educational, business, or sales pro-
motional use. For information, please e-mail the Special Markets Department at
SPsales@harpercollins.com.

FIRST EDITION

Designed by William Ruoto

Library of Congress Cataloging-in-Publication Data has been applied for.

ISBN: 978-0-06-240570-8

16 17 18 19 20   OV/RRD   10 9 8 7 6 5 4 3 2 1

To my father, who at age seventeen joined the navy
and sailed with the Seventh Fleet to help defeat
fascism in the Second World War

CONTENTS

PART II: LEADING THE CHARGE

PREFACE

A warm summer night on the Jersey Shore

I am a little kid in the backyard, swatting mosquitoes off my legs and waiting for Dad to flip a burger onto my paper plate. A neighbor barks to my dad, "If Nixon wins, I'm moving to Canada." Several years later, a different guy in our backyard threatens, "If Carter wins, I'm going to Canada." Four summers pass. This time a college dean asks, "You don't think it's possible that Ronald Reagan could ever, ever become president, do you? I'm looking at Canada."

I figure by now Canada must be a pretty crowded place. But it's not.

These neighbors were just bluffing, pumped up on mai tais, whisky sours, Rheingold beer, and whatever else people drank in the *Mad Men* and the disco days. The wives were teachers and nurses. Most of the husbands had served in World War II, Korea, or Vietnam. They were not going to give up the ship of state. You don't shield your buddy from bullets at Guadalcanal or Pork Chop Hill and then bug out to the Great White North the moment the "wrong" guy wins the vote in the Electoral College.

I hear the same kind of conversations today. Friends tell

me about properties they've bought in New Zealand and even Panama, "just in case." One explained that if she moves to New Zealand, she and her husband can raise their kids like it's the Eisenhower '50s, though none of us was alive in the 1950s. I've heard this kind of bluffing before. I have written this book because for the first time in my life, I'm not sure it's a bluff. In 2015 over forty-two hundred Americans renounced their citizenship, quadruple the number of a few years earlier, even though the State Department has quintupled the filing fee to $2,350.[1] Yes, it's a tiny trickle and many did so to avoid taxes, but we should feel a whiff of worry when anyone willingly surrenders a US passport and the privileges it brings. Throughout the twentieth century—through world wars and a cold war—the value of a US passport was incalculable. In 1939 a Jew in Berlin with a US passport escaped concentration camps. In 1965 a black man in Soweto evaded apartheid. In 1979 a Catholic in Leningrad with a US passport eluded the gulag.[2]

Many people have written about poor countries that have fallen apart, for example, Haiti, Syria, Sudan, and Somalia. But it occurred to me that rich countries can fall apart, too. Many have. When was the last time you met an Ottoman or a Habsburg? As I dove deeper into economic history, I realized that in many cases countries were more likely to fall apart after they reached prosperity. As an economist, an entrepreneur, and a student of history, I have advised government leaders on policy and counseled billionaire hedge fund managers on the latest twists in financial markets. But one cannot understand financial twists or government policy choices without grappling with the past. After all, today's world economy is not simply made up of everything going on at this precise moment—it's also made up of everything that has ever taken place before. In an earlier book on the history of economics, I wrote about three intellectual giants who opined on the problem of growth: Karl Marx, John Maynard Keynes, and Joseph Schumpeter. Marx wrote screeds, pamphlets, and a thick tome on the inherent contradictions of capitalism. He got much of it wrong and could not grasp, for example, the value of entrepreneurs or of intellectual property, or the rising standard of living that capitalism would bring to downtrodden proletarians, who now own smartphones, flatscreen TVs, and two-car garages. In the twentieth century archrivals Keynes and Schumpeter took the opposite tack. Keynes forecast that the economy would grow so abundant that by 2030 his grandchildren would be bored, bathed in luxury, and barely needing to work. Keynes saw the four-hour workweek eighty years before the guy who wrote *The 4-Hour Workweek*. Keynes suggested his descendants take up gardening and admire lilies in the field.[3] Schumpeter thought that the grandchildren of wealthy people would turn on capitalism and twist the world to socialism.[4] Sure enough, the parents of many '60s radicals belonged to tony country clubs and today the Occupy Movement is more popular within Oxford University than among field hands near Oxford, Mississippi.

But as I plunged deeper into economic history, I became dissatisfied with all three of these scholars. Marx thought capitalism's contradictions would "immiserate" the majority.[5] He was wrong. Keynes and Schumpeter surmised that capitalism's success would bore its beneficiaries and drive them either batty or to pick up brickbats and hurl them in protest. Their conclusions sound more like the musings of college dons cradling cognac snifters and less like rigorous analysis.

In this book I search for the forces that threaten to unravel wealthy countries. To do so, I will explore the economics and history but also the political and cultural dynamics of other countries. Sometimes a musical note will carry more weight than a statistic. I'll explain how Cio-Cio-San's high B flat in the second act of *Madame Butterfly* tells us more about the Meiji Revolution in Japan than any data point on the value of imports.

I was lucky—or not so lucky—to have a front-row seat at some of the key economic and financial crises in recent years, at the White House, on Wall Street, in corporate boardrooms, and in the halls of academia. In these positions, I've traveled the world, seeking out ideas and trying to understand the forces that shape nations. I've lectured on the beaches of Abu Dhabi, only to be interrupted by fireworks and the arrival of the emir; and in remote Kalgoorlie, Australia, where corrugated metal brothels have beckoned miners since the gold rush of 1893.[6] In Anchorage, Alaska, a spooky hotelier interrogated me about UFOs in Area 51 (since I worked in the White House and had taught at Harvard, he figured I was in on the conspiracy). I've been screamed at by a White House chief of staff and the governor of Idaho thanked me by handing me a thirty-pound box of raw potatoes. I hope to share with you what I've learned and to do so with suitable humility.

This book is ambitious and possibly quite foolish. On the other hand, it might just explain why those blustery neighbors who once threatened to renounce their citizenship and skip across borders might actually mean it this time. And it might show us what we can do to preserve and renew a nation.

THE PRICE OF
PROSPERITY

INTRODUCTION: THE PARADOX OF PROSPERITY

In *Casablanca*, Major Heinrich Strasser invites Rick to sit down and join him for a drink at the Café Americain.

"What is your nationality?" the Nazi commander asks.

"I'm a drunkard."

"That makes Rick a citizen of the world," the French captain Renault jokes.

The witty, sardonic lines fit the scene: a war-riven city in 1941 and a mass of desperate refugees figuring out how to fake their way to freedom. Rick was, of course, an American, but he was either too tipsy or too shrewd to cough up an honest answer to the Nazi. Who could blame him? But what about us today, who live in relative peacetime and prosperity? Do we feel a great emotional tug for our country? Many Americans seem to feel a greater emotional attachment to other things. If asked, "What are you?" their hearts might answer, "I'm an iPhone guy." Or "I'm a fantasy football fanatic." Or "I'm gluten free. And proud." If an airplane skidded on the runway and passengers had to evacuate quickly, how many would first save their iPhone, their football picks, or their tasty gluten-free muffin instead of an American flag? After a burst of flag-waving following 9/11, polls show that patriotism has drifted steadily lower, especially among young people. While 64 percent of senior citizens say they are extremely proud to be an American, only 43 percent of young adults agree, and nearly half of Millennials say the "American dream" is dead.[1] Other wealthy countries face the same trends.

Rick Blaine was a "citizen of the world" because he was a drunkard. But in a globalized economy, even sober types are citizens of the world. Bono of U2, who claims great pride in his Irish heritage and still speaks with a brogue, skipped out of Dublin so that his band could reincorporate in the Netherlands and pay lower taxes on their music royalties. Roger Moore—007 himself—has mostly lived in a Swiss chalet or in tony Monaco. And the guy who funded Facebook, Eduardo Saverin, hopscotched from Brazil to Harvard to Silicon Valley to Singapore after renouncing his US citizenship in 2012. Not only drunkards and superstar musicians and actors, but just about anyone who works in international sales or computer software development might naturally feel more anchored to ephemeral cyberspace than to some cobblestoned Main Street with flags flying from the lamp poles and local merchants scrambling to compete against Amazon.com.

This book is not a long lament about patriotism and its enemies. Nor is it an attack on the modern economy. In fact, it turns on their head many traditional notions about patriotism and the stability of countries. It is a diagnosis, a history, and a manifesto aimed at prosperous countries. Do not despair, for I will end on a note of optimism, with a road map that could help us avoid the shattering of nations. In the Conclusion I will introduce a new term, *patriotist*, which I define as someone who affirmatively believes that it is a good thing to be patriotic about one's country. Theodore Roosevelt said, "We want to make our children feel . . .

that the mere fact of being American citizens makes them better off. . . . This is not to blind us to our shortcomings; we ought steadily to try to correct them."[2] How many people agree only with Roosevelt's statement about shortcomings? Contrast Roosevelt's view with the University of North Carolina professor who teaches a course on "The Literature of 9/11" and calls the United States not just a superpower but a "*necro*power," adding the Greek prefix that means "death or corpse."[3] The professor does not mean that the United States is dying; he means that it delivers death to others through torture and other military means.

Virtually every advanced country from Japan to Italy faces similar economic and cultural land mines. This book is not solely aimed at Americans. As I write this, millions of refugees from Iraq and Syria stream across European borders, sneaking onto and even on top of trains and buses. Will they become Germans? Or Brits? Or Frenchmen? Or eternal refugees, the shrouded "Invisible Men" of the twenty-first century? Or worse? In 2014 the British Ministry of Defence reported that twice as many British Muslims traveled to Syria and Iraq to wage jihad than had joined the British military over the past three years."[4] Among British Muslim students, 40 percent support introducing sharia law. We might think of France as a fairly unified state, but early in its history France struggled to stop Normans, Bretons, Alsatians, Gascons, Savoyards, etc., from setting up their own countries. More recently, Charles de Gaulle wondered, "How can anyone govern a nation with 246 different kinds of cheese?" Like the France that de Gaulle bellyached about, the United States no longer coheres. We have a thousand television channels, 1 billion websites, and 330 million citizens with no reason to listen to each other. Talking heads on MSNBC and Fox News shout as if they are attending UFC wrestling matches. It is hard to get a country to "rally around the flag" when everyone stomps off in his or her own direction. Though President Obama won a clear reelection victory in 2012, he gathered votes from fewer than 28 percent of the adults in the country. Our official "national tree" is the oak, but perhaps our national symbol should instead be a splinter. The splintering is even more profound in the United Kingdom, France, Germany, and other "advanced" nations.

Many commentators blame an obvious villain for polarizing civil society: new technologies, especially the Internet, which offers infinite choices and distractions. The Internet raises two separate threats: it can radicalize loners and it can also fracture communities. An NYPD white paper proclaims that the "Internet is a driver and enabler for the process of radicalization" by luring weak-minded and strong-minded people into fringe groups. Former Obama official and Harvard Law professor Cass Sunstein warns that when "like-minded people get together, they tend to end up thinking a more extreme version of what they thought before they started to talk."[5] At the same time, new technologies enable a splintering of society. Picture an old black-and-white photo from the 1930s, with grandparents, parents, and children gathered around one RCA family radio in the living room listening to the revered voice of President Franklin Roosevelt. Even RCA's mascot, a terrier named Nipper, perked up his ears to listen. Now look around a home today, with each individual tuned to a personal smartphone or iPad. We have all seen families gather together at restaurants, ostensibly to share a meal and conversation, but each holds in hand an electronic device that literally packs more computing power than Apollo 11. At the same time community institutions have broken down, including thousands of city and village newspapers that have folded, at a rate of about 150 per year.

Clearly, technology can play a role in unraveling communities. But to blame technology is too simple, convenient, and recent an explanation. In the chapters ahead I will show that throughout history prosperous nations have suffered from a powerful tendency to fissure, splinter, and lose their unifying missions— even without the help of electrons zipping through wireless devices. This entropy explains why nations have collapsed, even when their economies looked relatively strong. *In fact, this book will show that nations are just as likely to unravel after periods of prosperity as during periods of depression.* I will uncover five key forces that tend to undermine nations *after* they have achieved economic success. Together these forces impose the price of prosperity. While Paul Kennedy's classic *The Rise and Fall of the Great Powers* hit bestseller lists with tales of countries overextending their military, I make the case that the rot begins internally, not from armies storming across borders trying to conquer others. Recent bestsellers like Thomas Piketty's *Capital in the Twenty-First Century* target inequality, while *Why Nations Fail* by James A. Robinson and Daron Acemoglu focuses on poor countries struggling to achieve prosperity. But we must also worry about "successful" countries that can no longer move forward or even stay in place.

I will also argue that a splintering among the population matters: it induces people to cheat, swindle, and focus more on the short term than on their long-term responsibilities, which ultimately undermines the economy and a cohesive civil society. The evidence jumps out from the headlines. A front-page story in the *New York Times* in 2008 reported that virtually *every* career employee of the Long Island Railroad applied for and received disability payments upon retirement. As a national spirit recedes, opportunism creeps in and shows up in everything from the housing market to school admissions to how congressmen handle national budgets. In the bubble years before the Great Recession of 2008 home buyers and brokers conspired to get subprime mortgages without putting any money down and without even showing tax returns to the bank. Bankers signed off anyway, since they were delighted to collect their hefty fees and pass the risk on to some faceless investor or taxpayer. Nobody had any skin in the game.

It is a common and dangerous mistake to think that societies are less vulnerable when they are relatively prosperous. Most readers and even some social scientists assume, for example, that economic downturns spark crime. But faltering spirits and a lack of faith in the future kindle kidnapping, burglary, and murder more than do falling incomes. During the 1930s, as families gathered around to listen to President Roosevelt's reassuring voice, they felt a greater sense of cohesion and mutual support. In contrast, crime rates exploded in the 1960s, even as paychecks got fatter and jobs got easier to come by. To explain how even relatively prosperous societies have a tendency to come apart, we will scroll back the pages of history and look at the story of the splintering of such powers as the Ming dynasty in the 1600s, Venice in the 1700s, the Habsburg monarchs and Tokugawa shoguns in the 1800s, and the Ottomans on the eve of World War I. In these examples, we will see how disintegrating national goals led to opportunistic behavior, an increase in cheating and theft, and a decrease in saving and investment. We will see how the five forces of entropy threaten nations, putting a price tag on prosperity. These empires were powerful and reached extraordinary heights of economic wealth, yet they all collapsed from within. In this book I have chosen examples that span cultural norms—from Confucian to Islamic to Catholic; geographic characteristics—from seafaring lowlands to mountainous highlands; and, of course, hundreds of years of history. The stories in this book will allow us to make inferences that are not anchored to one specific time, place, region, or religion.

BUBBLE WRAP AND BUBBLES

A more complex international economy disintegrates traditions and a community ethos. Globalization has ignited the forces of entropy. What is entropy? Of course, it's a word plucked from the hard sciences as a measure of disorder and randomness. So let's illustrate with a simple science class illustration:

Imagine a sheet of bubble wrap. Let's say there are 193 bubbles (the number of UN member states), each self-contained and filled with a different colored and flavored syrup, for instance, Canadian maple, Mexican agave, Peruvian yacon, and Chinese oyster sauce. The molecules in each bubble maintain an equilibrium state of density, color hue, and taste. Now let's grab some sharp darts and hurl them at the bubbles so that the syrups begin to travel and blend with others. Of course, this may sometimes be a very good thing. New combinations may suddenly seem appealing to the eye and even tasty to the tongue! But this is certain: *our ability to predict behavior has collapsed.* Once we've punctured the bubbles, the syrups have fewer boundaries, more freedom, and less certainty.

What if, instead of syrup, we imagined packing into those bubbles the characteristics of peoples and nations? For example, divergent beliefs in religion, magic, the rights of women, the use of violence, and obligations to parents. Here, too, leakages and mixing incite a more volatile, combustible situation. No wonder our globalized world has witnessed more terrorism, religious furor, broken states, and anarchy in the last twenty years than in the period from World War II to 1990. Even if we put aside global politics and limit our vision solely to economic and financial explosions, we can tick off a staggering list of crises and bubbles that have punctured lives and wiped out families over the past twenty years: Mexico bankruptcy and bailout (1995); East Asia crash (1997); Russia bankruptcy (1998); dot.com stock crash (2000); Argentina crash (2002); housing bubble and crash (2004–9); commodity bubble (2007–8); world stock market crash/collapse of Bear Stearns and Lehman Brothers (2008); Iceland bankruptcy (2009); Portugal, Ireland, Iceland, Greece, and Spain crash (2009); Cyprus bankruptcy (2013); energy crash (2014–2015); China stock market crash (2015). All these bubbles and crashes were fomented by the entropic forces addressed in the chapters ahead.

At the same time that nations feel themselves in an exhausting free-for-all struggle to understand globalization, many also struggle with internal immigration debates. How can a country feel stable and sustainable when so many diverse newcomers are unpacking their bags?

In part I of this book, I will set out the five potent forces that can shatter even a rich nation: (1) falling birthrates, (2) globalized trade, (3) rising debt loads, (4) eroding work ethics, and (5) the challenge of patriotism in a multicultural country. In part II, I will dive into fascinating historical case studies of individuals and countries that faced almost insurmountable odds in weaving together a frayed nation. In the conclusion, I will, among other things, do the unfashionable thing and praise corniness. Even the word *corny* sounds, well, corny, and recalls your great-granny's handmade quilt smelling of mothballs. So be it.

THE WELCOME MAT ROLLS UP

The global economy saps patriotism. Reckless financial markets encourage people to gamble with other people's money. A coddling culture in schools removes the stigma of a slacker's attitude. In the United States, community traditions like American Legion cookouts and patriotic parades are tossed aside as corny or jingoistic. In 2010 the Welcome Wagon company rolled up its welcome mat and sent its two thousand "hostesses" packing. The hostesses (later called representatives) used to knock on the doors of newlyweds and newly moved-in neighbors to offer neighborly advice, gift baskets, and coupons from local merchants. Now the remaining Welcome Wagon employees dump advertising circulars into mailboxes and the post office delivers them with other colorful junk mail. An explosion of media splinters national cultures. More media is not all bad, of course. YouTube, Netflix, Facebook, Snapchat, Google, and Instagram have ignited a supernova of creativity and freedom of expression. Within a split second you can learn of the history, current weather, and traffic jams in Split, Croatia. But there has been a price for creating millions of media websites. Back in the days of yore, when families could tune into just ten stations, television delivered a greater feeling of unity. When President Kennedy, Johnson, Nixon, Ford, Carter, or Reagan appeared, even if you changed the channel, you couldn't get away from his image. The State of the Union address appeared on nearly every channel. In 1970 an NBC Bob Hope Christmas Special attracted nearly two-thirds of viewers and his jokes were stale even by 1970 standards. In 1983, 77 percent of televisions were turned to watch a single show—the last episode of *M*A*S*H*. Television was once a unifying, community-building institution. But in the last twenty years, only Super Bowls have cracked the all-time top-twenty list of most-watched programs. We thirst for new unifying institutions or seek to rebuild old ones.

Here's the challenge: How do you keep community in a world that seems so different from the one faced by the so-called Greatest Generation and its children, the boomers? "To each his own" has morphed into the "Age of Whatever."[6]

Amid our examples from history and from pop culture, I will occasionally draw on literature, music, and art to illustrate key points. When we think about a modern country and its people, we can conjure up all sorts of metaphors: melting pot, salad bowl, mosaic, etc. I want you to think about standing too close to a painting, let's say Georges Seurat's pointillistic *A Sunday Afternoon on the Island of La Grande Jatte*. You simply see dots of color. They may be pretty, but they make no sense. Now back up slowly. Eventually the cheerful scene by the River Seine envelops you and you can make out figures. Wait, that's a dog! There's a sailboat! A very large bustle! Now you realize that each point of paint had a larger point, after all. But what if you backed up and all you saw were those same dots and they never formed a portrait or scene that made any sense to you? I am afraid that in the shattering of nations, the atomistic scattering of people, jobs, and hobbies no longer amounts to much else. Here's another way to look at it: In the past our political system and our culture might have alternated between waves of classicism and romanticism, times when we prize order and a legalistic structure and other times when we may feel more idealistic and sense a natural, romantic attachment to our homeland. You might consider the late 1800s a classical, Victorian period, when schoolmarms in buns smacked unruly kids with a hickory stick. In the 1920s flappers and romantics broke free and smashed rules of fashion and dating. Cole Porter wrote and Ethel Merman blared that in olden days a "glimpse of stocking was looked on as something shocking," but now anything goes. But how can a country survive if it starts to reflect, not classicism or romanticism, but a more modern chaotic trend, for example, expressionist art? Or a Jackson Pollock painting, where the drips do not clearly cohere? I once attended a lecture by the great actor Vincent Price, who loved art even more than movies. A woman in the audience complained that she had just visited a Picasso exhibit and could not understand the distorted figures, where heads were misaligned with bodies and legs twisted and detached from hips. She told Price, "Those Cubans were terrible!" Price laughed. She meant Cubists, of course, but what would it mean to have a country whose socioeconomics and politics reflected Cubism? We literally cannot make head nor tail of each other. Maybe that's what our county has evolved into. We've gone from admiring the classical structure of *Washington Crossing the Delaware* to worrying that we're just moments away from another *Guernica*.

REPAIRING AND REBUILDING

A hundred years ago life expectancy was just fifty years of age. There were virtually no antibiotics and only crude dentistry and yet young people felt more confident that they could get a job and support a family, in a local mill, a factory, a farm, or a mine.[7] If they stumbled into trouble, their neighbors or their church would step in to lift them up, offering a bed to sleep in or a chair at the breakfast table. Traditional "old economy" jobs have faded away and so has the community spirit that encouraged people to take risks and dream big dreams. Entropy, exacerbated by globalization, threatens to unravel communities, as it did the powerful dynasties of the Tokugawa shoguns, the Venetians, the Habsburgs, and the Ottomans. Is it inevitable? Can a community spirit be restored in the United States and in Europe today? In the pages ahead I will share the lessons of history to show that it can. We cannot retrieve the old mill and mine jobs of our grandparents, but we can embrace uniquely American traditions while building new foundations for new prosperity. Using the latest research in neuroscience and economics, we can identify policies that will make kids smarter and grittier, better able to carve out a good paycheck and a happier life in a confusing, apersonal, high-tech world.

From the footsteps of Alexander the Great across Egypt to the Turk who toppled a sultan to the former terrorist who turned Costa Rica into a durable democracy to the video-crazed kid in Cleveland who ranks as a commander in his avatar world but struggles to figure out how to get off his mother's couch in the basement—we will cover thousands of miles of bumpy, rough, and sometimes smooth terrain. It's a race to renew a nation.

PART I

SHATTERING FORCES

CHAPTER 1

The Paradox of Borders, Diapers, and Golf Courses

RICH NATIONS HATE BABIES

America has more golf courses than it has McDonalds. But this is not a story about Americans preferring manicured grass to grass-fed beef. It's a story of 40 million retiring baby boomers looking for a place to take a walk and exercise. They wield more influence and have more money than Generations X or Y. It's not a terribly disturbing trend. But now hear this: Japanese retailers sell more adult diapers than baby diapers. These two facts—about golf courses and diapers—tell you all you need to know about demographics in first-world nations.

Let me explain a big problem in seven simple sentences. As countries grow rich, their birthrates fall and the average age of the population climbs. In order to keep up a lofty standard of living, citizens need workers to serve them, whether as neuro-surgeons in hospitals, waiters in restaurants, or manicurists in nail salons. This requires an influx of new workers, which means opening up the gates to more immigrants. Unless a country has strong cultural and civic institutions, new immigrants can splin-ter the dominant culture. Thus countries face either (1) declining relative wealth or (2) fraying cultural fabric. Prosperous nations cannot enjoy their prosperity without becoming multicultural. But if they become multicultural, they struggle to pursue unified, national goals. Let's see how wealth and birthrates conspire to splinter nations.

AN AMERICAN FOLKTALE: WHERE HAVE ALL THE BABIES GONE?

During the 1960s a sad but popular folk song asked, "Where Have All the Flowers Gone?" Pete Seeger's plaintive lyrics seemed to imply that the combination of the Vietnam War and the pros-perous 1950s and 1960s had created a world where American males were either (1) dressed as soldiers and blowing up flower fields with napalm in Southeast Asia or (2) wearing hard hats and ordering bulldozers to trample flower fields in order to pave asphalt highways across American meadows. In either case, it was not a good time for innocent daffodils.

In a way, flowers were just a metaphor. The 1960s "countercul-ture" implied that the post–World War II boom posed grave risks for children, whether from air pollution, the threat of nuclear weapons, or the commercialism of too many plastic Barbie dolls and Hot Wheels cars. And it wasn't just Pete Seeger and Peter, Paul, and Mary singing such lyrics. An assortment of scientists and social commentators began warning of a "population explosion" that could doom the planet. Biologist Paul Ehrlich, formerly an acclaimed expert in butterflies, showed up on Johnny Carson's *Tonight Show* twenty times, urging "zero population growth," and forecasting that during the 1970s and 1980s hundreds of millions of people would starve to death. Even the Disney company got into the act, producing a short film in which Donald Duck helps explain that if families have too many children, the mothers will be "tired and cross . . . the children will be sickly and unhappy," and there will be "no money for modern conveniences," at which point the film shows a clunky, old-fashioned radio.[1] Thankfully, Ehrlich's worldwide mass starvation forecasts proved faulty. The world did not simply run out of food.

But around the same time that Ehrlich and Donald Duck urged fewer babies, parents in the United States, Japan, and Western Europe did affirmatively decide to bring fewer babies into the world. The baby boom fizzled out and, after 1960 (coinciding with the Food and Drug Administration's approval of the birth control pill), US birthrates began a long and powerful 47 percent plunge. In 1962's *Silent Spring*, Rachel Carson wrote of the death of robins and other songbirds; it turned out the rarest bird would be the mythical stork delivering babies.

Though folksingers might influence things like sales of tambourines and harmonicas, it would be wrong to give Peter, Paul, and Mary much credit for the enormous demographic shift that began in the 1960s. Likewise, it would be wrong simply to credit the birth control pill. More convenient reproductive technologies merely made it easier for parents to enact their childbearing choices; the technologies did not actually make the choices. In this chapter, I will argue that economic and cultural forces behind the demographic shift revealed themselves much earlier than the America of the '60s. *My historical findings suggest that the trend toward fewer babies shows up almost whenever a large middle class begins to form in a society.* For example, we will see the shift in the '60s of ancient Sparta—approximately 460 BC. And later in the '60s of Victorian England, the 1860s. But before looking back at history, let us take a look at the current trends and the predicament they create for modern nations.

No one in America ever recorded a song called "Where Have All the Dogs and Cats Gone?" That's not because popular music shuns pets. Back in 1953, "How Much Is That Doggie in the Window?" hit number 1 on the *Billboard* chart and stayed there for eight weeks. No one has recorded "Where Have All the Dogs and Cats Gone?" because the number of pets owned by Americans has soared higher over the past fifty-five years, just as the baby birthrate has plunged. We have about 75.5 million children in the United States but 90 million cats, 75 million dogs, and 170 million freshwater fish. Together Petsmart and Petco sell $10 billion in pet goods. The largest children's retailer, the Children's Place, earns just $1.8 billion in revenues, pretty much equivalent to what Americans spend on snakes, turtles, and lizards. Now, it is true that the Children's Place competes with Walmart, Target, Nordstrom, and other clothing sellers. But pet owners also buy from Walmart, Target, and grocery stores. A few blocks from my house, I can find stores that specialize in dog bathing and grooming, both the do-it-yourself type and the hired guns equipped, of course, with customized blow-dryers and the promise to return the pooch smelling of mango, coconut, or lemon verbena shampoo. It is more difficult to find someone else to wash and dry your kid's hair. Last year when my dog required surgery, the veterinarian, a caring and gentle doctor who had emigrated from India, referred to my dog as "my kid." I asked him whether that was a common expression in his birthplace. No, he said, he picked it up in the California suburbs. By the way, the surgery was performed using a high-tech radiation system called CyberKnife—which the veterinary hospital shares with the human hospital at the University of California. Presumably, a human patient may have had to wait a day for his surgery because my dog was poised on all fours on the operating room table. I am not making a judgment about priorities, just an observation of changing tastes. We have developed a relatively greater preference for pets and a lesser preference for children.

The average American woman is likely to give birth to 1.89 babies. That is below the 2.1 replacement rate for a stable population (which takes into account disease, infant mortality, war, etc.). Remember, this skimpy 1.89 data point comes at a time when surrogacy, in vitro fertilization, and other even more heroic fertility treatments allow millions of infertile couples to have children. Each year over sixty thousand babies are born with the help of a laboratory assistant, a syringe, and a petri dish. Still, 17 percent of white American women are childless, almost as many as in the 1980s, compared with 15 percent for black women, 13 percent for Asian women, and 10 percent for Hispanic women. Some proportion of these childless women would prefer to bear children. But given the advent of new technologies and legal options we can assume that a greater proportion of the childless are childless by choice compared with prior periods in history.

Though overall fertility rates fall when countries grow wealthier, upper and middle-income earners are especially slow to reproduce. US families earning over $75,000 per year have fewer than fifty-five babies per thousand women. This is half the birthrate of families earning less than $10,000. Apparently, attaining a college degree is a wonderful contraceptive. College-educated American mothers average only 1.6 babies, not much higher than China's (noncollege)

1.54. The difference is that until 2015 China's government dic-
tated an official one-child limit, whereas in America many couples
choose to impose their own one-child policy on themselves.[2]

Why would Americans in their childbearing years choose not to
have children? Ask any parent! Children are messy, loud, worrisome,
and expensive. Veterinary visits cost dog owners an average $378
per year.[3] The cost of medical care for a child is $990.[4] The cost of
personal dog training might reach $50 per hour. The cost of a four-
year college can exceed a quarter of a million dollars. Putting the
economic burden aside, even the most embittered, talking mynah
bird will not scream "I wish I were never born!" and slam shut its
cage door. Of course, children can provide moments of rapturous
love and affection. And, of course, children might take care of a
parent in old age or in sickness, in a way that birds, cats, and dogs
might not. It is difficult to get even the most intelligent schnauzer
or dexterous monkey to fill out a Medicare reimbursement form.

Yet children have always been messy, loud, and expensive. In
1900 the average white woman in America was ringed by three or
four whining, crying, and loving children. Each year since 1936
Gallup pollsters have asked, "What is the *ideal* size of a family?"
That ideal number slumped from 3.6 in 1957 to 2.5 children in
1978, where it remains today.[5] But as with so many other things in
life, people do not always achieve their ideal, leaving average actual
birth numbers below two. So what has changed to explain the declining preference for children? And why is it so widespread? For
most Western European counties, fertility rates are even skimpier
than for the United States: for example, 1.4 for Germany and
1.39 for Italy. German's speak of *schrumpfende Stadt*, the shrinking state of Deutschland. In 2014, 17 percent more Italians died
than were born and the number of new bambini fell to the lowest
since Garibaldi and Victor Emmanuel unified north and south

and declared the Kingdom of Italy in 1861. Italy's health minister looked at the most recent statistics and declared, "We are a dying country."[6] But Italy does not rank first among shrinking lands. Japan's fertility rate dropped to 1.3, as a 2015 government survey covering 7,000 people showed that 40 percent of singles in their twenties were "not looking for a relationship," thinking "romance is a hassle" or that they would rather pursue other hobbies. The Japan Family Planning Association reported that 21.6 percent of men in their late twenties "have no interest in" or "despise" sex.[7]

While Japan's Millennials prioritize texts over sex, the old people are hanging around longer. In 1963 the Japanese government decided to send an exquisitely wrapped silver sake bowl to anyone who turned one hundred that year. In 1963 the health ministry delivered 153 bowls. In 2015 about thirty thousand Japanese turned one hundred and the health minister announced that the dwindling number of young taxpayers can no longer afford to pay for all those silver bowls.[8] Future centenarians might get tin or zinc. Eventually those old people will pass on, and in two hundred years the "vanishing Japanese" might deserve their own exhibit at the Smithsonian in a wing devoted to "lost civilizations." Here is a thought experiment: swoop down and point to a random baby born anywhere in the world today. There is a 97 percent chance that the baby lives in a country where the fertility rate has fallen below replacement.[9]

TRADITIONS AND THE BABY IMPERATIVE

Why the choice? Here's the two-word answer: Blame prosperity. But the subject deserves a more nuanced answer. So before further explaining why birthrates have dropped, let's first ask, "Why were birthrates so much *higher* in past eras?" In poorer centuries, children served as crucial working assets who were needed to help harvest and thresh grain, lug sacks of wheat, or in the nineteenth century crawl on their bellies into coal mines. Though some might find it distasteful to look at children as economic beings, a family with many children would have a more diversified portfolio of human assets. One child might be very smart and help ensure that the parents were not cheated when they measured sacks at the trading station. Another child might prove very strong and help lasso cattle or corral sheep or have the stamina to kneel in the fields picking strawberries. A third child might grow to be very attractive and entice a neighboring suitor, who might come from a wealthier family and would diversify the DNA of the family. A fourth child might win a wrestling contest and grow up to become Abraham Lincoln (a recent *Sports Illustrated* article called Lincoln "A Skilled Wrestler and World-Class Trash Talker").[10] A fifth child might chase his wanderlust and escape the home region, but later send money back home to Ma and Pa. Even today, remittances from family members living abroad bring in 21 percent of the GDP of Armenia and 19.7 percent of Liberia's.[11] In the modern world, we think of children as needing insurance, in case something goes wrong. In earlier times, children *were* the insurance.[12]

Often a young man who played one role in his family's portfolio would marry a young woman who played an opposite role in another. Together they would create a more talented, durable, and diverse family. Much of romantic literature is based on a clash of opposites who "meet cute." In *The Taming of the Shrew*, Petruchio wanders in from Verona to "wive and thrive," with a taste for beauty and an even stronger thirst for money. He meets Kate, who is very smart but prone to angrily hurling pots and pans. Her father is desperate to get rid of her. Eventually, they all live happily ever after. Contemporary "rom-coms" throw opposites together, whether in animated Disney versions like *Beauty and the Beast* or racier Judd Apatow films like *Knocked Up*.

Maybe love and romance have not changed much. But what about when the young couple decides to have children? Here the traditional world does not sync well with the twenty-first century. In traditional societies, love would follow the playground song: "First comes love, then comes marriage. Then comes the baby in a baby carriage." Marriage was supposed to quickly lead to a baby carriage. If a young couple decided not to bear children after twelve months, rumormongers would whisper of health defects or a bad sign from the gods. (Less than nine months suggested loose morals.) After my wife and I had been married for a year, my grandfather Sam (born in London in 1901) called us on the phone to announce:

"Your grandmother and I have been talking. We're ready to become great-grandparents. Now—get to it!" Click. Hang up.

The age-old bias toward high fertility sounds like a cult, but it is found in nearly every traditional society. The Bible, of course, encourages couples to "be fruitful and multiply." If a traditional society was to survive storms, drought, invaders, and horrendous infant mortality, it needed many newborn babies. Culture fostered baby making. Even the disdain for premarital sex fostered baby making because it incited young couples to anticipate their wedding night, not just with nervousness but with a great deal of pent-up lust. Traditional Irish brides would carry a bouquet of flowers in a "magic hanky." Ten months later the new mother would use that same handkerchief as a christening bonnet for her firstborn child. In an ancient Chinese custom, the day before the wedding a bridal bed would be set by someone with "good luck," defined, of course, as someone who had given birth to many children. The "good-luck relative" would scatter on the bed symbolic fertility foods like pomegranates and lotus seeds.

In ancient cultures, more children implied more virility and higher status. Men of high stature would boast of more wives and more children. Higher status also implied more midwives and nurses to take care of the brood. Laura Betzig, an anthropologist who studies despots, examined data from six early civilizations: Mesopotamia, Egypt, the Aztecs, the Incas, imperial India, and ancient China. She discovered very stable patterns of behavior over a span of four thousand years and four continents. In 2600 BC, the Chinese emperor Huangdi had twelve hundred women available for his pleasure. Betzig found a descending number of children lining up neatly with a descending level of power. Princes each had hundreds of wives and concubines. Generals could claim about thirty and upper-class men fewer than a dozen. A middle-class man would keep just a handful.[13] In the Americas, an Inca lord in Peru kept at least seven hundred wives "for the service of his house and on whom to take his pleasure." A petty chief might have just seven.[14] With so many women came even more children. A higher-ranking male could also expect a greater proportion of his children to survive infancy, since they received more nourishment than the children of an impoverished peasant or tribesman.

The genetic markings of eminent ancient rulers still show up today when people test their DNA. When Genghis Khan faced his enemies, he wielded a mighty fierce sword. Apparently, he possessed another tool in the bedroom and with it he sired lots of little Mongols. A recent chromosomal study showed that today about 16 million people can trace their roots to Genghis Khan.[15] In Ireland, one in twelve may be descendants of a fifth-century warlord known as Niall of the Nine Hostages.[16] In Rogers and Hammerstein's classic *The King and I* (based on the real nineteenth-century King Mongkut of Siam), theater audiences in the 1950s oohed as the king boasted of 106 children and were charmed as dozens of adorables scurried and kowtowed at his feet.

In traditional societies, men would be expected to protect their family. A man who could not shield his wife or wives would be emasculated, symbolically if not literally. In his role as a protector, a man would tend to favor those children who resembled him most, for they assured him of paternity. The genetic link to children proves very strong to this day. A fascinating study of 635 men and 1,169 children who had attended college in New Mexico showed that fathers spend much more time and money on genetically linked children than on stepchildren or on children about whom they doubt paternity. Children of men who had low confidence in their paternity were 13 percent as likely to receive any money for college as those whose fathers were convinced they were the genetic parent.[17] Similar inquiries in Cape Town, South Africa, and in Tanzania showed similar results.[18]

The idea of a portfolio of children and the sexual liberties given only to men clearly show a gender bias. Traditional societies discriminated against females, through inheritance, investment in education, and sometimes allocation of meals. In our own time, subtle slights can still shine through. My father had one sibling, a sister named Rhoda. I will never forget that when my grandmother died, one of the mourning neighbors whispered to another, "Well, at least she left a son," never mentioning my Aunt Rhoda. A desire for sons can lead to all sorts of dastardly behavior. In China, after the communist government imposed a one-child policy in 1979, many families simply aborted female fetuses, while others committed infanticide after the girls were born. Throughout Asia demographers have reported the phenomenon of "missing females." Traditional Hindu culture honors boys above girls, since the religion requires that parents be buried by a son. The economist Thomas Malthus, whose dire population forecasts predated Paul Ehrlich's by nearly two centuries, quoted an Indian law, stating that "by a son a man obtains victory over all people; by a son's son he enjoys immortality; and afterwards by the son of a grandson he reaches the solar abode . . . the son delivers the father from hell."[19]

WHEN WEALTH BREEDS LESS BREEDING

How does prosperity foul up traditional ways? As societies grow relatively richer, children stop looking like nifty manual workers and obedient field hands and instead begin to resemble luxury goods, much like pets or handbags. Even our perception of animals changes when we get more comfortable. Consider: in 1900 a hardworking Alaskan trapper might have wanted six hairy, well-insulated malamutes to haul his sled through the snow. Today a resident of modern Anchorage might be happy with one Pomeranian to sit on his lap while he watches Netflix in his toasty warm home, heated by natural gas pipelines. In the eyes of potential parents, modern children have turned from working malamutes into Pomeranians. Times have changed, along with status symbols. Whereas traditional societies might have gauged a man's status by counting his children, elite status today may come from counting the number of Rolex watches in his drawer, his accumulated frequent-flier miles, or the number of his followers on Twitter and Instagram.

Nobel laureate economist Gary Becker asserted that parents see a trade-off between the quantity of children and the quality of children.[20] Middle- and upper-income parents expect their children to achieve much. That requires parents to invest time and money in their offspring. Since childrearing may require tutoring, carpooling, and paying for college, parents often choose to have fewer children of higher achievement than more children of middling accomplishment. Furthermore, more money spent on children means less money left over for ski vacations and fancy cars. Joseph Schumpeter, who ran the Austrian Finance Ministry before he ran Harvard's Economics Department in the 1940s, asked, "Why should we stunt our ambitions and impoverish our lives in order to be insulted and looked down upon in our old age?"[21] Schumpeter knew that successful people could be rather self-involved. He was known for strutting around Harvard dressed in jodhpurs and riding boots and famously said he had three ambitions in life: to become the greatest economist in the world, the greatest horseman in Austria, and the greatest lover in Vienna. He boasted that he had achieved two of three before leaving his homeland for Massachusetts.

From all around the world, data show that more education has meant fewer children, perhaps because more educated people feel more comfortable with the Beckerian "opportunity cost" choice framework. And more highly educated people are less prone to embrace peasant traditions. In countries as different from each other as Yemen and Brazil, a woman with a high school education is likely to bear half as many children as a woman with no education.

A century ago some commentators foresaw falling fertility. In George Bernard Shaw's 1903 play *Man and Superman*, Don Juan in Hell worries that "lovers of money and solid comfort, the worshippers of success, of art, and of love, will all oppose to the Force of Life the device of sterility." Shaw, a Fabian socialist and sometime eugenicist, saw a risk in prosperity and peasants climbing out of the fields, washing their hands, and waltzing like swells into salons and parlors.[22] But signs of this phenomenon appeared long before even Shaw's day. Let us turn back the calendar quite a few pages.

WHERE HAVE ALL THE SPARTANS GONE?

We use the word *spartan* to signal a gritty willingness to make do with bare-bones necessities and without luxuries. Back in the 1970s Bud Grant, the coach of the Minnesota Vikings football team, refused to allow his players to warm their hands on the sidelines with an outside heater—in Minneapolis in the winter. That was spartan. Their aggressive defensive squad was called "The Purple People Eaters." Those were the days. For most of the past thirty-five years, the Vikings have played inside, under a dome. And they have not made it to the Super Bowl since 1976, when they played outside under Grant's spartan style.

Like the Vikings of the 1970s, the ancient soldiers of Sparta sported a brutal offense and a nearly impenetrable defense. The recent movie *300* focuses on the true story of the three hundred Spartan soldiers who in 480 BC (along with soldiers from other Greek city-states) fearlessly battled a force of Persians under Xerxes the Great that outnumbered them perhaps 20 to 1. The Spartan army was efficient and ruthlessly effective. Soldiering began almost literally in the cradle. In Sparta, it was survival of the fittest. A public committee would inspect a newborn to determine whether he or she should be nourished or killed. Assuming the baby made it through this first test, if the mother suspected her toddler acted cowardly, she had the right to kill him. Starting at age seven, young men would leave home and begin battle training, eating in military mess halls and living communally under austere conditions. They did not talk much either, which probably made them even more intimidating. The word *laconic* comes from the Spartan region Laconia. Dressed in red cloaks, marching in intimidating phalanx formations, swinging bronze shields and bronze spears, Spartan forces were nearly untouchable during the fifth century BC.

After they conquered Laconia and Messenia, they dragged their victims back to Sparta to work as slaves on the farms or to perform day-to-day labor. Spartan men no longer had to work the farms; Spartan women no longer had to perform housework. Spartan women became educated and gained the right to inherit, own, and bequeath property, rights not known in Athens.[23] Relieved of heavy lifting, Spartan women could manage the farms because the tasks required brains, not brawn. They did not have to lift bales. Instead they handled assignments like choosing breeding livestock or bargaining for seeds. By conquering neighbors, Sparta gained wealth. With more wealth, the Spartans had more control over their time and their bodily labor.

So where are the mighty Spartans today? Gone. They did not leave much of a written record. Most of what we know about them comes from other Greeks, including Aristotle. Where did the Spartans go? The short answer is that the Thebans trounced them at the Battle of Leuctra in 371 BC and invaded Sparta the following year. But how could the Thebans defeat the invincible Spartans, who were trained from the cradle to kill and to live on skimpy rations? The answer: the Spartans either forgot to or chose not to have enough sex and babies to continue populating their society and their army. Aristotle indicated that the Spartan population began to shrink *following* their victories in war: "although the country is capable of supporting fifteen hundred cavalry and thirty thousand heavy-armed troopers, they numbered not even a thousand."[24] The population shrank because *after* their victories, the Spartans began to rely on captured slave labor. Wealthy families decided to have fewer babies, which concentrated land and money into fewer hands. Aristotle explained that "the defective nature of their system of land-tenure has been proved by the actual facts of history: the state did not succeed in enduring a single blow, but perished owing to the smallness of its population."[25] With land under the Spartan's control and slaves ordered to perform the work, the labor of one's own child became less vital and the opportunity cost of bearing another child rose. Another child meant less time to manage the estate and less time to travel or enjoy luxuries. It meant possibly sharing property with numerous sons-in-law and daughters-in-law. By the early fourth century, Sparta's citizen population had shrunk by about 80 percent. With a meager population, the mighty phalanxes of Sparta's army thinned. By 371 BC, Thebes was no longer intimidated and conquered Sparta, liberating the Messenian slaves who had been "lying in wait for their masters," as Aristotle put it.[26] Sparta evaporated because Sparta gained wealth and lost the need and urge to procreate.

How did these ancients avoid giving birth to children? Birth control consisted of celibacy, coitus interruptus, abortion, using plants like silphium with contraceptive qualities, and, sadly, infanticide. If an infant made it past all of these obstacles, he could be sent away (fosterage) or abandoned and left to an orphanage or to starvation.

Early in the first century AD, the geographer Strabo, whose life straddled ancient Greece and ancient Rome, looked at the remnants of ancient Sparta and remarked in his masterwork *Geographica* that it is "a country the most of which is deserted . . . now short of population as compared with its large population in olden times, for outside of Sparta the remaining towns are only about thirty in number, whereas in olden times it was called, they say, 'the country of the hundred cities,' and it was on this account, they say, that they held annual festivals in which one hundred cattle were sacrificed."[27]

You might think that the triumphant Thebans and Athenians would learn the lesson of Sparta. As we will see in chapter 6, the roaring success of Alexander the Great put more land and slaves under Greek command. With land, labor, and booty, the Greeks lay back but did not procreate. If you visit Athens today, you will wait in a line for a crowded tour bus or walk behind rows of backpackers in order to get up to the Parthenon on the Acropolis. It's a magnificent site, of course, and assures you for at least a few moments that there is a thing called "Western civilization." Strabo, too, surveyed the site and its surroundings. In his day he did not wait in a long queue, however. He witnessed an Athens that appeared nearly deserted, noting that he saw *more statues than people.*

I am not trying to reduce the entire rise and fall of civilizations to one factor, of course. Reckless military campaigns, rebellious slaves, lethal plagues, thuggish invaders, crop failures, and incompetent governments demolished nations. My point is not that a lower birthrate always dooms a nation. My point is that a lower birthrate can come from economic and political success, which then creates new, sometimes insurmountable obstacles to that nation continuing its reign.

The Greek historian Polybius (200–118 BC) understood that the fall of nations has multiple causes. He did not usually blame bureaucrats, plagues, or faulty physicians. Instead, he followed the prevailing paradigm of the era and blamed the gods. Polybius implored his leaders to respond to droughts, frosts, and epidemics through "sacrifices to appease the wrath of heaven, and . . . ask[ing] the gods" for a respite from "the evils which are afflicting us." But in other matters, Polybius takes a more modern turn. After describing "a dearth of children and generally a decay of population, owing to which the cities were denuded of inhabitants, and a failure of productiveness resulted, though there were no long-continued wars or serious pestilence," Polybius places the blame on the mortals, not gods: "Our men becoming perverted to a passion for show and money, refusing to rear children . . . or at most one or two . . . for the sake of leaving them well off or bringing them up in extravagant luxury. . . . The house must be left heirless: and like swarms of bees, little by little the cities become sparsely inhabited and weak."[28]

Eighteen hundred years later in the American South, where the porches of grand plantation homes bore Ionic columns (and where nineteen hundred years later William Faulkner penned his echoes of Greek tragedy), slavery had a similar impact on fertility. As the South's economy expanded in the early 1800s, slaves displaced white children in the fields. Rising incomes focused wealthy families on preserving and showcasing their horses and footmen, not their baby strollers. White fertility underwent a 20 percent plunge from 1800 to 1850.[29]

Business managers and economists often cite ratios such as the retail ratio of "sales revenue to square foot" of space; or in hotels, the "revenue per available room." Following Strabo, I would suggest a new and useful ratio for interpreting the sustainability of a nation: *statues per young citizen*. Like the Greeks, the Romans ultimately watched this ratio go up and their prospects go down.

The Emperor Augustus led Rome to remarkable prosperity, boasting that he found Rome a "city of brick but left it as marble." Economic historian Peter Temin at MIT estimates that Augustus's Rome in 20 BC was as wealthy as England or Holland seventeen hundred years later! Augustus built aqueducts, lauded trade, and promoted literacy. We know that Rome was fairly literate because the graffiti and business signs in Pompeii tell us so. I have toured Pompeii several times, for every few years more discover-

ies are unearthed and cataloged. The Lupanar is a favorite stop
for tourists, located near the corner of Vico del Lupanare and
Vico del Balcone Pensile. *Lupanar* comes from the Latin word for
wolf (*lupus*) and, of course, the myth of Rome's founding derives
from the babies Romulus and Remus nursed by a she-wolf. But in
Pompeii the Lupanar is the famous brothel. A prostitute's written
advertisement offers "I am yours for two asses cash," while a business offers sixty-five sesterces for the "return of a missing copper
pot." Incidentally, *asses* refers not to donkeys, but to a Roman
bronze coin, known as an "A."

But Rome's wealth and literacy among the well-off ushered in
one unwelcome trend: a falling birthrate among citizens. Augustus grew so concerned that in 18 BC and 9 BC the Senate passed
laws penalizing the unmarried, the celibate, and the childless.
Under the law, a man without children would lose 50 percent
of his inheritance (*Lex Papia Poppaea*). Historians have blamed
Rome's low birthrate on everything from lead poisoning among
the upper classes (from lead crockpots) to males lounging around
in baths so hot that the water killed off their sperm. Though these
environmental explanations may have some merit, clearly Augustus and the Senate believed that well-to-do Roman citizens were
deliberately choosing to bear fewer babies and therefore enacted
laws that tried to reverse the trend. Pliny the Younger complained
that most Romans believed that "an only son is already a heavy
burden and that it is advantageous not to be overburdened with
posterity."[30] The term *proletarius* had once been an honorable
term for a "child-producer." But that badge of honor apparently
slipped into the gutter. Meanwhile, marriage seemed more like
a sport or privilege than a sacred act with any purpose. Juvenal
wrote a satire of a woman who was married and divorced eight
times in just twelve months.

Polybius lamented that this lack of sexual and procreative action would foil Rome's foreign policy. He noted that with a dwindling population, the Romans might have been "the masters of the world [but] . . . they could not" staff enough "ships, nor put to sea with such large fleets" a big enough force to maintain mastery of their own domain. To man the army and navy, Rome was forced to enlist Germanic tribesmen. But these "barbarians" bucked the discipline of Roman generals. In the western part of the empire, barbarians made up almost half of the fighting force. And they were not so eager to fight for Rome.

And so here lies the paradox: had the Spartans, Greeks, and Romans not achieved wealth and power by conquering their neighbors, they might not have conquered their own drive to reproduce.

POST-NAPOLEONIC FRANCE AND VICTORIAN ENGLAND AND THE RULE OF TWENTY-FIVE

The Industrial Revolution brought rapid growth to France and England. Finally, eighteen hundred years after Augustus, Roman achievements and wealth were eclipsed by modern Europe. But almost as soon as France began enjoying higher income growth following the Revolution, French wives began producing fewer offspring. At the time of the French Revolution, France was the third most populated country in the world, after India and China, and there were nearly 40 percent more Frenchmen than Germans. But by 1850 slower-growing Germany had caught up. With better medical care (such as it was), personal hygiene (such as it was), better nutrition, and less frequent pandemics, a smaller proportion of French infants died, which meant fewer needed to

be born. But the French economy was changing too. An industrialized economy required working parents to be mobile, which
made inconvenient those little hands yanking on the parents'
bleus de travail when the parents wanted to head out the door to
work in a factory. Religion and culture counted, too, of course.
After the Revolution, the church lost authority and "natural birth
control" lost some of its stigma as an "unnatural act." And, finally, as in Sparta, the rules of inheritance impacted fertility decisions. Under the ancien régime, primogentiture held sway, so that
regardless of the number of children, the oldest male generally
got the estate. However, under the Napoleonic Code, all children
got a share. That diluted the estate and made the parents think
thrice about having more than one or two heirs. The proportion
of young people under the age of fifteen stagnated between 1750
and 1800 and then slipped for the next 150 years![31] When the
actor Maurice Chevalier sings "Thank Heaven for Little Girls" in
the movie *Gigi*, he is not really making a religious statement. He
may, however, be lamenting how few young female children one
saw in Paris in 1899. The Belle Epoque had few belles, it turned
out.

As in ancient Greece and Rome, the wealthiest and highest-
status French families were first to put the brakes on their breeding.[32] George Finlay, a nineteenth-century American historian of
Greece and Rome, pointed to the population parallels between
nineteenth-century France and the ancients. He observed that in
ancient times the oligarchs failed to increase their flock, while in
contemporary times this same tendency "affects . . . the two hundred thousand electors who form the oligarchy of France."[33] And
it did not take too long before the common folk followed the lead
of their relatively infertile aristocrats.

Across the English Channel, it took a bit longer for the Brits to curb their procreation. Yet during the last decades of Queen Victoria's reign, the middle- and upper-income English began celebrating their rising incomes by having fewer babies. When Victoria ascended to the throne in 1837, the UK birthrate was fairly stable, about 170 babies per 1,000 women. As the new queen was crowned, England was just becoming the "workshop of the world," a powerhouse in manufacturing. Over the next forty years, its share of world manufacturing climbed from about 10 percent to 25 percent and the size of its economy nearly tripled. Then *following* this ferocious economic growth, something dramatic happened: around 1880 birthrates began to plunge. By the eve of World War I, birthrates had collapsed by 70 percent! This was not a matter of government mandate, or plague, or global climate change. This was a matter of choice: British families decided (with the benefit of crude contraception) that they would be happier, healthier, and wealthier with fewer mouths to feed.[34] Since fewer Britons were working on farms, fewer children were needed as farmhands. In the minds of middle-class social climbers, more than two or three baby buggies or prams parked in front of a door marked a slip in social status.

My research suggests the following rule of thumb: *In modern times (following industrialization), if a nation exceeds a 2.5 percent annual average growth in GDP for two consecutive twenty-five-year periods (two generations), the fertility rate will drop to just over the replacement level, that is, to 2.5 children per female. If GDP continues to grow for a third consecutive generation, the fertility rate will tend to drop below 2.1 and the nation will require immigration to maintain a stable working population.*

In the past few years some countries like France, Singapore, South Korea, and Russia have tried to convince young couples to spend, frankly, more time in bed, offering everything from free motel visits to more time off for "whoopee." The Russians promised new parents a chance to win a new refrigerator! I cannot think of anything less sexy than a government minister dimming the lights and turning up a Frank Sinatra tune. It doesn't inspire blissful evenings and it could lead to nightmares. In recent years some fertility rates have moved up a bit, for example, Japan's rose to 1.43 and, aided by immigrants, France's has moved close to 2.0. Still, pushing fertility rates well over the replacement rate seems close to fruitless.[35]

WHAT DIFFERENCE DOES IT MAKE? HERE COMES THE PARADOX

When nations grow wealthier and begin to brake their birthrates, they see a lot more wrinkles and gray hair, or buy a lot more Clairol coloring solution. And if scientific advancements like blood-pressure pills, MRI devices, and pedometers extend life expectancy, the older population can grow very old indeed. Life expectancy has jumped from roughly forty-seven years of age in 1900 to about eighty today in most industrialized countries. If you gathered together all the world's people sixty-five and older, they would constitute the third most populous nation on the planet.

Here's another twist that comes from longer lives: the mere fact of living longer might actually induce people to have fewer children. Consider: if you know you are going to live to be ninety, you might feel less pressure to marry early, which means delaying marriage until after the prime baby-bearing years have passed. The age of first marriage in the United States has climbed in the past century, from roughly twenty-one years to almost twenty-seven years. At age twenty-seven, the chance of a female getting pregnant begins to slip, so that a twenty-seven- to twenty-nine-year-old has a significantly smaller chance of becoming pregnant than a nineteen- to twenty-six-year-old.[36] But here is a different way to look at the data: the proportion of one's life spent in marriage has soared. A hundred years ago, when people died sooner, Americans waited about half their expected lifetime before marrying. Today, Americans marry after just 35 percent of their expected lifetime has passed. Across the globe, as incomes have risen, so has the average marriage age. UN data show that between 1970 and 2005 the marriage age for women climbed from twenty-five to almost twenty-nine.[37] Of course, many women give birth without wearing a wedding ring or even living with the father. But if we look at the average age of an American woman bearing a first child, that number leaped from 21.4 years in 1970 to 25 years in 2006. And waiting is not a stupid decision. A study by Amalia Miller at the University of Virginia showed that not having babies pays, at least in the short term. For every year an American woman delays childbirth, she earns 9 percent more in the workplace as she gains more experience and enhances her nonchildrearing skills.[38] In sum, rising life spans and rising incomes dampen the tendency to bear more children.

As the industrialized world ages, the future starts to resemble a vintage postcard of Miami Beach circa 1980, where elderly people look for a nice park bench or shuffle to their cars at 2 p.m. for the early-bird dinner special, where waitresses serve soft food in exchange for a 2-for-1 coupon. While a population with a median age near senior citizenhood might be a good thing if you resent screaming babies and abhor teenagers blaring loud music, it is a challenging demographic transition, if you want the economy to both (1) keep growing and (2) maintain its character and traditions. Who will drive the senior citizens' buses? Draw blood for their cholesterol tests? Or deliver the meals on wheels? Who will pass on local traditions like Memorial Day parades and community band concerts?

Miami Beach is no longer aged and stooped. But why? Because in the 1990s the elderly demographic vibe got shaken up by an influx of young Latin Americans migrating from places like Venezuela, Colombia, and Argentina, adding to the already substantial Cuban-born population.[39] Miami Beach was aging and slowing down until non–Miami Beach citizens arrived. We see this phenomenon throughout history and throughout the world: older, affluent populations requiring an influx of younger people from abroad. I confess that I enjoy Miami Beach as a tourist. There are few nicer strolls in the world than along South Beach on a starry night in front of pastel-colored Art Deco hotels built in the 1920s, as palm trees sway and local bands play a samba. The pedestrian shopping boulevard called Lincoln Road bustles, and it is sometimes hard to get a table at an outdoor café or a ticket to the gleaming Frank Gehry–designed New World Symphony Hall. My good friend Jimmy Morales, who is the son of a local school janitor and who graduated from Harvard Law School, is the proud, popular, and very effective city manager of Miami Beach. As Jimmy and I recently walked down Lincoln Road, I was stunned by the energy and entrepreneurship. With Jimmy by my side, a Cuban restaurant served us a tender and tasty *boliche* (beef roast). Jimmy taught me that black beans and white rice are called "*Moros y Cristianos.*" The translation is "Moors and Christians." That's a nice metaphor for the cultural mix of the city: people from many cultures and countries tossed together.

But this wonderful lunch for a visitor and all this cultural fusion do not mean that Miami has, on average, grown more prosperous. In the city of Miami, one-half of the population, 1.1 million, is now foreign born, chiefly from Spanish-speaking countries. Miami ranks second lowest among US cities in median income and second highest in poverty. Though wages are relatively low, Miami residents do share their income, but not necessarily with each other. The city ranks high in remittances sent by immigrants to their countries of origin. Each year about three-quarters of Cuban Americans in Miami send money to their relatives in Cuba, totaling about $1 billion.[40] Cuban Americans are not alone in mailing money to the Caribbean. Salvadorans and Dominicans send home even greater proportions of their income. Given the relatively low wages earned by average Latin American immigrants, this is an extraordinary sign of generosity. But the generosity is aimed across the Caribbean, not across the street or across town.

A recent study of volunteerism ranks Miami dead last in the country, with just 14.8 percent offering to regularly help others. Miami competes with Las Vegas for the bottom rung. While one might understand Las Vegas, a transient place proud of its vices, it is hard to defend Miami's low standing. Since Las Vegas and Miami escape wintry weather, is it possible that good weather makes people less likely to help others? Perhaps. About 37 percent of chilly Minneapolis–Saint Paul residents volunteer, as do about 35 percent of damp Seattleites.[41] Still, drier and warmer Oklahoma City dwellers also volunteer at high rates. I suspect the answer has more to do with the culture that has been established in those regions. And by culture, I do not mean Catholic Hispanic versus Germanic Lutheran. I mean the constellation of religious, community, school organizations, etc. Are parents expected to volunteer at PTA events? Do neighborhoods foster parades, historical reenactments, farmers' markets, and charity runs?

Here's the question in this chapter: "Do the lower birthrate and aging of the general population lead to more immigrants, which leads to either a breakdown or a downward shift in the spirit of community?" If the answer is yes, that does not imply that the policy response should be to block immigrants from landing at airports or docking at ports. As we shall see in the Conclusion, the answer is in building better community institutions and more durable traditions.

Who does the work when a rich country gets older? Using Department of Labor Statistics and census data *U.S. News & World Report* calculated the fastest-growing sectors for job growth in the next decade: (1) health care, (2) business, (3) construction, (4) technology, and (5) social services. But when we look into the data, the *three fastest-growing jobs* are (1) personal care aide, (2) home health aide, and (3) interpreter/translator.[42] What do we know about these jobs? Immigrants are vastly overrepresented in these jobs. In health care, for example, 2.5 million people care for the elderly in their homes and 23 percent of those aides are foreign born.[43] This, of course, does not include the children of recent immigrants who may work as health aides or nurses. Bricklayers and construction workers show up high on the list of fastest-growing jobs, too. Here, too, foreign-born workers make up 23 percent of the construction workers, with over 82 percent of those coming from Latin America. And nearly 27 percent of construction workers speak a language other than English at home.[44] Immigrants may have heard that America's streets were paved with gold. Now they are finding out that *they* will do the repaving. For who else is young and hungry enough to want to lean over 275-degree asphalt concrete as it pours from a hot mixer? Only 14 percent of the US-born population is made up of men between the ages of eighteen and thirty-nine, the prime candidates to shovel hot asphalt. But 35 percent of undocumented workers (and 18 percent of legal immigrants) fit into the young male category.[45] Americans did not see many Hispanic immigrants when the United States was young and when its population was younger and more fertile. In 1820 the average age of an American was just 16.7 years.[46] How many Mexicans immigrated to the United States in 1820? Just one.[47] Not one million or one hundred. Simply one.

Let's finally return to our example in Victorian England, which will lead us to themes in chapters 2 and 5, the role of foreigners and resentment against them. With a collapsing birthrate, Victorian England increasingly turned to immigrants to pull the levers in the workshop of the world. Foreign factory workers, craftsmen, and entrepreneurs remade the East End of London, which changed from Irish to German to Jewish between Queen Victoria's coronation and the start of World War I in 1914. Fleeing pogroms in Russia, about 120,000 immigrant Jews found homes in England, sparking tensions and conflicted emotions among unionized English workers. The leader of the dockworkers, a devout socialist named Ben Tillett, who was himself the son of an Irish migrant, scratched his head and told new immigrant workers: "Yes, you are our brothers, and we will do our duty by you. *But we wish you had never come.*"[48] That's quite a welcome mat to roll out.

CHAPTER 2

Melancholia Madeleine and the Paradox of Trade

A few years ago, California pistachio growers asked whether I would speak at their convention near Carmel-by-the-Sea. I love pistachios, and since Magnum-toting Clint Eastwood once served as mayor, it seemed a safe assignment. The audience was friendly and many of the attendees were true farmers, wearing caps emblazoned with the name John Deere, Caterpillar, or Sunkist. In my talk I discussed globalization. I grabbed a bottle of FIJI Water resting on the lectern shelf and raised it high: "Imagine, it is economical today to import water from the South Pacific, all the way to California! That's the miracle of new transportation technologies—containerization, advanced logistics." As I praised the forces of globalization and the sleek design of the rectangular

FIJI bottle, I noticed a rather elegant man in a fashionable suit jacket sitting in the front row nodding, smiling, and paying close attention. Then I paused and looked at the FIJI bottle the way Hamlet looks at Yorick's skull and said, "Now, I've never been to Fiji. I'd love to go there. But I'm pretty sure these bottles are filled by some guy in his boxer shorts standing in his backyard, holding a garden hose." The audience roared. I felt good. Then they kept laughing and some whistles got added to the sound mix. Finally, the master of ceremonies stepped onto the stage, put his arm around me, and pointed to the elegant man in the front row.

"Todd, let's call up here the owner of FIJI Water!"

Gulp.

The man's name was Stewart Resnick, and he was also the co-owner (with his wife, Lynda) of the POM Wonderful pomegranate and pistachio company. I also love the taste of pomegranate. Resnick, who has given generously to medical research, could not have been nicer. He and the rest of the audience assumed that I had the nerve to deliberately tease him from the stage.

This is a new world, where nothing on earth is far away from our grasp. No longer do we step off the treadmill at a gym and stumble to a rusty water fountain. Instead, we may depend on a guy named Stewart, who lives in Beverly Hills, to send us bottles designed by a talented graphic artist and filled with water from the tropics. Bottled water is a $12 billion industry and consumers are devoted to their favorites—even though the basic ingredient is supposed to be pretty tasteless. I intend neither to exalt nor to pick on FIJI Water, or any other brand. After all, the story of human survival is closely tied to finding sources of drinkable water.

We are evolutionarily driven to discover good water. And the more recent one-hundred-year story of modernization is closely linked to a desire for and an ability to obtain nonpolluted bottled drinks, whether Coca-Cola in Africa, Pepsi in the Soviet Union, or Pabst Blue Ribbon in Guangdong. It is easy to forget the power of Coca-Cola and Pepsi as symbols for developing nations in the twentieth century. If a government—whether dictatorial or parliamentary—could deliver American fizzy drinks to its people, that government had a better chance of clinging to power. Coca-Cola created its own foreign department in 1926, mirroring the US State Department. In 1959 at a trade exposition in Moscow, which turned into the famous "Kitchen Debate," a Pepsi executive managed to sneak a cup of cola into the hands of Nikita Khrushchev and Richard Nixon, while photographers snapped away. With that icebreaker, Pepsi later arranged to swap soft-drink concentrate for Stolichnaya vodka to be sold in the United States. But at first communist governments despised such symbols of Western wealth and leftist critics called it "Coca-Colonization." To compete with Coca-Cola, Khrushchev's henchmen came up with their own bubbly dark drink based on the traditional *kvass*, a sour, cloudy brew made from fermented brown bread. In *War and Peace* soldiers call it "pig's lemonade." The Soviet state version probably went down well with joy-riding local commissars who cruised around town in rusty, sixty-five-horsepower Ladas. Their expectations were low. In 1959 Romania's hard-core communists spied their national fencing champion sipping Coca-Cola while in Krakow, Poland. They threw him into jail for this sin and denounced the drink as the official "beverage of capitalist sports." Eventually, the barriers to Eastern Europe collapsed. In Romania after protesters toppled the brutal and comically egotistical Ceaușescus in 1989 (see Conclusion), the swirl of Coca-Cola's red-and-white stripes popped up on kiosks across the country, symbolizing freedom and access to global goods. James Cagney's character predicted all this in Billy Wilder's 1961 comedy *One, Two, Three*: "Napoleon blew it; Hitler blew it; but Coca-Cola's gonna pull it off."[1]

The old Roman motto coined by the poet Juvenal was "bread and circuses," meaning that Caesar could stay on the throne so long as he provided entertainment and the daily necessities. In Ethiopia, Coca-Cola became the Roman bread. As recently as 1999 the BBC reported that a "Coca-Cola shortage is being treated as a national emergency," as the East African Bottling Share Company ran out of bottle tops and laid off one thousand workers. In a national credit crunch, "[s]treet children have reportedly been collecting the much-needed bottle tops from the streets of Addis Ababa."[2] In the 1980 cult movie, *The Gods Must Be Crazy*, a Coca-Cola bottle falls out of an airplane and lands in the Kalahari Desert near a naïve and unworldly Bushman named Xi. Xi had never seen such a sparkling, entrancing thing. It must be holy, a gift from the gods! Eventually, the gift ruins his tribe's harmony and Xi races across the Kalahari trying to hurl the bottle off the ends of the earth.

Now we ask ourselves, how does globalization impact the harmony of a nation? Be careful here, for even if we answer that globalization harms the harmony, we must also ask, can a nation live *without* globalization? Which brings us to the paradox of this chapter: *Nations cannot grow and stay rich without trading with others. But trading with others eventually shakes the customs and character of the nation.* At some point, we all feel like the early Xi who marvels at the bottle of Coca-Cola. Maybe we are not bedazzled by a soft-drink bottle. Maybe for us it is the supersharp photos of a Samsung Galaxy phone or the painted, colored dots that emerge from Damien Hirst's art factory in London. Still, we marvel. But at some later point, we also feel like the older, disenchanted Xi and ask ourselves, "Have these global marvels interrupted our lives and disrupted our relationships with our neighbors?" Those Galaxy photos are sharp, but maybe we miss the guy who used to run the photo shop down the street before he was put out of business.

Nostalgic feelings are not new. In Proust's *Remembrance of Things Past* (1913), the middle-aged narrator (Marcel) shudders with a flood of feelings when he tastes a baked madeleine dipped in tea. He yearns for the memories of his youth: "after the people are dead, after the things are broken and scattered, taste and smell alone . . . remain poised a long time, like souls, remembering, waiting, hoping amid the ruins of all the rest."[3]

Sounds sentimental and dreary. But it is worse for us today. Unlike Marcel, we miss the cookie because Nabisco has displaced the baker! We miss the taste of an earlier time—*and* the very neighbors and artisans who created those tastes! Most of us occasionally feel a nostalgic twinge at the costs of modernization. I call the feeling *"melancholia madeleine,"* for we were all like Marcel or a Kalahari Bushman at some point in our personal history. *Melancholia madeleine* is a syndrome that makes it very difficult to keep a country together.

It is true that nowadays "artisanal" bakers, "craft" olive oil bottlers, and "local" kale growers do crop up to command premium prices from affluent consumers. Often, however, the most skilled and successful artisans quickly sell their businesses to bigger brands desperate to show their cutting edges to the public. There's nothing wrong with brave and noble artisans selling their shops, but it is tough to conjure misty-eyed nostalgia for a company like 10 Barrel Brewing that had been brewing beer in Bend, Oregon, "since 2009" and in 2014 snuck the whole operation under the sign of its acquirer, Budweiser.

Let us, like the Proust narrator holding his madeleine, go back in time again. In this chapter, I will show you old nations like Ragusa and Venice that grew rich by trading and then fell apart. We will see one of the most powerful empires of the nineteenth century, the Habsburg Dynasty that ruled Austria-Hungary, crumble like a stale linzer torte. We will also see how a globalized economy can sap patriotism. It's not all bad, though. These very same forces that ripped apart nations brought us longer, healthier lives and so many good things from lifesaving penicillin to the lowly pencil.

IT'S HARD TO GET RICH WITHOUT TRADE

I have spent much of career extolling the virtues of trade. I am proud to say that Milton Friedman endorsed my first book, a history of economic thought entitled *New Ideas from Dead Economists*, and when I served in the White House I debated opponents of the North American Free Trade Agreement, including one boisterous union leader who literally took off his shoe and pounded the lectern, eliciting cheers and whistles from the crowd gathered at a massive, dingy hotel in Chicago. On the book jacket of his classic *Free to Choose*, Friedman holds up a pencil as a symbol of the wonders of free trade. No single person, Friedman insisted, knows how to make a pencil.[4] To construct a pencil you need to be able to get to a place like Oregon and learn how to chop down a big tree. But first you would need steel for the saw. So you would need to fly to an iron mine in Brazil and strap on a miner's helmet. Then make your way to Pittsburgh to figure out how to turn iron ore into steel. Do not forget the pencil's metal tip, graphite center, and rubber eraser. They require trips to Sri Lanka and Indonesia. After all that traveling and learning all the chemistry, engineering, and foreign languages necessary for the transactions, do you think you could churn out a single pencil for the thirteen cents that Dixon Ticonderoga charges—a pencil which also comes in a handy cardboard box with attractive graphic printing and which attracts faithful fans? (George Lucas wielded a Dixon Ticonderoga before he gave Luke Skywalker a lightsaber and Willie Wonka's creator, writer Roald Dahl, would sharpen half a dozen each morning before his first morning scribble.)[5] Remarkably, not the iron miner, the tree chopper, the rubber farmer, nor the graphic artist ever has to gather together in a conference room to conjure up the miracle of the pencil. No central planning bureaucrat needs to direct the operation. The price system and the "invisible hand" of the market coordinate all of this. And in your lifetime, have you ever heard of a shortage of pencils? Or price-gouging by pencil makers? Pencils are, of course, a trivial matter (unless you show up without one on the morning of your SAT test). But far more sophisticated examples, from an aspirin pill (one penny for each pill) to an airline jet engine ($11 million) come to us through the same mechanism. Over time, markets deliver to consumers better products and better prices.

Perhaps the best way to look at the benefits of trade comes from asking, how many hours does an average person have to work in order to earn enough money to live and buy the stuff he wants? By this standard, over the past 150 years life just got grander and grander. In 1870 children were expected to start working at age thirteen. The retirement age was death, and in addition to three thousand annual hours "on the job," Americans performed eighteen hundred hours of home chores. They spent 61 percent of their waking hours working. By 1950 young people joined the workforce at 17.6 years and adults spent only 45 per-

cent of their waking hours working. Today, we start working at
twenty, can expect to live sixteen years in retirement, and spend
only 28 percent of our waking hours working.[6]

Look now at how purchasing power has soared. When I was
a kid, I loved to flip through the Sears Christmas "Wish Book"
catalog. I don't know if Santa caressed the same catalog, but it
seemed pretty magical. When I was thirteen years old (and no
longer believed in Santa) and wanted to learn how to develop
and enlarge film photographs, I discovered in the Sears catalog a
Kodak package that sold for roughly one hundred dollars. That
seemed expensive to me. So I wrote a letter to the president of
GAF (Kodak's competitor) describing the Kodak system and
asking whether it seemed like a good starter kit for a kid like me.
Sure enough, a few days later, a brown UPS truck drove up to my
house and the driver handed my mom a red box. Inside was a free
GAF kit and a very nice note from the president wishing me good
luck in my budding photography career (I did not have much luck.
When you are growing through the awkward "wonder years," it's
easy to trip and spill toxic chemicals in a makeshift darkroom
that is actually your parents' laundry room.) Economist Mark
Perry has done us the favor of flipping through old Sears catalogs
to compare prices over time. In 1959, for example, an average
worker would labor for over a hundred hours to afford a washing
machine. Today, it takes less than one-fourth as many hours. A
vacuum cleaner would require over a week of labor; today it takes
less than one day.[7] And despite the recent debates about inequality, note how poor households have benefited. In 1971 only about
20 percent of American homes owned a dishwasher and about 40
percent watched television in color. By 2005 about 40 percent of
poor families had a dishwasher and nearly *all* had at least one color
television. Other countries enjoyed similar wonders. As recently

as 1965 one-third of British families lacked a refrigerator, which explains a lingering tolerance for room-temperature beer.[8]

Countries that shun trade end up stagnating or sinking. After the Soviet Union splintered in 1991, I took a few days off from my job at the White House and visited Saint Petersburg, Russia. Strolling through the flaking halls of the Hermitage, I realized that communism's problem was not failing to keep up with the rising standards of 1980s America but failing to keep up with the standards of 1917 Russia. Before Fidel Castro's 1959 revolution, Cuba's GDP per capita was near the top of Latin America's rankings. In the decades that followed, as Cuba's leaders banned or confiscated private property and entrepreneurial profits, Cuba slipped to the bottom. Castro's supporters might blame the plunge on the US embargo, but that makes my point: countries that are cut off from trade (whether voluntarily or not) at best stagnate. On average, since 1959 the standard of living in Latin America has doubled. Cuba's per capita GDP has hardly budged.[9] And when you see photos of skinny peasants pushing their vintage 1956 Chevy Bel Airs, you see who has to do the budging. Now that the United States is beginning to lift the trade embargo, we might expect a more prosperous Cuba, provided Raul Castro permits a more active entrepreneurial class.

We will see in chapter 8 that in the 1800s Japan's fearsome Tokugawa shogun rulers were shocked, awed, and panicked when they saw English and Portuguese traders steam into their harbors under a black cloud of coal-fired power. The leaders had cordoned off Japan for hundreds of years, but instantly realized their country was economically and militarily retarded.

We can compare pairs of countries that chose starkly divergent paths in the 1980s and 1990s. The first of the following pairs opted to globalize; the other stayed within its own bubble:

Vietnam versus Burma; Bangladesh versus Pakistan; and Costa Rica versus Honduras. On average those countries that opened up grew at a 3.5 percent annual pace in the 1980s and 5 percent in the 1990s. The insulated economies grew by merely 0.8 percent in the 1980s and 1.4 percent in the 1990s.[10] Over time, when a country folds itself into a self-contained bubble, the economy grows stale and fetid, much like a badly aerated terrarium. Or a dank prison, which pretty much describes North Korea. In 1953, after fighting subsided in the Korean War, the north was slightly wealthier than the south. The Japanese had built factories north of the thirty-eighth parallel and in the 1950s and 1960s the USSR, China, Poland, and even Albania delivered massive aid to rebuild North Korea. Despite such kind communist assistance, today the south is seventeen times wealthier and South Koreans live ten years longer and stand several inches taller. The Koreans call it "the Miracle on the Han River."[11] North Korea does lead in a few categories, for example, executions without trial and infant mortality rate (six times higher). South Korea produces supersharp Samsung flatscreen televisions, supersmart LG refrigerators, fine Hyundai and Kia cars, and charismatic K-pop singers that elicit raving standing ovations around the world. What does the North produce? Death threats against Hollywood actors who star in stupid movies (like *The Interview*). And, presumably, those silly jumpsuits worn by Kim Jong Il.

Free trade brings vast benefits to most people. Since the time of the Phoenicians, trading nations have prospered most. Commentators, including some economists, make a big mistake when they think that a country's wealth rests on its natural resources (or in fancier words, its "factor endowment.") Look around the world. Hong Kong is a pile of rocks. And now a very rich pile of rocks. The Netherlands was a swamp. Israel was a desert without a sprig of parsley, much less oil. Now it hatches more NASDAQ technology companies than countries ten times its size and its coastline is dotted with research buildings bearing all the familiar names from Silicon Valley, including Google, Apple, Cisco, Microsoft, and Facebook. These countries believe in trade, not just in trinkets and electronic devices that you can hold in your hand, but in the free exchange of ideas.

THE FREE MARKET IS NOT A PAIN-FREE MARKET

But the free market is not a pain-free market. And we should admit that some people lose when a country opens its markets. It is hard to find a shoe that is made in America. In 2015 President Obama visited Nike's headquarters in Oregon to explain why a new global trade agreement would help Americans. If Obama looked at his wristwatch in order to time his speech, he probably would not have seen "MADE IN USA." The United States does not have a booming wristwatch industry anymore, having fallen first to the Swiss, then to the Japanese, then to the Chinese, and then to the Swiss again. Maybe Detroit's Shinola or Apple's iWatch will bring it back (though most components come from Asia).

The paradox of this chapter squeezes tight: countries need trade but trade can crumble loyalties.

WHAT IS RAGUSA?

Even to most highly educated people, the name Ragusa means nothing today. Perhaps it sounds like a popular brand of spaghetti sauce (Ragú) that an immigrant husband and wife couple from

Naples started bottling in their New York basement in the 1930s and later sold to Unilever, Lipton, and Best Foods. During Renaissance times, the Republic of Ragusa was a glorious place of riches, tucked behind beautiful rocks that drop sheer down to the sea, boasting a calm harbor, marble streets, and the most pleasant weather this side of San Diego. In *Twelfth Night*, Viola may be speaking of romantic Ragusa when she washes up along the shimmering Adriatic Sea and asks with wonder, "What country, friends, is this?" Today, Ragusa has a different name, Dubrovnik, and each year 15 million tourists trample each other and hold out selfie sticks to photograph themselves leaning against baroque buildings and pointing to the blood-orange-colored terra-cotta roofs.[12] A sixteenth-century Dominican monk named Serafino Razzi described Ragusa's tasty wines, sweet pears, fat watermelons, and fresh fish leaping atop the Adriatic. Before most of Europe, Ragusa built sewer and drainage systems and it suffered fewer plagues and famines. From 1358 to 1806 Ragusa displayed the word LIBERTAS on its flag and was virtually the only town along the Dalmatian coast not governed by Venice. Ragusa was run by a confident magistrate who, when traveling abroad, donned red stockings and red shoes, a symbol the Greeks had used to show supreme power. The Ragusa magistrate would stroll through foreign ports to the drumbeat of martial music, though he was "protected" by a dozen *unarmed* guards.

Ragusa was not entirely a paradise, though. The country was plunked down in a rough neighborhood, frequently threatened by Turks, Venetians, and brigands of all sorts. (In chapter 9, we will read of Costa Rica's leadership in a similarly rough neighborhood from the 1950s to the 1990s.) Ragusa built walls to protect itself not just from the navies of princes and sultans, but also from neighboring feudal lords and pirates. To keep its independence the Ragusa republic relied on bribes, spying, trickery, and feigning. Here is a sample of obsequious and somewhat devious missives sent to foreign chieftains:

The Ragusa Senate delivered a dispatch to the ruler of Austria: "We the sworn servants of your majesty are bound by duty to inform you of everything we learn that the Venetians are doing against your lands."

To the Holy Roman Emperor Charles V: "We are always devoted to you."

To the sultan of Turkey: "Twelve galleys of the Pope have united with 49 of the King of Spain . . . to unite with the Venetian fleet."[13]

The Ragusans explained to the Habsburg emperor Ferdinand that they pay tribute to the sultan not to preserve "our private goods, but in the name of the whole Christian Republic . . . under the banner of Christ." By paying money to the sultan, we "keep alive the religion of Jesus Christ in these parts." But then Ragusa's ambassador turns to the sultan and declares, "We care more for the lowest of the servants and slaves of your Highness than for all the Christians."[14]

Ragusa instructed its ambassadors to Constantinople: "When the pasha tells you that the Sultan wants to increase our tribute, fall on your knees, pour tears, and with most humble words beg him to desist." The ambassador was then instructed to offer a bribe of five thousand ducats to back up the tearful plea.[15]

This duplicitous yet understandable strategy worked quite well as Ragusa navigated among threats from the Turks, Venetians, Spaniards, et al. But in 1806 Ragusa collapsed before Napoleon, and the Republic had to take down the flag on its fortress that proclaimed "*NON BENE PRO TOTO LIBERTAS VENDITUR AURO*" (Liberty is not well sold for all the gold). Ragusa did not fall because it was *too poor*. Ragusa fell because it was *too rich* to stay a free republic. First, following the same tendency we saw in the prior chapter, Ragusa's surging standard of living pushed down the birthrate, especially among the bickering and intermarried aristocracy. Starting in 1500—during the "Golden Years" when Ragusa erected more buildings than it would ever construct again—Ragusa's population began to drop, from almost ninety thousand to just twenty-six thousand in the late 1600s. The average number of persons per household plunged from ten to five.[16] In a sign of upward mobility, commoners received 42 percent of bank loans and owned an overwhelming proportion of ships compared with the nobles. Ragusa's historical record does not show a national debt default crisis, as we see in Greece today.[17] The culprit was not poverty.

Despite the Latin motto on the flag, Ragusa's *libertas* was indeed undermined by gold. As Ragusa residents accumulated wealth, who remained loyal to the Ragusa Republic? From throughout the world, sacks of spices, crates of armaments, and legions of itinerant merchants arrived in port, each quite aware of his escape route. In the streets vendors squawked in Latin, Arabic, Russian, and a variety of African dialects. Catalans arrived with wool to sell. Egyptians showed up with wheat. From Saxony came miners. The standard of living went up, but communication grew tougher and loyalties frayed. As Charles V, the Holy Roman Emperor, once remarked, "I speak Spanish to my God, Italian to my women, French to my men, and German to my horse." The merchants resented the aristocrats, and the aristocrats found their numbers dwindling. Ragusa was not willing to defend itself and spent (proportionally) about one-fourth to one-half as much of its budget on its defense as other nations did. As Napoleon's soldiers stepped ashore and conquered, a contemporary witness decried the "blindness of the people and the bourgeoisie who receive the

French with open arms."[18] On the night that French troops seized the palace in 1808, Ragusa's burghers gave a ball to celebrate the end of it all.

WHERE HAVE ALL THE HABSBURGS GONE?

Like a chopped-up Magritte painting, all that is left of the Habsburgs is a homburg hat. The Habsburgs ruled much of what we now call Austria, Hungary, Poland, Romania, Czech Republic, Slovakia, Ukraine, and the Balkans. Perhaps one in ten American can trace his or her heritage to a town or hamlet ruled by the family. At one point the Habsburgs reigned over most of Mitteleuropa, along the Adriatic through Ragusa down to Montenegro, and as far to the east as Dracula's castle in Transylvania. These days the Habsburgs seldom show up in popular culture, save for appearances in Peter Shaffer's play (and later movie) *Amadeus*. In the movie, the Habsburg emperor Joseph II tells young Mozart that he likes the genius's latest opera, but he's afraid there are just "too many notes. Cut a few and it will be perfect." A sarcastic Mozart turns on the ruler and says, "Which few did you have in mind, Majesty?" History has mostly cut out the Habsburgs. Not because they were particularly evil, greedy, or musically vulgar. The Habsburgs could not hold together an empire made up of too many peoples, too many customs, and too many lands.

Like their Ottoman rivals—we'll explore them in chapter 7—the Habsburgs disintegrated with World War I. But they were on their way out before the war—following their strongest growth in four hundred years! The empire straddled Vienna and Budapest, and the last powerful monarch of the dynasty, Franz Joseph I, and his successor Charles were both emperors of Austria and kings of Hungary. Franz Joseph had a stoic, military bearing, a love of uniforms, and a very tough family life. Listen to this sequence of woes: although he escaped (with the help of a highly starched collar) an assassin's knife aimed at his neck in 1853, his brother was assassinated by a firing squad during a revolt in Mexico in 1867; his son and only heir Rudolf killed himself and his seventeen-year-old mistress in a Romeo and Juliet lovers' pact in 1889; an Italian anarchist stabbed his wife Elizabeth in the heart in Geneva in 1898; and the 1914 assassination of his heir and nephew Franz Ferdinand launched the world into the Great War. The economy of the emperor's domain was much more promising than his family life. The economy had been growing fitfully in the late 1700s and early 1800s. Then in the early 1800s Austrian weavers began to import British machines for cotton and flax, boosting productivity. In 1851 the government lifted tariff barriers that separated Austria and Hungary. In 1859 the government abolished guilds, which then made it easier for new entrepreneurs and tradesmen to compete with established businesses. A surge in modernization, which began in the 1830s, accelerated sharply between 1850 and 1873.[19] The Austrians called the period *Grunderzeit* (literally, the "founder epoch"), and it brought to Vienna a new opera house, town hall, and parliament building, as well as many migrants and merchants who moved into new tract housing. If you visit Vienna, you might drop by the Café Landtmann, which opened in 1873 and has served *Apfelstrudel* to the brooding likes of Sigmund Freud and Gustav Mahler. The opening of cafés symbolized rising disposable incomes. Between 1870 and the 1914 assassination of Archduke Franz Ferdinand in Sarajevo, per capita incomes rose much faster in the empire than in England and France. Finally, amid the galloping GDP, internal population growth slowed down, fitting the pattern we saw in the last chapter. The fertility rate decreased from 1850 to 1910 compared with the period from 1817 to 1845.[20]

Between 1870 and 1910 the Austrian-Hungarian economy roared, expanding by 128 percent.[21] You might think that a richer country could afford to calm internal tensions. But rising incomes sparked more ethnic conflict than stagnant incomes did in prior eras. In 1897 ethnic riots broke out from Vienna to Prague to beautiful Salzburg, where Mozart had learned the violin and where Maria von Trapp later yodeled. When Prime Minister Badeni, a Polish count, proclaimed that all bureaucrats must speak German and Czech, even newspapers six thousand miles away could hear a violent rumble. The *Los Angeles Herald* reported that "Unrest continues in Bohemia . . . troops patrolled the streets of Prague . . . a bomb was found last Thursday evening near the royal German theater . . . the prisons are so full . . . collisions between the students and the police have occurred at Prague, Cracow and Qrats . . . thirty newspapers have been confiscated."[22]

Visiting Vienna, Mark Twain wrote an entertaining (and politically incorrect) account of fights in parliament. He describes a "wild and frantic and deafening clamour as has not been heard on this planet since the last time the Comanches surprised a white settlement at night." Twain then describes a legislator aptly named Wolf:

"Trim and handsome . . . black hair roughed up . . . hospitable with a sword and pistol; fighter of the recent duel with Count Badeni, the head of the Government. He shot Badeni through the arm, and then walked over in the politest way and inspected his game, shook hands, expressed regret, and all that." Twain reports Wolf demanding the floor of parliament to proclaim that "we intend to find out, here and now, which is the hardest, a Pole's skull or a German's!" After catcalls, Wolf demands "an adjournment, because I find myself personally threatened. . . . Not that I fear for myself; I am only anxious about what will happen to the man who touches me."[23]

Though an overwhelming majority of the empire was Catholic and the emperor himself was personally popular and spoke many languages, the empire could not hold. With easier trade flows across borders, the population of Vienna multiplied fourfold between 1850 and 1910 as immigrants and farmers rushed to the very civilized city of Strauss's waltzes. Despite the prosperity, few champagne corks were popped. In fact, even before World War I, the Viennese complained of a siege—but from *fellow* Austrians purportedly carrying diseases and lower wages. Anyone not from Vienna (including Salzburgers, Czechs, Poles, and Hungarians) was deemed a "political unreliable." Police reported fistfights among shoppers because newcomers "touch the merchandise, put it back, haggle over the price and then don't buy it in the end." No wonder that when the Great War broke out, Austrian generals protected their troops by stationing them *outside* the city, far from the civilian wars *within*!

Viennese who traveled elsewhere within the empire faced similar sneers and a similar siege mentality. Here is an extraordinary observation from 1902 by Karl Wittgenstein, a steel tycoon friend of Andrew Carnegie and father of the philosopher Ludwig Wittgenstein: "When Viennese musicians and singers perform in Budapest, it is a cause of public annoyance." *The Magic Flute* and "The Blue Danube" so annoying that their melodies can spark a riot? Therefore, Wittgenstein points out, "the children of our country emigrate . . . to America, whose culture and language is closer to them."[24] Imagine, Austrian children in the Austria-Hungary Empire packed up their belongings to board boats and cross the stormy North Atlantic because they found they had more in common with Americans than their own "countrymen."

SCOTLAND THE BRAVE AND CONFUSED

The two powerful paradoxes explained in this and the prior chapter—(1) rich nations have fewer babies and therefore require immigrants, and (2) to get rich and stay rich, nations must trade with foreigners—are sparking nationalist and separatist movements across the globe today: the Basques and Catalans in Spain; the Kurds in Turkey; Northern League supporters in Italy; and Walloons versus Flemish in Belgium. A few years ago while visiting Rome, I heard an angry nationalist declare himself against cultural diversity: "We don't want your United Colors of Benetton!"

On September 18, 2014, the Scots rushed into voting booths to decide whether to declare their independence from the United Kingdom. Even Sean Connery—who served Her Majesty the Queen as the first 007—campaigned for separatism. The independence movement received about 45 percent of the vote, an impressive performance considering that the Tory and Labour parties battled on the same side to fight against a yes vote. Moreover, major Scottish banks and businesses threatened to flee their home offices if the yeses won.

You might think that poverty and despair drove many Scots toward breaking away from the English. But in fact, Scotland is far wealthier than it was in 1970 or 1950, when the blaze of independence was just an ember. Scotland's per capita GDP stands at about $47,000, beating the average for England and Germany. Nonetheless, a large proportion of Scots believe that this wealth has come at too high a price: too many foreigners, too many English seeking to share North Sea oil revenues, too many able-bodied adults on the dole, and too many weapons on Scottish soil, ready to be deployed in the affairs of foreign countries. Scotland's Bard, Robert Burns, wrote, "We are bought and sold for English gold." The resentment has intensified as Scotland has grown wealthier. Many Scots no longer recognize their homeland. In *Macbeth*—"the Scottish play"—Macduff asks, "Stands Scotland where it did?" The worrisome answer:

> Alas poor country!
> Almost afraid to know itself.

The splintering forces of entropy, not economic desperation, provoked the Scots to kick up their kilts.

FROM "MADE IN USA" TO "MADE WHEREVER IT'S CHEAPER"

> *My father was fired. He was technologically unemployed. He worked for the same firm for 12 years. They fired him and replaced him with a tiny gadget that does everything he does. Only it does it much better. The depressing thing is my mother went out and bought one.*
> —WOODY ALLEN, 1968

If they fired Woody's father today and replaced him with a smooth-talking engineer from Punjab, would his mother go out and get herself a svelte Sikh in a turban? We have grappled with the idea of machines replacing people ever since the first ancient

Roman winemaker used a plank and heavy stones to crush a vat of grapes instead of asking women to stomp on the grapes with their calloused toes. In 160 BC, Cato the Elder wrote a treatise on agriculture, the oldest surviving book of Latin prose, in which he explained how rocks can replace feet in winemaking. The debate on machines and computers stealing jobs away continues today with great passion. Taxi drivers do not like Uber swiping their customers away by deploying sophisticated GPS technologies and ratings systems that leave rude drivers on the side of the road. Soon Uber drivers will resent Google's self-driving vehicles. The man-versus-machine debate will rage on, but in the case of taxi versus Uber, both sets of drivers are wrestling in the same time zone and in the same country.

Workers feel threatened by a combination of foreign machines and foreign people. Further, a more globalized, trade-based economy threatens to bleed patriotism out of nations. Let's consider the United States today, which exports more goods and services than ever in history ($2.4 trillion), making up 13.4 percent of GDP. Boeing has a backlog of over five thousand unbuilt jets valued at $489 billion, most of them purchased by customers outside the United States. Hurray for Boeing. But the United States also exports jobs. If you look under the hood of Boeing's new 787, you will find that 70 percent of the aircraft is "MADE OUTSIDE THE USA" (compared with 2 percent for the original 747 in the 1970s). The wingtips flew in from South Korea, Sweden shipped Boeing the cargo doors, and Japan made the toilets and those pesky lithium-ion batteries that kept catching fire a few years ago. We have moved from "MADE IN USA" to "MADE IN WHEREVER'S CHEAPER." ABC News once asked me to visit a Best Buy store, followed by a camera crew. I flipped over radios, TVs, and DVD players like a clumsy juggler. We were hoping to find at least one gadget stamped "MADE IN USA." We found China, Malaysia, Taiwan, and Japan. Only after buying some batteries did I find "MADE IN USA." But it was not on the batteries. It was on the bright yellow plastic bag that the cashier handed me. I asked Best Buy shoppers whether they hesitated to buy from abroad. Of course they did not. A few even confessed that a "MADE IN USA" stamp might worry them, for fear of lower quality. How ironic! Back in the 1960s Sony got in trouble with US customs agents because it tried to hide "MADE IN JAPAN" by using the smallest possible font.[25]

At first the outsourcing boom of the 1990s hurt only uneducated Americans who lost factory jobs because a peasant in Guangdong could wield a screwdriver on an assembly line just as well as a Clevelander. Then call centers in India wiped out Dell Health Care clerks in Rhode Island. But the story broadens, deepens, and moves up the income ladder. It turns out that Indian radiologists can read a cancer screening just as well as an American, and a Filipino accountant can fill out a 1040 tax return without missing a decimal point. International Paper, a 117-year-old company, had roughly the same total number of employees—61,500—in 2008 as it did in 2012. But in those four years the paper company sent pink slips to eight thousand US workers and hired eight thousand outside the United States.[26]

In the long run, outsourcing likely helps the US economy by boosting productivity and increasing the available sources of intellectual and physical capital. McKinsey estimates that for every dollar of U.S. corporate spending in India, the United States gains $1.14.[27] When Walmart opens a new store in China, it hires lots of Chinese workers, but then needs more US workers to help with logistics, international marketing, and human resources. Let's conduct an extreme thought experiment. Let's say that Santa

Claus began delivering free toys and clothing all across the United States. Would the United States be better off? Yes, because we could spend our time making other things, while our kids enjoy the gifts. Here's the unavoidable follow-up question: would *everyone* be better off? No. Employees of Mattel and Hasbro might find Santa a particularly unfair trade competitor as they are laid off and sent to stand in line at state unemployment offices.

While *outsourcing* may be a new word for the twenty-first century, history shows many examples. After the Civil War, for example, many New England textile factories slinked off to the South, taking jobs with them. Not every instance of outsourcing threatens a nation's integrity. But when the outsourcing country hires another to perform its most valuable work, the outsourcer grows hollow, shaky, and vulnerable. Consider Venice at its peak, officially known as Serenissima Repubblica di Venezia. The very name boasts of serenity. And yet from the 1400s to the 1700s Venice battled the Ottomans to control the Aegean and Adriatic and occasionally skirmished with the Holy See, Austria, France, and numerous neighbors along the Dalmatian coast. Despite foreign threats, Venice managed to bring riches to its citizens through shipping, banking, the spice trade, bookbinding, and glassblowing (which can still be admired on the island of Murano). Venice was the hinge that linked Asia and Europe. Indeed, without Venice, Marco Polo might not have brought lo mein noodles from China.

So what sector did Venice outsource, plunging the republic into mortal danger? Certainly not noodles or glass. That would have been tolerable. Instead, the doges of Venice outsourced their safety, their military. The maritime republic was beholden to mercenary marines from France and Holland. And the problem with a mercenary navy is obvious: if your enemy is willing to pay more, your sailors will turn their cannons on your own forts and piazzas. And so when the Ottomans dangled more gold in front of the Venetian navy, the navy simply switched flags. The Venetian senate then hiked taxes on workers and businessmen to buy back naval loyalty, which then squashed the economy. Assaulted by pirates, in 1600 Venice's shippers were forced to pay higher insurance premiums, which rose from around 5 percent to 35 percent of the value of the cargo. In 1615 French mercenaries plotted to seize and blow up the doge's palace and murder the senators.

Just a few years earlier Shakespeare wrote of Venice's mercenaries in *Othello*. When the play opens, the brave Moor has just repelled a Turkish attack on Cyprus. The play, of course, revolves around the lies of "honest Iago," who enmeshes the tragically gullible, "erring barbarian" Othello in murder. But the real tragic history of Venice came from believing that military loyalty can be bought and secured, even if your well-funded foe incites a bidding war.

WHAT'S AN AMERICAN BRAND?

Outsourcing may make companies more efficient, but Americans pay a high price when an icon like Coca-Cola announces it is no longer an "American" brand, and when Kentucky Fried Chicken focuses more on selling drumsticks in Da Nang than in Louisville. Some CEOs even look at the US consumer as a "wasting asset," whose value inevitably declines over time, like an old metal lathe gathering dust and rust. They see 31 percent of eighteen-to thirty-four-year olds living with their moms and dads, which helps explain why only 43 percent of Millennials consider themselves "very patriotic," according to Gallup.[28] No wonder the *New*

York Times reports that only 54 percent of Americans think that the United States should have a basic "American" culture and a set of values, a percentage that slipped from 59 percent in 2004.

In some cases, US-based companies find themselves stuck in a paradox of their own. Foreigners perceive them as distinctly American companies, even as they target more and more of their business outside the United States. By placing bigger bets on foreign consumers, they become more susceptible to how foreigners view the American government and American people. Consider YUM, parent of Kentucky Fried Chicken and Pizza Hut. A few years ago, YUM was humming, with half its sales and most of its growth coming from its 4,260 restaurants in China. The share price doubled between 2009 and 2012, mostly on the Asia story. I asked a top executive why YUM triumphed. He explained that Kentucky Fried Chicken enjoyed two advantages over other chicken sellers, following its first Beijing outpost in 1987. First, Chinese consumers like eating chicken served on the bone, which McDonalds's breasts did not provide. Second, the grandfatherly image of Colonel Sanders reminded them of revered ancestors and tapped into a collective Confucian memory. But Chinese no longer look at Colonel Sanders with such affection and the brand's "desirability" dropped from 42 percent in 2012 to just 19 percent in 2015. In the first quarter of 2013 alone, sales fell 20 percent. The faltering colonel may be linked to trade and military tensions between the United States and China. When I first visited Beijing I was surprised to see Colonel Sanders's beaming face looking down from a convenient perch in Tiananmen Square, sharing almost equal billing with Mao Zedong. For a long time Kentucky Fried Chicken occupied a four-story building the size of a small palace. The company did occasionally stumble, for example, when it translated "finger lickin' good" as "we'll eat your fingers off."

But more serious trouble bit YUM in 2012 when the state-run media accused the company of injecting unsafe antibiotics in the chickens, even though subsequent testing showed no such additives.[29] Later YUM sued three Chinese firms that claimed that KFC had genetically modified its birds to grow eight legs.[30] Suddenly, with the American restaurant chain hobbling on its dubious chicken legs, Chinese-owned poultry sellers gobbled up KFC's market share. In October 2015 YUM announced it was splitting up the company, divorcing the Chinese operation from the American so that it will be called YUM China.[31] YUM tripped into its own paradox: it had grown richer by targeting China and becoming less American, but then became poorer because its new customers in China perceived it as too American.

The global economy breaks apart the concept of "Made in USA" or "Made in England" and the pride that used to accompany such logos. In a clever stunt Ralph Nader in 1996 and again in 2013 wrote to the CEOs of one hundred large corporations asking whether the CEO would stand up at the next annual meeting and on behalf of the company "pledge allegiance to the flag of the United States of America and to the Republic for which it stands . . . with liberty and justice for all." Only one company, Federated Stores, thought it was a good idea. It is easy to picture nearly every general counsel and top tax official dissuading his or her CEO from complying with Nader. Why risk their global sales, licensing, and leasing agreements? Nader then challenged twenty top unions. None of them complied.[32]

The answer to our challenges is not, of course, to discourage American companies from fighting for market share in foreign markets nor to prohibit Americans from buying foreign-made goods. Either would be a disaster. But it does require us to build other institutions that can bring people together in spirit and work.

There is good news. US companies still reign in many key fields. Apple, Google, IBM, Boeing, and Facebook top the list of the world's most admired firms. In Shanghai, police had to close down an Apple store when riots broke out over which customers would have the right to buy a new iPad model. This wasn't looting and theft; this was violence in the pursuit of paying for American technology. Nonetheless, a smaller sliver of America is producing more and more of the wealth. The problem goes beyond the usual "99 versus 1 percent" income-inequality debates. The distribution of self-confidence and work ethic is skewing sharply and dangerously. For every Mark Zuckerberg in his dorm room, thousands of young men in hoodies are sitting on a sofa in their mom's basement, bravely chasing avatars in *World of Warcraft*, but not gritty enough to climb the steps out of the basement to sign up for a training session to get a machinist's license in the world of reality. They may rank as a Supreme Commander in the basement but a zero outside the house. The maldistribution of income and work ethic breeds resentment and selfishness at both ends of the spectrum. The rich believe they are carrying an ever-heavier load, since the top 10 percent pay over 70 percent of the taxes. Meanwhile, the bottom 90 percent fear they will never achieve the middle-class standard of living that even high school dropouts could muster in the 1950s and 1960s.

Young people *and* older people have lost confidence. The Pew Research Center reports that only about 50 percent of Americans believe the future will be brighter than the present. Most startlingly, *even their view of the past* has changed. Baby boomers are growing nostalgic, so perhaps it is understandable that only 29 percent think life has improved since the 1960s. But over 50 percent of Millennials think they would have been better off if they were adults forty years ago. These perceptions are powerful and persistent. Life expectancy has been extended by almost ten years since the 1960s but somehow that shorter life of the 1960s appears to be a better life.

Feelings of *melancholia madeleine* have broken out across America and across the globe. We will need more than a cup of tea and a shell-shaped, cakey cookie to feel good again.

CHAPTER 3

The Problem with Other People's Money

DEBT

Polonius is a windbag. Though he proclaims that "brevity is the soul of wit," he drones on with all sorts of advice to his son Laertes, including his most famous: "Neither a borrower nor a lender be." This was not very original advice, even in medieval and rotten Denmark. Laertes, being a college boy, would have already known that the Bible frowns on debt and that *Leviticus* sets forth a jubilee year when debts are forgiven.[1] The ancient Hebrew word for *interest* on a loan derived from the word for a snakebite.[2] Medieval priests reinforced the message and, of course, Shakespeare crafted Shylock as a moneylender seeking his pound of flesh.[3] Religious and classical sources send a clear message: debt hurts. When we think about debt problems, we easily conjure up images of a "FORECLOSED" sign on a home, a boarded-up storefront, a pawnshop with the traditional three golden balls hanging in front, a nineteenth-century debtors' prison, or the ragged clothes of an indentured servant. This chapter will not present a thorough history of debt and bankruptcy, for you can easily find that in treatises, journals, and spoken words emanating from pulpits. Instead, I will make claims that you probably will not find in such sources. First, debt may be positively good for an individual and for a country—depending on the kind and the degree of debt. Second, as countries get richer, they are *more* likely, not less likely to get into trouble with debt. Third, as countries grow richer, they build bigger bureaucracies, aggravating their debt problem.

As nations develop, their view of indebtedness seems to go through a transformation that is like a parody of the Alcoholics Anonymous credo. Here are the three stages of viewing indebtedness:

1. Preindustrial country: debt is bad
2. Industrialized country: debt is okay, but bankruptcy is bad and carries a stigma
3. Postindustrialized country: debt and bankruptcy shed their stigma.

By the time a nation passes through all three stages, attitudes evolve from Polonius's "Neither a borrower nor lender be" to a line better suited for a contemporary comedy about slackers: "What the hell, we all screw up, don't we?" You might recognize stage 3 as a pretty good reflection of the United States in 2016.

CAN DEBT BE GOOD?

Of course, debt can be good. It is not always bad for an individual to borrow money nor is it always terrible for a government to borrow money from its citizens or its neighbors. Let's start with a quick primer on lending to businesses and individuals. Then we can move to the problem of governments. If I am running a shoe business and want to attract customers in search of black stiletto high heels, I'd better have some black stilettos to display. Naturally, the guy who makes the stilettos wants to be paid before he delivers the shoes to my retail store. Therefore, I may borrow in order to pay for the privilege of putting inventory on display. But I fully expect to sell those black stilettos and pay back the inventory loan, as well as earn a profit when my customers stumble out of the store door trying to balance on high heels. If I fail to sell the stilettos and go bankrupt, at least the lender can take back the inventory and walk around in new, unsold shoes (lawyers call this a "security interest"). This kind of lending has been going on since the first rug merchant unfurled a berber in the grand bazaar of Constantinople.

Now let's say I am an individual who has a job and wants to buy a Ford Mustang. I might have trouble coming up with thirty thousand in cash. I suppose I could try to buy the Mustang on a literal installment plan—this week I buy a steering wheel, next week a seat belt—but it would take years to accumulate all the parts and I am not a skillful enough mechanic to pull off this trick. In an episode of the old television series *M*A*S*H*, the character Radar O'Reilly mails an army jeep to his parents in Autumna, Iowa, one part at a time. Iowans tend to be more mechanical than Californians. Instead of coming up with all the money at once, a bank or an auto company will lend me funds for the car that I will pay back over, say, the next five years. If I lose my job and my ability to pay during that period, the dealer or bank can repossess the Mustang, which will still have value (unless I drive as badly as my nineteen-year-old cousin). There is nothing wrong with this kind of lending and borrowing, so long as my job is secure and I have not borrowed $300,000 to buy a Lamborghini on the salary of a short-order cook at Chili's. Similar guidelines can be cited for borrowing responsibly to buy a home.

Without any borrowing, it is hard for a country to move forward. Lending at interest creates a way to place a value on tomorrow, which promotes investment. When I first visited the island of Crete, I could not understand why I saw so many partially built homes. Did a real estate depression or a tsunami wipe out the families? It turned out that mortgages were not available and so families could build a home only to the extent they had cash on hand. Each month the family might return to the construction site with the cash needed to pay for a window, a door, or a roof. Only when the family had accumulated the entire sum needed to build the house could they move into a finished home. Of course, they would have no place to sit down, since they would wait longer to buy a sofa or chair. This seems extraordinarily cautious and, indeed, economically primitive.

If borrowing often makes sense, why do we so often hear of people and financial institutions tripping into financial trouble? The dodgy words to look for are *leverage* and *extrapolation*. *Leverage* (or *gearing*, as the Brits and Aussies call it) is borrowing money for an investment because you are convinced that the value of the investment will go up more than the interest on the debt. Leverage particularly appeals to people who think they are smarter than everyone else. Leveraged borrowers often believe in the "greater fool theory." Even if they make a foolish mistake in buying an overpriced asset, they convince themselves that an even bigger fool will come along to take it off their hands. Imagine you see a framed crayon scribble and become convinced it is the undiscovered work of Jackson Pollock. The owner will sell it to you for $1 million.

You borrow $1 million at a 10 percent interest rate because you are sure that within a year someone will pay you more than $1.1 million for the framed crayon scribble. Stranger things have happened. In the meantime, you have taken a large risk. Remember, the painting does not spin off any income while you wait for its value to go up and while you stare at it hanging above your Ping-Pong table. Also, you might consider what happens if the value of the painting plummets because, for example, art connoisseurs figure out that your Pollock was actually the work of a kindergartner named Pollak. You would still owe the lender $100,000 in interest after the first year, in addition to the $1 million in principal, which you will never recoup.

Extrapolation is another dangerous trap for the greater fool. I have often seen even investors deemed "sophisticated" jump aboard an investment idea simply because a chart displaying its price trend has consistently pointed up and to the right. From 1995 to 2008 many college endowments and pension plan trustees became convinced that commodity prices could only climb higher. Why? Because China and India would need more zinc, oil, and corn. It was a sure bet! Only a dummy could argue against the trend. The dummies eventually won the bet. The "sure bet" was a double extrapolation: rapid, endless Asian growth fueling rapid endless demand for raw stuff from the ground. Herb Stein, the droll former economic adviser to Richard Nixon and Gerald Ford (and father of actor Ben Stein), once declared, "If something cannot go on, it will stop." Rabid commodity investors ignored Stein's tautology. During 2008 and 2009 a basket of commodities lost half their value. When the Great Recession ended, commodity prices tried to climb higher again, only to flounder and flop again in 2011. When leverage and extrapolation come together they often appear both alluring and deadly. Around the time that Shakespeare penned Polonius's words, another British author named John Bridges wrote that a "foole and his money is soon parted." When I see a greater fool and his money, I wonder, "How did they get together to begin with?"

WHEN GREATER FOOLS COZY UP WITH GOVERNMENT

In the old days, when Polonius pontificated, bad debts carried a terrible stigma. A bankrupt individual could be dumped into prison, sold into slavery, or even forced to surrender his children to slavery. The British Bankruptcy Acts of 1604 and 1623 permitted certain bankrupts to be pilloried or have an ear chopped off. In a more charming punishment, some debtors in Italy would be shamed in the public square and required to bang their bare buttocks against a special rock (presumably a rock with a rough surface).[4] I am against all of these. They are cruel. Moreover, in our era of the "selfie," forcing people to bang their bare buttocks against a rock in public might even encourage narcissistic borrowers to go belly up on their debts.

In any economy that permits borrowing and lending (and we should), some borrowers will stumble because of bad luck or bad judgment. This chapter is focused on how rich nations tend to foster more reckless borrowing among the citizenry and by the government itself. Here is the key phrase to focus on: "Skin in the game." Skin in the game means that an economic actor has a personal stake in the outcome of an event. Skin in the game helps create bonds of trust in a society. For example, a borrower with skin in the game has an incentive to pay back a loan. In olden days, the risk of giving up a pound of flesh or a fleshy ear tended to inspire debtors to honor their debts. Pride and reputation also mattered. But bankruptcy has lost much of its stigma. Even before the Great Recession hit in 2008, California bankruptcies had soared 85 percent in just a few years. The concept of walking away from a home was shameful to prior generations. But today, it may be sound advice. Witty debtors even came up with a cute phrase: "jingle mail"—sending the bank an envelope that holds the keys to the abandoned house.

During the Great Recession we learned what happens when real estate borrowers do not have a big enough personal stake in the outcome of their lending arrangements. In the 1980s a couple buying a home would typically come up with 20 percent of the money needed (the down payment). If the couple failed to make mortgage payments, a sheriff would force them from the house and they would forfeit the 20 percent equity they invested. Over the next twenty years down payments shrank and the federal government created incentives so that banks stuffed more and more money into the hands of more risky borrowers. For example, in 1995 the US Department of Housing and Urban Development required Fannie Mae and Freddie Mac (government-chartered finance firms) to purchase riskier mortgages, known as subprime mortgages. By pressuring Fannie Mae and Freddie Mac to purchase shaky loans, the federal government essentially told bankers: "Don't worry, we'll take the blame if your home buyers turn out to be deadbeats, or merely imprudent." The government in Washington, DC, deliberately made it cheaper for banks to lend more money to borrowers who seemed to be poor risks. By 2006 nearly one in four new mortgages was considered subprime and in the state of California 90 percent of new mortgages were of the adjustable rate type, which could quickly backfire on home buyers.[5] Borrowers got more access to more credit, with less reason to worry about paying it back. That is, less skin in the game.

Here is the nature of what took place in San Diego, where home prices doubled from 2001 to 2006 and then plunged by 40 percent in just one year, 2008.[6] We start with "Mr. and Mrs. I Deserve Four Bedrooms and a Jacuzzi, Even Though I Never Saved a Dime in My Life." They visited the mortgage broker, who wanted to collect his fee, and the banker, who knew that Fannie Mae and Freddie Mac would probably take the mortgage loan off his hands. "Mr. and Mrs. I Deserve Four Bedrooms and a Jacuzzi . . . " did not put any money down, and in some cases, did not even show their income tax return to the bank. I asked bankers how they could explain granting mortgages without inspecting tax returns. They explained that in a bubble environment, fueled by the dangerous yet enticing combination of (1) easy lending standards, (2) great fools, and (3) extrapolation, local bankers simply could not keep up with the paperwork. Everyone was making money on the deals. Advertisements on radio stations claimed that ordinary laypeople could "earn" millions flipping homes. One banker confessed to me, "We didn't want to ask for a tax return, because we didn't want to embarrass our customers." Embarrassment was not the great risk. The great risk was that the loans would fail and the American taxpayer would be caught losing, not an ear, but confidence in a rigged system.

Despite a stock market crash, millions of jobs lost, and endless congressional hearings following the Great Recession, the federal bureaucracy does not seem to have learned many lessons about leverage, extrapolation, greater fools, or skin in the game. In October 2014 Mel Watt, the head of the federal agency that oversees Fannie Mae and Freddie Mac, proclaimed that the agencies should once again back mortgages with down payments as low as 3 percent. Even home building executives, who must maintain good relations with government regulators, were surprised.

Robert Toll, chairman of Toll Brothers Inc., called Watt's plan "really dumb."[7] Where did Watt deliver his speech proposing a return to skimpy down payments? The Mandalay Bay Hotel in Las Vegas. A choice venue for rolling the dice.

As social bonds fray and people act as if they have less skin in the game, trust goes down. What goes up? The appeal of get-rich-quick schemes. Drive across the country listening to AM radio and you will swear that many stations stay on the air simply by selling advertisements to companies that hawk investments in gold and shout about the inevitability of a collapsing dollar. Sure enough, the price of gold skyrocketed during the Great Recession; but then it collapsed over the past two years. While staying at a New York hotel recently, I turned on the television and was surprised to see Ed Kranepool on camera. When I was a little kid, the lumbering Kranepool played first base for the Mets. What was Ed telling me through the television speakers? "Buy gold." I looked at the screen and thought, "Ed, why should I listen to you? You were a lifetime .260 hitter. Maybe if the gold company hired Pete Rose, I'd listen. Rose was a crooked gambler, but at least he hit .300." The ultimate theme of the gold ads is this: the future is bleak, everyone is ripping you off—so you'd better get rich quick or you'll go broke before the next commercial break.

WHY PUBLIC DEBT IS WORSE THAN PRIVATE DEBT

In many important ways, public debt is more dangerous than private debt. Let's say your dad is a deadbeat, who turns out to have been a compulsive shopper on the Home Shopping Network and eBay. When he dies you inherit nothing, except funeral instructions to bury him in the slightly overdone casket he acquired, featuring Liberace-like lamps bolted to the lid. At the funeral, as the pallbearers lower the coffin into the ground, a lawyer representing grieving and aggrieved retailers pulls you aside and says, "Sorry for your loss, but your father racked up millions of dollars in shopping debt. We insist that you pay us." Your legal reply: "Hop in the hole with Dad, 'cause I'm not responsible for his debts." Debts die with the parent.[8] You can inherit your father's eye color, droopy lips, or heroic square jaw, but you will not inherit his debts. If he finagled or inveigled department stores or auto dealers into extending credit, they can share the blame and shoulder the burden for their lax investigative skills. In most cases, creditors are more sophisticated than debtors and are in a good position to check credit ratings, property deeds, and income tax forms before lending.

When congressmen and presidents rack up debt, however, the debts do not die when they leave office or when they shuffle off this mortal coil. In many cases, the debts multiply themselves, creating an even larger burden on the generations to come, generations who do not yet have the right to vote. Since 1961 the United States budget has been in deficit every year except for five. This is not just a string of bad luck; it is the logic of the system. The American Revolution was fought, in part, under the banner "NO TAXATION WITHOUT REPRESENTATION." But who represents future generations who cannot find their way to the ballot box because they have not yet been born? Future generations, whether they like it or not, must rely on patriotism, ethics or, as Tennessee Williams called it "the kindness of strangers." Williams, incidentally, died drunk and alone. In Washington, DC, and political capitals throughout the world, one frequently hears speeches dedicated to the "youth of tomorrow." Aren't today's politicians and voters motivated to protect the interest of their descendants? Yes, a bit. But not a lot.

HAMILTON VERSUS HAMILTON

Alexander Hamilton was a scrappy fighter born out of wedlock who made his way from a shipping clerk's job in Saint Croix to treasury secretary of the United States in 1789. He understood competition and ambition. But he could also be a bit idealistic, as when he suggested that citizens would choose "fit men" as legislators who would somehow rise above petty self-interest:

> A man of virtue and ability, dignified with so precious a trust, would rejoice that fortune had given him birth at a time, and placed him in circumstances so favorable for promoting human happiness . . . to do good to mankind, from this commanding eminence, he would look down with contempt upon every mean or interested pursuit.[9]

Hamilton envisaged noble leaders and urged the federal government to issue debt. He even pushed for the federal government to pay off the $25 million in IOUs that the states had accumulated during the Revolution, in addition to a $70 million national debt, and about $7 million in IOUs issued by George Washington and his generals during the Revolutionary War. At the time, many of the state debts were trading at perhaps fifteen cents on the dollar. Hamilton believed that paying off state debt would lift the stature and reputation of the US federal government, allowing it to borrow in the future on more favorable terms. By issuing debt, Hamilton thought that he could align the moneyed class with the new nation. In other words, lenders would be on the same hook as the borrowing country. Hamilton stunned the crusty Whigs by declaring that "a national debt if not excessive will be to us a national blessing."[10] Hamilton did set forth limits on borrowing, of course, suggesting a kind of "sinking fund," whereby the United States would not incur new debts before paying off old debts. Further, the country's budget revenues would not be exceeded by its spending, including interest on the debt.

Hamilton's idea worked pretty well while the United States was a relatively poor country. The country paid off the massive Revolutionary War debt by the 1830s and Civil War debt shrank by the turn of the twentieth century. But as the country grew richer in the twentieth century, the discipline of paying off debt subsided. Today, US federal debt held by the public equals 75 percent of GDP, and over 100 percent if you add money owed to the Treasury by government trust funds, for example, Social Security. Which raises the following question: if a rich country sheds its philosophical bias toward fiscal discipline and shreds a powerful strain of patriotism, how strongly will politicians and voters protect future generations? Instead of Alexander Hamilton we can turn to the twentieth-century biologist William Hamilton for some sobering clues.

When governments are given the power to borrow they are given authority to bind future citizens, who are strangers to them. Yet human beings are not designed to care a great deal about strangers and especially about the unborn children and grandchildren of strangers. Our biology favors our immediate family and the present time. In an earlier chapter I pointed out that fathers are far more willing to pay for their own child's education than for a stepchild's. In the 1940s a twelve-year-old British boy named William Hamilton was playing with a few leftover items that his father had used in World War II. Unfortunately, the items were not canteens or maps of the Rhineland. They were hand grenades. One grenade exploded, blowing off several of the boy's fingers. His mother, trained in first aid, rushed young William to the hospital, where the doctors saved his life, though they could not save all of his fingers. The boy later went off to study at St. John's College, Cambridge, and spent much of his career investigating how families look after each other. Hamilton developed brilliant and original insights into the theory of evolution that we can apply to political economy. Hamilton realized that the caricature of a selfish, Darwinian "survival of the fittest" was too harsh to explain many behaviors. It does not explain why a parent sacrifices for a child. Some of these sacrifices may be dramatic and fatal, for example, jumping in front of a car to push an endangered child aside. Others may be less thrilling, for example, a mother saving money that will be passed down as an inheritance after she dies.

Hamilton showed that people may make tremendous sacrifices but those sacrifices will be in proportion to how closely they are related to the person who benefits.[11] A parent shares 50 percent of her genes with her child. A grandparent shares 25 percent, a first cousin 12.5 percent, a second cousin 3.125, and a stranger 0. Before going through a mathematical example of Hamilton's theory of *inclusive fitness*, we can summarize the conclusion in this offhanded way: a man would gladly die to save two brothers or four first cousins or eight second cousins. Hamilton used the equation $c < br$, meaning that a person will sacrifice for someone else, if the cost (c) of the sacrifice is outweighed by the benefit (b) multiplied by how closely related (r) the beneficiary is. A simple example: Your brother Josh asks you for ten dollars because he is convinced he can swap it for twenty-five dollars. Your sacrifice (c) is ten dollars. You share 50 percent of your DNA with Josh. Since $25 times 50 percent equals $12.50, which is more than $10, you would likely cough up the $10 for Josh. Now let us say second cousin Rusty stumbles along asking for $10 and expecting the same $25 swap. In his case, $25 times 0.03125 equals just 78 cents. Sorry, Rusty, but your second cousin is not that into you. Hamilton (though he had played with hand grenades) was no dummy. He realized that his mathematical rule did not apply to everyone and was too precise. Many people donate to charities and anonymously drop dollars into tip jars and Salvation Army pots at holiday time. My wife and I have sponsored theater performances at schools and I snap up cookies when Girl Scouts come knocking at my door, not so much because I love all the cookies but because the process brings back fond memories of my sister and my daughters in their Brownie uniforms. Nonetheless, for looking at large swaths of populations, Hamilton's basic approach has merit. Of the Thanksgiving pilgrims in 1620, 50 percent died after the first winter. Those who died had fewer genetic relatives than the survivors. A more recent study of three hundred old women in Los Angeles asked, "Who helps you the most when you have trouble?" The most frequent answer: close kin. Even squirrels are kinder to kin. Field biologists have reported that when a squirrel sees a coyote, he will warn his nearby brethren and risk bringing attention to himself. But if there are only strangers about, the squirrel will simply slink off and save his own skin.[12]

In the Conclusion, we will see how nations can create bonds that go beyond DNA in order to elicit sacrifice, inspire savings, and engender a spirit of brotherhood. Without these new bonds, people may act more squirrelly, rather than charitably or heroically. The Alexander Hamilton imperative to borrow turns out to be more dangerous in a rich, William Hamilton country of large, diverse populations and fewer familial relations.

PARADOX OF THRIFT VERSUS PARADOX OF THEFT

John Maynard Keynes was a quick-witted, sharp-penned bon vivant from Cambridge University. He was also the most influential economist in the world from roughly 1930 to 1980. During the Great Depression he devised a clever concept later called the "paradox of thrift." In Keynes's model, savings could be a bad thing. If suddenly everyone began to spend less on autos and stuff more into their bank accounts, the economy would tip into recession. He pointed out that, paradoxically, people will end up with less extra income to save. Keynes said, "The more virtuous we are, the more determinedly thrifty . . . the more our incomes will have to fall."[13] This claim was a punch in the gut to everyone from Polonius to Ben Franklin. In Keynes's world a penny saved is a penny *ruined*. Keynes's followers, notably the Nobel laureate Paul Samuelson, brought the paradox of thrift into textbooks across the world and later used it to justify fighting recessions with government spending rather than tax cuts.[14] Certainly, if all shoppers suddenly go on strike, the economy will wobble badly. But the paradox of thrift has its own flaws. For example, if savings go up, interest rates decline, which may spur more investment. Empirical evidence appears to show that higher national savings rates are correlated with stronger, not weaker, growth.[15]

Our task here is not to debate the validity of Keynesian economics. Please go to my *New Ideas from Dead Economists* for that discussion. Our task is to look at the flip side of the paradox of thrift, which I will call the "paradox of theft." Typically, as a family grows wealthier, it is less likely to fall into deep debt, default, and bankruptcy. A family in the top 5 percent of income typically owes half as much as a typical family in the bottom

95 percent (the ratio of their debt to income). Now we have all heard of exceptions, from Ulysses S. Grant (whose face appears on the fifty-dollar bill) to the bankrupt singers Meat Loaf and 50 Cent (whose faces do not appear on any currency). But on average affluent people sleep more soundly and happiness surveys show that money does buy some peace of mind. So what's the paradox? My research shows that the opposite is often true for the finances of individual countries—*wealthier nations may pile up proportionately more debt than poorer nations!* Amid the onslaught of the Great Recession in 2010, developing countries like Mexico, Vietnam, and Russia had smaller debt burdens than the United States, Japan, and the Eurozone. While the United States stacked up debt equal to about 75 percent of its annual output, Russia owed only 10 percent. When the US annual budget deficit soared to over 10 percent of GDP, Russia's deficit was less than 4 percent, Mexico's was less than 3 percent, and Indonesia boasted of a balanced budget. Why do you think in February 2014 Vladimir Putin could simultaneously (1) strut bare-chested through Crimea; (2) scoff at UN condemnations; and (3) goad vicious Russian separatists in Ukraine but then sit back to watch Russian bond yields rise just 0.55 point over the next two months, from 4.65 to 5.2 percent? Because Russia—a far less wealthy nation than the United States—did not borrow as much from foreigners as the United States and its "rich" allies.[16] On the eve of the Great Recession in 2008, when the US debt ratio was 39 percent, Mexico's was under 17 percent, and Russia's was about 10 percent.[17]

Now, I am not arguing that it is better to live in a poor country than in a rich country, or that poor governments are smarter or more honest than rich governments. They are not and many do sometimes stumble into debt crises. (When commodity prices imploded in 2014–2015, so did the Russian economy.) Still, we must grapple with the paradox of theft, and ask, why do richer nations often pile up more debt? Why is this the logic of rich nations? Three reasons emerge.

First, because rich nations *can* borrow more. Banks and bond buyers are more comfortable lending to rich nations. Rich nations tend to pay back their loans. Alexander Hamilton was right: by demonstrating a history of paying back debts, a nation builds a stronger reputation, which then allows it to take on more debt. A rich nation also has real assets to back up loans: trains, planes, tollbooth revenues, railroads, etc. And since the US dollar is still considered the world's prime currency of exchange, bankers willingly accept promissory notes denominated in dollars. In fact, the US government makes money every time it simply prints a piece of paper with "$100" engraved on it (a practice known as seignorage). People around the world give the US Mint one hundred dollars of value in exchange for a slim six-inch piece of paper that costs just about nothing. Weaker countries such as Mongolia do not issue much debt in their native currency. Few lenders will accept the Mongolian tugrik as collateral. Instead, Mongolia promises to pay back its debts in US dollars.

Second, rich nations begin to pile up more debt because their fertility rates fall, as we saw in chapter 1. As the ratio of retirees to workers increases, they must access more goods without actually producing those goods. In an extreme example, Japan's debt-to-GDP ratio has soared from about 50 percent in 1980 to 245 percent today. *If the fertility rate falls below the replacement rate, it is almost impossible to pay down accumulating debt.*

Third, as nations grow richer, the bonds that tie future generations frequently begin to fray. Who is burgled in the paradox of theft? Young people. Consider two Americans: (1) a baby boomer turning sixty-five this year and (2) an infant just riding home from the maternity ward at the hospital. The boomer will rake in $327,000 more in lifetime Social Security and Medicare benefits than he paid in federal taxes. The newborn had better brace herself. She will pay $421,000 more in federal taxes than she will ever receive in future benefits.[18] To fund government programs, her lifetime tax will need to be nudged up to about sixty cents on every dollar earned. And those earned dollars will be harder to come by.

One of my daughters recently asked me to buy our family an electric scooter. I wasn't sure what she meant.

"You know," she explained, "the scooters you see people ride at Costco."

I didn't like the idea. "That's ridiculous. First of all, we all need more exercise. Second, electric scooters are expensive. I'm not paying for it. Forget it."

She had a retort ready. "Don't worry, Dad. I saw it on TV. Medicare will pay for it!"

The television advertisement does not, of course, explain who will pay for Medicare.

In a scary way, many politicians today are willing to sacrifice young people, not merely to pay bills for old people, but for their narrow and near-term political reputations. Here is a simple example. The US government borrows money by issuing bonds, bills, and notes. Lots of them. But how long do those IOUs typically last? Seventy percent of US debt has a duration of less than five years. Much of it will be rolled over when it comes due, possibly at much higher interest rates. Today's politicians are like game-show contestants playing with someone else's future. Now, it is true that America has been the land of the game show since Groucho Marx dangled a toy duck in front of the faces of contestants in the 1950s. Whether watching *Jeopardy*, *Let's Make a Deal*, or *Wheel of Fortune*, at some point just about all of us have screamed at a contestant, "Don't be stupid—take the money!" That's what American citizens should have been screaming at the US Treasury Department over the past few years. Between 2009, when President Obama moved into the White House, and 2015 the federal government racked up $7.5 trillion of debt. Prior presidents had together amassed about $10.6 trillion.[19] We do not know how we are going to pay it back. And yet the world was willing to lend us ten-year money at rates substantially below 3 percent, in some years, as low as 1.6 percent.

So why did the US Treasury not give tomorrow's children a break by taking a deal and issuing fifty- or one-hundred-year bonds, locking in those puny rates for a lifetime? You might think that no one would trust that a government would be around in fifty or a hundred years. But corporations have successfully auctioned long-term bonds. Disney issued "Sleeping Beauty" bonds and the market scooped them up. According to the *Los Angeles Times*, "demand proved greater than the company had anticipated." Norfolk Southern enjoyed a similar reception in 2010 when the railroad issued hundred-year bonds. CBS News reported that "institutional investors bought them like crazy, leading Norfolk Southern to more than double the issue." Imagine, buying hundred-year bonds from a railroad. Will rails even exist in the twenty-second century? Dozens of other companies, including Coca-Cola, IBM, Federal Express, and Ford have also issued hundred-year debt.

It doesn't take a mastermind to understand the benefit of issuing ultra-long bonds, but institutions of higher education— including the University of Pennsylvania, Ohio State, the University of Southern California, and Yale have also issued hundred-year bonds. Governments across the globe are also grasping the concept. In 2010 buyers even grabbed Mexico's hundred -year bonds, despite a pockmarked history of devaluations and defaults that stretch from 1827 to 1994.

Japan, France, and the United Kingdom already sell bonds with durations of forty years or more.

Instead of taking Disney's and Mexico's lead, the US Treasury recklessly borrowed short-term funds that must be rolled over. The average maturity of UK debt is three times longer than US debt. The Obama administration claims that it has taken advantage of low yields and has in fact extended the average duration of debt. But it is a flimsy boast. Yes, duration has moved up to just about five years, but that is still short of the early 1990s and well below the 2001 record of about six years. And let's put the 2001 comparison in perspective. In 2001 ten-year Treasuries yielded 5.16 percent. In 2012, the ten-year hovered just above 1.60 percent, before climbing above 2 percent in 2015. If policy makers were more prudent and more committed to future generations, they would have smashed the 2001 record, not gazed up at it. According to the minutes of the Treasury Borrowing Advisory Committee, the acting director of debt management stated that the Treasury wants to "remain flexible." Sometimes flexibility is good, if, for example, you are a rubber band, a Slinky, or a clown at the Big Apple Circus. But if you're a debt manager with the opportunity to lock in borrowing rates that will help avoid a financial catastrophe, it's better to be firmly in place.

So why did the administration choose to play the role of the feebleminded game show contestant? The answer probably does not come from feeblemindedness. Round up the usual suspects: shrewd political self-interest and a bias toward the short term. Because short-term debt yields are typically the lowest on the yield curve (a graph that usually shows that it costs more to borrow for a longer term), borrowing short gives the illusion of a lower budget deficit, flattering the president's fiscal profile. With a generous Federal Reserve squeezing short rates down to zero, the interest cost of existing debt looks pretty meager at 1.4 percent of GDP.

But this is a terrible trade-off that made President Obama look better while almost guaranteeing that our children are worse off. Issuing hundred-year bonds, or at least fifty-year bonds, would have required a higher interest rate, perhaps 3 or 4 percent. Sure, that would put more pressure on near-term deficit reports. But leaders should be willing to let their personal image accept a dent, if it clearly helps their constituents. Locking in a hundred years of borrowing at a 3 or 4 percent rate would have been the biggest bargain since Michelangelo agreed to paint Pope Julius's ceiling.

President Obama's advisers should have admitted that our relatively short-term debt imperils American citizens. If yields jump back to normal levels, deficit estimates would soar by $4.9 trillion over the next ten years.[20]

Would you advise a friend who's buying a home to accept an adjustable teaser-rate mortgage that could catapult higher in a few years? In today's environment, teaser rates are for fly-by-night salesmen. The United States should not be a fly-by-night country.

The stakes and risks are clearly much higher than anything Bob Barker or Drew Carey ever offered on *The Price Is Right*. One of these days when the government tries to roll over America's paper, rates will have catapulted much higher, and the world's financial system will look at the US taxpayer and announce: "Game over. You lose."

To tackle the paradox of theft we need new institutions that can link society both vertically and horizontally, not just people of diverse ethnicities and job titles, but people of different generations. What voice do infants have in the backslapping back room of Congress's Ways and Means Committee? Politicians will often show off photos of themselves looking hale while climbing mountains or fording streams in national parks. They say they favor conservation so that future generations will enjoy camping under the stars or snapping photos of bald eagles perched in tall cottonwood trees. What a shame if an avalanche of our debt buries our grandchildren so deeply that they have to sell off national treasures to make ends meet.

THE RISK OF HOT MONEY

In our modern high-tech era of finance, bad debt management grows even more dangerous. "Hot money" speeds up markets across the world, as if a wild fire hose started spraying crystal methamphetamine on trading desks. In Martin Scorsese's *The Wolf of Wall Street*, the main character boasts that he swallows and snorts "enough drugs to sedate Manhattan, Long Island, and Queens for a month." A great line. But based on my experience in the hedge-fund world, this is a total misrepresentation. Wall Street, London, Frankfurt, and Beijing are not overly *sedated*. That might be better. The problem is they're amped up on Adderall, Red Bull, and oolong tea.

To understand hot money flows, let's start with a simple domestic scene: In the old days of black-and-white television shows like *Leave It to Beaver*, moms and dads wanting to buy a home would drive to their sleepy local bank. They knew the banker and he knew whether they were good credit risks. Their kids got lollipops. (I remember those lollipops.) Even in *The Beverly Hillbillies*, the poor-mountaineer-turned-millionaire Jed Clampett knew his comic banker, Mr. Drysdale. If the Cleavers or the Clampetts borrowed money, the bank would be on the hook. Therefore, the banker had a big incentive to keep an eye on the monthly payments. In later decades Wall Street teamed up with Fannie Mae to turn loans into tradable securities and sever the connection among saver, banker, and borrower. By 2006 a local bank that issued a mortgage might send 98 percent of the debt to Wall Street, leaving the local banker with almost no incentive to monitor the loan. As we saw earlier, the banker no longer had skin in the game. This distance propelled the housing price explosion of the 2000s and the bust of the Great Recession. But that's not the whole story. The international hot money problem doubles the trouble.

Across the world today, investors' eyes sweep across computer screens seeking the "next next thing." It could be a tech stock, an oil rig, or even a particular country's stock market. Investors stand ready, locked, loaded, fingers on the trigger. Walking across any trading floor, you can hear the chatter: "Costa Rica's ready to fly!" "If Facebook crosses eighty bucks, I'm all in!" "Get me *all* the Panama bonds!" When short-term investors get a whiff of a potential boom, they squeeze the trigger, firing billions of dollars at the target. As the barrage strikes, the price of the asset shoots higher. So what's the problem? Many of these stocks and even many of these countries are *simply too small* to safely absorb billions or trillions of dollars worth of enthusiasm. (When I served as a managing director of the legendary $15 billion Tiger hedge fund, we actually bought two-thirds of Canada's bond auction. And Canada's a pretty big country!) Remember, enthusiasm can wane. Maybe it's a sour headline about a crooked politician or a canceled inventory order from a big player like Walmart. If those trigger-happy investors start feeling nervous about their stakes and begin to pull their money out, what happens? Of course—a bloody crash.

During the 1990s Thailand, Indonesia, Malaysia, and South Korea were roaring. "You just can't lose on the 'Asian Tigers,'" Wall Street advisers shouted: "They are unstoppable export superstars!" In 1996 private investors stuffed $93 billion into those four modest-sized countries. Malaysia's stock market doubled in just one year! But stuffing so many billions into those countries drove up the value of their currencies, which then made it tougher for them to export cheap stuff. So in 1997 suddenly everyone seemed to get queasy and investors yanked out over $12 billion. The about-face equaled more than 10 percent of their combined GDP. Their currencies started crumbling and their citizens could no longer afford lunch, much less automobiles and homes. Deadly riots broke out, killing a thousand civilians in Indonesia, while headlines screamed of looting, mass rape, and finally a xenophobic metaphor, "the rape of Asia by Wall Street traders." The violent swings of the entropic world economy devastated common people who never realized their lives depended on the whims of amped-up wolves on Wall Street.

Though this book does not focus on environmental downfalls, we can also see how the modern economy can more easily spread disease. For most of human history, men and women did not travel more than a few miles from their homes. As scientist and best-selling author Jared Diamond points out, flora, fauna, and people kept their distance, separated by mountains, oceans, and seas. But travelers, whether in diasporas, crusades, or migrations, carried infections to vulnerable populations. Until World War II, more war victims died of microbes accidentally introduced by the enemy than from battle wounds.[21] Globalization has opened up the world to free trade for services, manufactured goods—and pathogens. Just as human mobility has increased a thousandfold since 1800, so has microbe and pestilence travel.

Dengue fever travels inside the Asian tiger mosquito, which sails across the seas in containers of used tires. In the ballast water of supertankers, aggressive zebra mussels find their way from Russia to the Great Lakes. With every jet that lands at Heathrow or JFK, an infinite number of microbes disembark, looking for new hosts. Thirty years ago brown tree snakes started arriving in Guam, where they've managed to kill off most of the forest birds. Now they hitchhike to Hawaii as stowaways in the wheels of Airbus jets. The USDA estimates that the traveling snakes could cause $600 million to $2.1 billion of damage in medical incidents and power outages each year. To beat back the snake invasion, the USDA sends helicopters over the forests, where they drop dead mice laced with acetaminophen (Tylenol), which poisons the reptiles.[22] Of course, the solution is not to ban airplanes. Those same airplanes that inadvertently transport nettlesome snakes may deliberately carry precious vaccines and lifesaving medical instruments in their cargo holds. We must face up to such paradoxes and figure out how best to deliver meds while blocking the snakes from coming aboard.

To rich nations like the United States and the United Kingdom, poorer nations used to seem remote. They were deemed beyond the pale or in the heart of darkness, seen only by daring explorers or salesmen for the East India Company. Now, the world has shrunk in size, microbes could qualify for frequent-flier points, the problems of the poor are visited on the rich, and the rich in turn churn out their own problems from within. And those problems get handed over to a new generation.

CHAPTER 4

The Problem with Work

About five years ago, an engineer working for an electric utility company in Florida asked for my advice on what her living-at-home twentysomething college grad son should do. He could not find work in Cocoa Beach, along the so-called Space Coast, and the state's overall jobless rate hit 10 percent.

"Does he have a mortgage?" I asked.

"No."

"A spouse?"

"No."

"Kids?"

"No, Joshy just graduated a few years ago."

"Then tell Joshy to grab a cheap flight on Southwest to Fargo, North Dakota. He'll have to change planes and hop the overnight Greyhound in Omaha, but the unemployment rate is just 2.9 percent. Joshy will nab a job as soon as the captain turns off the fasten seat belt light." I also asked if Joshy liked skiing or maple syrup, since Vermont's jobless rate was just 4.5 percent.

My conversation with Joshy's mother encapsulates the challenges of a rich, indebted, over-bureaucratized country. When a rich nation begins to shatter, people do not go hungry. They simply stop waking up as early to fix breakfast. When rich nations begin to shatter, everyone has a comfy bed—but fewer people have a reason to get out of it. As confidence ebbs and debt piles up, the work ethic suffers. Each month the Department of Labor publishes a nerdy number called the Labor Participation Rate. That's the proportion of adults who want to work. It has been falling for the last seventeen years to about 63 percent and is now beneath the level of the late 1970s. Why is that shocking? Because in the 1970s millions of women had not yet figured out how to enter the workforce; many called themselves "homemakers" or faced insurmountable discrimination. Since women now have more opportunities to work, the overall adult participation rate should trounce the '70s level. It does not. And in West Virginia, fewer than half the adults now work, about the same as forty years ago.[1]

I should point out that many of the statistics I cite in this chapter pertain only to men. During the twentieth century, the employment trends for women were contorted by discrimination and cultural norms, which dramatically dampened the ability of willing females to get jobs. Beginning in the 1950s female labor participation began to soar, doubling from 35 percent to 75 percent in the 1990s. Since 2000, though, even the likelihood of a female working began to slip.

So why has the proportion of adults working slid so sharply during the past fifteen years? Retiring baby boomers explain only a part (and their impact began to hit only since 2010), according to the Federal Reserve Boards of Chicago and of Philadelphia.[2] Many Generation Xers and Yers, who are nowhere near retirement age, have shed their ambition to take full-time jobs. About 11 million Americans have quit and have successfully filed for disability payments. That's double the 1995 number and odd since, as I will discuss later in this chapter, jobs are safer and less physically strenuous than ever before. We cannot just blame the feeble recovery from the Great Recession for the dropping Labor Participation Rate. In the spring of 2015 the Department of Labor reported 5.4 million job openings, the highest since it began compiling the series in 2000.[3] Granted, not every job opening is well-matched for a job seeker. We need more software engineers and more respiratory therapists aiding medical patients rather than more mortgage brokers baying for borrowers. A report by Deloitte found that 600,000 jobs in manufacturing went unfilled in 2011, even though the overall unemployment rate averaged over 8 percent.[4] Now, perhaps the wages for these jobs were not attractive enough. More likely, though, we are seeing a structural swing, almost like a shift in tastes. Just as people have decided they prefer low-fat milk to full-fat milk, tens of millions have decided that they do not care much for the idea of showing up for work in the morning and staying on the job till the end of the day. While news reports tout the amazing success of Mark Zuckerberg, Sergey Brin, Elon Musk, and other entrepreneurial wizards, the sad truth is that even the level of entrepreneurship in America has reached a thirty-year low.[5]

ONCE UPON A TIME EVERYONE WORKED

If we scroll back the calendars to a poorer time, from 1850 to 1900, an overwhelming majority had no choice but to work or to starve. It was a bleak choice. About 90 percent of males over the age of sixteen worked.[6] For how many years did people work? The average retirement age was "death," since life expectancy was so much lower than today. In poorer southern states, even children were often expected to hold jobs. In Alabama and North Carolina over 50 percent of the children aged ten to fifteen worked full-time.

Immigrants toiled even harder and were more likely to be working than the native-born. This makes sense, since foreigners (unless they were rich) often had to prove they had strong backs and calloused hands in order to qualify for a rocky boat trip to the United States. Only the wiliest slacker could sneak aboard a ship crossing the Atlantic or Pacific.[7] The *Titanic* was a real ship in 1912 and the steerage decks were jam-packed with hundreds of immigrants seeking jobs, but the scamp played by Leonardo DiCaprio in the blockbuster film was fiction.

Before the twentieth century societies had to grapple with what to do with old people who were too feeble to earn their keep but too hungry to skip lunch. We hear ancient tales of Inuits sending old people out to sea on ice floes or grizzled Hindus in the former Madras region in the south (now known as Tamil Nadu) deliberately forced into renal failure by drinking too much coconut water. In his dystopic novel *The Fixed Period* (1882), Anthony Trollope imagined a breakaway colony of Britain called Britannula. It is 1980 and the parliament passes a law that any citizen reaching the age of sixty-seven must be sent to Necropolis and cremated at age sixty-eight. The protagonist, a farmer named Crassweller, is still robust and hearty in his sixties. So he does the heroic thing: he lies about his age. In a more recent satire, the 2015 television series called *Younger* depicts an over-the-hill forty-year-old woman lying about her age and claiming to be twenty-six in order to land a job in publishing and to avoid psychological death. The lead character is played by Sutton Foster, who earned Broadway's Tony award for playing heroines who break social rules in two different Roaring 1920s–era shows, *Thoroughly Modern Millie* and *Anything Goes*.

Trollope's *Fixed Period* found a fan in the turn-of-the-century "founder of modern medicine," Sir William Osler. In his farewell retirement address at Johns Hopkins Hospital in 1905, Osler suggested mandatory chloroform at age sixty, stating that the "effective, moving, vitalizing work of the world is done between the ages of twenty-five and forty." His textbook on medicine called pneumonia "the old man's friend," a disease that Osler himself succumbed to at age seventy.[8] Was Osler serious about forcible chloroform? Probably not. He was known as a practical joker and once tricked the editors of the *Philadelphia Medical News* into publishing a fake paper on *penis captivus*, a very rare disease in which intercourse resembles a Chinese finger trap prank. Osler's backing of Trollope's *Fixed Period* was likely just for laughs. But until the last hundred years, few others found the plight of old people comic or the source of any relief.

If you tally up the most remarkable feats of rich nations in the twentieth century, this one stands out—*they generated enough wealth so that old people could stay alive even if they did not work*. Scary ideas like the Hindu coconut cocktail and Osler's chloroform were shoved off the table. In the twentieth century from 1900 to World War II, as standards of living began to rise sharply, labor participation began to trail off a bit for men. Men who reached age sixty-five began to utter the word *retirement*, a term unknown to their fathers and grandfathers. After Franklin Roosevelt's administration set up the Social Security system in the 1930s (inspired in part by Otto von Bismarck's 1889 social insurance program in Germany), about half the sixty-five-year-olds stopped working. Eleanor Roosevelt imagined they would sit around in rocking chairs. She could not foresee shuffleboard on cruise ships or today's inexhaustible senior citizens engaging in extreme hang gliding and white-water rafting. Her wish was merely that old people could comfortably loll about and avoid poorhouses. In a speech to the Monday Evening Club, a Washington group dedicated to social causes and going out on Monday evenings (Monday Night Football did not begin until 1970 and one strains to picture Eleanor Roosevelt on a sofa next to Howard Cosell), she observed, "Old people love their own things even more than young people do. It means so much to sit in the same chair you sat in for a great many years, to see the same picture that you always looked at!"[9] With the help of Social Security most elderly people stopped working, but many of them had ambitions greater than simply plopping themselves down on a plastic-covered couch and staring at the wall.

Swelling incomes allowed individuals to purchase for themselves not just meals but leisure time. Ask yourself, why did the game of baseball take off in the 1920s? Because tens of thousands of people in major cities had the economic freedom to take off two hours in the daytime to cheer Lou Gehrig and Babe Ruth (this was before ball games stretched to over three hours and before night games). Picture in your mind those black-and-white photos of American presidents throwing out the first ball at baseball games, starting in 1910 with William H. Taft, who somehow managed to get his arm around his well-fed, barrel-chested 340-pound body. Rising incomes made all that possible—Taft's gut and the thousands of fans watching the Washington Nationals play the Philadelphia Athletics. During the 1920s and 1930s the game of golf spread beyond the wealthiest meadows of Long

Island and Chicago's North Shore. The number of golf courses tripled, inspired by Bobby Jones, who in 1930 won the US Open, the British Open, the US Amateur Championship, and the British Amateur Championship. Tennis reached a heyday as champions like Bill Tilden and Helen Wills became household names. My grandpa Bobby was the New York City tennis champion of 1927 (I have the trophy to prove it), becoming a household name, at least in the Buchholz household.

THE GO-NOWHERE GENERATION

In recent decades, amid the shattering of nations, we are seeing a new phenomenon: young and middle-aged people acting more like retirees and avoiding work. A test: do you know any recent high school graduates who do not have a driver's license? In the most startling behavioral change among young people since James Dean and Marlon Brando started mumbling, an increasing number of Gen Yers are not bothering to get drivers' licenses. A few years ago in a widely shared essay in the Sunday *New York Times* entitled "The Go Nowhere Generation," my daughter and I showed that young people today are 25 percent less likely to get a driver's license than their parents or grandparents were at the same age. Don't blame the drop on more expensive cars: households own more cars than ever before and it takes fewer workweeks to buy a car today than in the early 1980s. Don't blame Uber, because the trend predates it.

Another test: do you know any young people who have moved to another state to take a job? The likelihood of an eighteen- to twenty-four-year-old moving to another state has dropped 40 percent since the 1980s. The stuck-at-home mentality hits not only college-educated Americans but also those without a high school diploma. This is another paradox of our era: as native-born people find themselves surrounded by foreign-born people, they become less likely to explore our own country or the world. They become homebodies. The proportion of young adults living at home nearly doubled between 1980 and 2008, before the Great Recession hit, and the trend continues to creep upward. *This is the Occupy movement we should really be worried about.*

What does not getting a driver's license or not moving to a new state have to do with entropy and national spirit? Each suggests a tendency to sit and wait, rather than get up and go and seek new opportunities when times are tough. In *The Grapes of Wrath*, young Tom Joad loads up his jalopy with pork snacks and relatives, as the family flees the Okie dust bowl for sun-kissed California. Along the way, Granma dies, yet the Joads keep going. But sometime in the past thirty years someone has hit the brakes and Americans refuse to climb out of their La-Z-Boy recliners. The timing is terrible. Even with a 10 percent jobless rate in the depths of the Great Recession and a foreclosure rate that would grab the attention of the Joads, Americans were less inclined to pack up the station wagon for sunnier economic climes, even if the station wagon came equipped with a Blu-ray DVD player on the back of each seat.[10]

Mobility can be crucial for poor people. A fascinating study by Raj Chetty, Nathaniel Hendren, and Lawrence Katz looked at a program that offers housing vouchers to randomly chosen parents so they can move out of very poor housing projects and into less impoverished neighborhoods. Ten years later the children of parents who moved were earning 31 percent more income than those who stayed behind.[11]

Generation Y is turning into Generation "Y Bother?" The

proportion of teens with summer jobs or part-time after-school jobs has plummeted since 1980. In 1994 two-thirds of teenagers worked during the summer. By 2007 (*before* the Great Recession) less than half participated. This radical shift is not just focused on white teens, rich teens, black teens, young teens, old teens, high-school-dropout teens, or college-attending teens. *All* teenage groups have basically gone on strike.

Now, I must admit that cooking hot dogs on the boardwalk and stacking pints of cottage cheese and yogurt at the supermarket hardly count as academic exploits. As teenagers growing up on the Jersey Shore, my brother and I performed both these tasks. What did we learn toiling in the dairy department? I am not sure, other than to wear a sweater (and that the freshest milk sits on the back of the shelf). Yet work teaches young people to show up on time and it also teaches them that they'd better develop new skills, lest they spend their careers grilling hot dogs in the hot sun or stacking cottage cheese in the chilly dairy department aisle. An after-school or summer job helps to build discipline and helps teens bridge the path to adulthood. If a kid has not done any work before age eighteen, he finds it much harder to understand how and why to put in a hard day's work at nineteen, twenty, or twenty-five years of age. A recent Northeastern University study found that poor high schoolers who worked (especially blacks and Hispanics) were more likely to graduate and that female teens who worked were less likely to get pregnant than their peers.[12]

Many teens cannot be bothered to stand in line at the DMV and even bicycle sales are much lower than they were in 1973. The millennial generation is *literally* going nowhere. All this turns American history on its head. The United States was a nation of movers and shakers. Pilgrims leaped onto leaky boats to get here. After World War I the so-called Lost Generation followed Ernest

Hemingway and Gertrude Stein to Paris. In the 1940s the Greatest Generation signed up to ship out to fight Nazis in Germany or, like my father, the Japanese imperial forces in China. The '60s kids joined the Peace Corps. Even Jack Kerouac put down his reefer to hit the road. We've gone from *What Makes Sammy Run?* to "Joshy, get off the couch!" But Joshy and his friends won't put down the *Mindcraft* magic wand.

A shattering of work ethic and of ambition shows up even in high school course selections, as native-born students display less ambition and avoid more difficult classes. Even though employers are handing out bonuses for graduates in science, technology, and engineering, white and black students have been throwing up their hands and essentially saying, "Let the Chinese and Indian kids do the math." It shows up in the numbers, of course. Among Asian American students, 43 percent take advanced algebra or calculus, twice the rate of white students and four times the rate of black students.[13] But laxity is contagious. By the third generation, Asian American students taper off in their enthusiasm for hard classes, essentially saying, "Let the guy who just got off the boat do the math." In a bad sense, they become more like the white and black kids next door.

HURTS SO GOOD?

A sagging work ethic is contagious. People who do not work do not pay income taxes. Those who do pay income taxes feel resentful. A splintering of the population drives people to cheat and focus on the get-rich-quick or quick-getaway. Earlier in this book I cited a 2008 report that virtually *every* career employee of the Long Island Railroad applied for and received disability payments upon retirement! The US attorney in Manhattan stated that "Employees, in many cases, after claiming to be too disabled to stand, sit, walk or climb steps, retired to lives of regular golf, tennis, biking and aerobics." The scandal goes beyond Long Island, of course. A recent NPR report stated that one in four adults in Hale County, Alabama, collects disability. On days when government checks come in, the Hale County banks stay open late. In New Mexico disability payments jumped 59 percent between 2003 and 2011. Since the late 1980s total applications have tripled. Between 2000 and 2013 disability awards in the United States rose 43 percent.[14] Even after the Great Recession ended, the number of Americans collecting disability kept climbing, by about 10 percent. The chance of a judge's approving one's application has jumped 50 percent since 1980. For every American working in a factory, another former worker is collecting disability. The United States is not alone. The Netherlands, Sweden, Great Britain, and Australia have also seen leaps in disability claims.

Are jobs really more dangerous than ever before? Is that really possible when rusty factories have shut down, replaced by employees merely sitting in front of telephones and laptops, and many working from home and avoiding the hazards of commuting? Since the 1990s workplace fatalities have dropped by one-third. Businesses and workers have incentives not to cut off hands or break bones. Working with the United Food and Commercial Workers Union, Tyson Fresh Meats reduced workplace injuries, including sprains and strains, by about 70 percent in the past twenty years through better ergonomics and replacing dangerous whirling blades with shielded, automatic loin trimmers.[15] But these improvements—jointly hailed by unions and employers—do not seem to show up in the soaring number of disability awards. Moreover, in recent years the claims seem based on

less palpable, less provable injuries. In 1961 just over 8 percent of
workers received disability payments because they suffered from
back pain or musculoskeletal problems. In 2011 over one-third
of the recipients did.[16] The number of people who are disabled
for mental illness doubled over the same period to 19 percent.
Soaring disability claims come not only from blue-collar employees. White-collar workers, too, are claiming disability at a higher
rate, even if they are more likely to be injured while swiveling in
a Herman Miller Aeron chair than while controlling a band saw.
The NPR report on Hale County described a hearing in which a
judge named Sonny Ryan asks from the bench, "Just out of curi-
osity, what is your disability?"

"I have high blood pressure," the man said.

"So do I," the judge said. "What else?"

"I have diabetes."

"So do I."

Many of our great-grandparents worked in construction and
they jammed shovels into the dirt to dig tunnels; today carpal
tunnel syndrome keeps a million Americans from performing any
kind of work, whether they developed the syndrome from fillet-
ing trout in a seafood factory or writing a blog in their pajamas.
And there lies the systemic problem: in the current environment,
when a person is diagnosed with a disability and begins receiving
Social Security payments to compensate for lost work, he or she
will likely *never* return to the workforce in *any* capacity. Someone
who injured his ankle as a crossing guard might still have the
physical agility to get a job sitting at a desk but the chances of his
even applying are slim. Of the roughly 10 million Americans collecting disability payments, only 2 percent tried working in the
past year. Only 0.3 to 0.5 percent try to find work each month.[17]
The overwhelming number of people who ever exit the disability

program do so because they reach retirement age and switch to other benefits or because they die. The US federal government has from time to time tinkered with the rules in order to nudge those on disability to rejoin the labor market. Nonetheless, the nudge has mostly been shrugged off, even by those who purport to be too injured to even move their shoulders in a shrugging gesture. A program called Ticket to Work has apparently helped one-tenth of 1 percent of disabled workers get back into the workforce, a pretty puny ticket, it seems.[18]

Getting anyone back to work is a challenge. Even for those who have not filed for disability, the economy's ups and downs can deplete their willingness to be flexible. Once laid off, many workers stay on the sidelines for a long time. Our state unemployment compensation system does little to spur an ethic of returning to work. When people are laid off, they typically receive twenty-six weeks of payments. When do they typically accept a new job? At the end of the twenty-six weeks. In a front-page proposal in the *Washington Post*, I suggested turning unemployment benefits into signing bonuses, to lure laid-off workers back into the workforce earlier.[19] Under the proposal, the sooner a worker accepts a new job, the more money he gets. A signing bonus, like the ones pro athletes and Wall Street guys get—albeit with fewer zeroes—could be a nice push forward at a time when the tendency is to slouch back.

NOT WORKING KILLS BRAIN CELLS

Human beings did not evolve as sloths. A sloth has a curved claw that can lock onto a pumpwood tree even when Caribbean winds blow at near-hurricane speed. But a sloth does not get more stupid if it spends its life simply hanging around and eating twigs and fruit. People do. A fascinating multicountry study showed that when people retire early, they lose cognitive abilities, even after controlling for age and other health issues. For example, researchers asked sixtysomethings in the United States and twelve European countries to look at a list of common words (*lake, car, army*, for example) and to recall those nouns five minutes later. In countries where people retire early, individuals could not recall the words as readily and were less competent at adding and subtracting numbers.[20] Americans and Danes tend to retire later than do French and Austrians. In the United States and Denmark, most men in their early sixties are still working. In Austria and France, over three-quarters have retired. The cognitive ability of a French or Austrian sixtysomething drops twice as much as an American's or a Dane's. If you ever appear on a trivia game show where you have the chance to "phone a friend," do not dial Paris or Vienna.

Not working shrinks the brain's capacity to think quickly and clearly. When people work, they are forced to handle new challenges, even if these are frustrating challenges like a broken photocopier machine or an annoying receptionist. When life becomes more rote, the brain slips into a more slothlike state. That is why retirees should challenge themselves physically and mentally. Whether taking a Road Scholar trip to Brussels or taking up the bassoon, they should keep moving and thinking. Retirement does not condemn retirees to stupidity. Of course, they can keep up their mental health, but they'd better exert energy to do it.

Perhaps more important, when able-bodied people do not work and do not stay active, they lose ambition and it dampens their ability to catch a few glimpses of happiness. Neuroscientists have shown that when we take action, dopamine and serotonin begin to flow, lifting spirits. Gray cells, which process information, become revitalized and the brain renews itself. Feeling ambition and action is like allowing your brain to sip from the fountain of youth. Arthur C. Brooks has reported data showing that if you take two people with the same age, education, and employment characteristics, but if one is collecting welfare, there is a 16 percent chance that person will have felt "inconsolably sad" at some point in the past month.[21] I suggest that *people who feign disability will actually become disabled* as they sap themselves of vital neurotransmitters.

Work builds and preserves nations. In chapter 9 I will discuss Golda Meir and the early Zionists, who were convinced that Israel could not be created and would not have the spirit to survive unless its people worked the land and tried to conquer drought, parched parcels, and scarce resources.

In the early 1930s in a small Austrian town called Marienthal just south of Vienna, a terrible thing happened. Faced with a worldwide collapse in trade, the town's textile factory, which started as a flax-spinning mill in 1820, slammed its doors shut. Men wielding axes and sledgehammers demolished the place. You can see the sad black-and-white photos of the destruction.[22] It was not only the building that was demolished. Twelve hundred laborers were thrown out of work and the town spun into a depressed state. Out of 478 households about four hundred were without a breadwinner. Only a few local shopkeepers kept going. Incomes plummeted and the most desperate and poor apparently swiped the pets of others for food. Yes, the depression was economic but it was also spiritual. Before the shutdown, the town boasted of libraries and social clubs. Without work, the spirit of living seeped away. Few borrowed from the library even though the fee for borrowing was zero. The theater club went dark along with the football and wrestling clubs. Three-quarters of the families received government relief aid but the state government actively discouraged Marienthal citizens from taking on any work projects. If bureaucrats spied anyone chopping wood or delivering milk, they would snatch the relief check from the offender's hands. According to a landmark study conducted at the time by Marie Jahoda and her husband Paul Lazarsfeld, one man lost his government aid simply because he pocketed some coins in exchange for blowing his harmonica.[23] The researchers quote one woman who recalled, "During the summer we used to go . . . [to] all those dances! Now I don't feel like going out anymore." This was truly the day that music died.

The Marienthalers lost a sense of themselves and they also lost a sense of time. Literally. Most of the families lived along Main Street and most people walked wherever they needed to go. The researchers began to observe and time the pace of walking among men and women. They discovered that the men seldom strode directly as they crossed the street. Two-thirds interrupted their ambling but without apparent reason. The women walked one and one-half times faster than the men. Remember, wives still had to organize the children and figure out how to put food on the table. They managed to do so but the men began to show up late for the meager meals. People chose to go to bed earlier, 9 p.m. instead of 11 p.m., but they reported feeling more tired even with more sleep. The children absorbed the dread and it stunted their ambition and their natural fantasies. The researchers arranged for a teacher to ask children, "What do I want to be when I grow up?" The once typical, optimistic boy themes were gone. None wanted to be ship captains or airplane pilots. One still wished to be an Indian chief but was not sure whether he could find an opening in the field. A large number longed for a factory job, the kind their fathers reminisced about.[24]

Not working impacts trust and honesty, too. As the situation turned darker, more Marienthalers accused others of cheating on their relief aid.[25] The incidence of actual cheating rose. But so did the incidence of false, unfounded accusations of cheating hurled by others. In 1928–29, when the factory was still operating (but with half its employees laid off), nine residents were denounced for unreported work. Three of these accusations turned out to be justified. Now we compare that with 1931–32, when the factory was demolished. During this more dire period, twenty-eight individuals were accused of cheating. Twenty-one were exonerated and seven were convicted.[26] Without work, the social fabric ripped. Of course the rip would soon become louder and joined by the jackbooted march of the fascists. In Germany and Austria support for the Nazi Party closely tracked the unemployment rate.[27] Dependent on government relief, Marienthal became fertile ground for mental disease and a deadly social disease called Nazism.

VENICE RECLINING AND DECLINING

Marienthal shows how economic collapse can extinguish spirits and a work ethic. But history also shows that during relatively healthy economic times, government bureaucracies can discourage employment, entrepreneurship, and innovation. Consider the Serene Republic of Venice in the 1600s. After the economic fireworks of the mid-1500s, marked by spectacular success in coloring glass, dying textiles, and tanning leather, the Venetian government began crushing merchants with tariffs, which doubled the cost of textiles and allowed the British to poach market share. Employers and workers grew discouraged and became less productive and less innovative. The guilds more tightly controlled

who was permitted to work, and the labor force grew older, closing off opportunities and demoralizing young people. Typically,
guilds and unions work hardest to protect senior members and
those who already pay dues, rather than the up-and-coming.
(That is why, for example, today most teachers' unions insist on
negotiating contracts that pay a ten-year veteran gym teacher
more than a calculus teacher with just five years' experience.)
Over the course of the 1600s young Venetians increasingly felt
blocked from the workplace, whether the potential employment
involved hammering against anvils, casting iron, or fitting shoes
on horse hooves. In 1600 only 15 percent of the workforce had
been over the age of forty-five. By 1690 nearly half were over the
age of forty-five. Remember, this was at a time when a fifty-year-
old was far less productive than today and typically hobbled by
rickets, syphilis, or worms.

In rushed a period that historians call Venice's "era of deca-
dence." Aristocrats and merchants became focused on renting land
and exploiting peasants rather than on expanding and inventing
new products. Businessmen preferred luxurious villas to grubby
countinghouses. Peasants buckled under heavy rents, even as guilds
blocked the young and ambitious from joining the workforce. Ambition ebbed and along with it the proportion of workers eager and
able to put in an honest day's labor. The Republic transformed into
a kind of theme park of gambling and debauchery, better symbolized by frivolous carnival masks and lecherous Casanovas than by
hard work and rising incomes. Eventually, the economy crumpled,
but not because of some environmental mishap like a rising tide in
the canals or even because of a shortage of silica sand to melt for
Murano glass. When a rich nation loses a desire to work, and when
those who happen to have jobs block others from competing with
them, an unraveling begins.

BUREAUCRATS CAN DAMPEN WORK AND DRIVE UP DEBT

You might think that as a nation grows richer, its citizens might be in a better position to take care of themselves. In this case, bureaucracies would shrink. That seldom happens. It has been easy to decry bureaucracies ever since Hammurabi placed wage-and-price controls on Babylonian cowboys 3,700 years ago ("If a man hires a herdsman for cattle and sheep, he shall pay him six gur of corn per annum," *Code of Hammurabi* 261; this wage would equal about twenty-six bushels). Today comedians can win laughs merely by pronouncing to audiences the acronym DMV. I do not believe that bureaucracies are intrinsically evil or unnecessary. But as nations grow more prosperous, they tend to become more encrusted with bureaucracies. These bureaucrats tap the brakes on the economy, which then short-circuits optimism. Large bureaucracies are symptoms of the entropy of rich nations. Large bureaucracies subvert nations because they create a wedge between citizens and leaders. The larger the wedge, the larger the risk that the nation will unravel.

CHINA: AFTER THE EUNUCH FALLS

This is not simply an American story from the twentieth century or a Venetian tale from the seventeenth. During the Ming dynasty (AD 1368–1644) the Confucians scorned Chinese merchants as parasites. No surprise, then, that they expanded the bureaucracy to oversee and ultimately stomp on the merchants, which strangled the economy and helped implode the dynasty. But how could Ming mandarins afford to expand their ranks, hiring and training more bureaucrats? Quite simply, *the economic growth came first*. Manning the massive bureaucracy came second.

In the early Ming period a visitor from Europe would marvel at China's riches and its technology, from gunpowder to movable type for printing to seed drills to four-hundred-foot-long ships that could carry a thousand soldiers. Chinese mariners used a magnetic compass hundreds of years before the Italians, and in the 1400s they figured out how to sail as far as the Red Sea and Zanzibar. One mission came back from East Africa with a tower of giraffes to delight the emperor. In contrast to a sophisticated citizen of Peking, a Londoner in 1400 might as well have been swinging from vines. When China referred to Westerners as barbarians, they weren't kidding!

But then in the mid-fifteenth century science and sailing skidded to a stop. In 1433, after the death of Zheng He, a leading palace eunuch who promoted trade, the bureaucrats banned shipbuilders from constructing seafaring vessels. The scholarly Confucians sneered at moneygrubbing merchants and periodically confiscated private property. They slammed shut the printing presses except for scholarly works and then banned those they deemed "illiterate" from holding public office. With each edict, each stoppage, and each embargo, the Chinese bureaucrats ended up building their own great wall separating the government from the people, which ultimately crippled public support for the emperors. Although the Ming dynasty lumbered along for another two hundred years, it stopped moving forward and became more vulnerable to invaders, rebellions, and economic crises made worse by government deficits and high taxes. Ming troops grew dispirited and angry. Overcome by treachery, in 1644 the last Ming emperor hanged himself from a tree as the Manchus crashed through the gates of the Great Wall of China. The stones of the Great Wall might have done a better job protecting the dynasty from collapse had the Ming bureaucrats not erected their own great walls severing themselves from the people.

WHO DO REGULATORS PROTECT?

In a brilliant book called *The Rise and Decline of Nations* (1982) Mancur Olson described how regulations and bureaucracies almost inevitably increase their power over time.[28] Groups from cotton farmers to dockworkers have an incentive to organize and lobby congresses, kings, and prime ministers to protect them from competition. This protection requires more government ministers and minions. In Washington you will find the American Dehydrated Onion and Garlic Association, which protects against imported flavorings, and the Balloon Council, which fights for a government helium reserve. Sometimes bureaucracies created to protect the public end up protecting the companies they oversee, as Nobel laureate George Stigler described in his "capture theory." An example: even though Frank Sinatra's "Come Fly with Me" album was a bestseller in 1958, by 1965 only one in five Americans had ever stepped onto an airplane. During the 1960s and 1970s few Americans could afford to fly because the Civil Aeronautics Board ruled over a cartel that kept prices sky-high and routinely turned away applications for new airlines to challenge incumbents. The board, founded in 1938, would specify which routes airlines were permitted to fly, often consulting old railroad maps, so that United would get the east-west routes from Chicago and TWA would dominate routes from Saint Louis.[29] Even upstart cargo carriers were discouraged from liftoff. Federal Express could not fly big jets until the airline deregulation acts of 1977 and 1978. Nowadays half of Americans take a round-trip flight every year.

Olson pointed out that countries grow faster after wars and revolutions precisely because such stormy events sweep aside the old regimes that restrained free commerce. He noted, for example, that Germany and Japan grew faster after World War II than before. Olson (who died in 1998) demonstrated that countries accumulate more bureaucrats over time. But my research shows that it is not just the passing time that attracts bureaucrats; prosperity itself does so.

America's bureaucracy grew rapidly during the Johnson and Nixon/Ford years from 1964 to 1975, when the number of non-defense US government employees climbed by 46 percent. This period was preceded by one of the most prosperous periods in US history, the post-WWII boom from 1945 to the 1960s. The postwar boom supplied the funds to pay for new cabinet departments including Health, Education, and Welfare (1953; it became Health and Human Services in 1979), Housing and Urban Development (1965), and Transportation (1966). (By some accounts US real weekly wages have still not regained the peak they reached in 1973, suggesting that new government bureaucracies might drag down economic growth.) After the recessions of the 1970s and early 1980s, the federal bureaucracy actually shrank by eleven thousand workers. After the meltdown of 2008, total government employment dropped by over half a million (though federal employment ticked up slightly). Here's the key point: bureaucracies often grow fastest *after* periods of prosperity. They do not grow as quickly during periods of stagnation or poverty.

When bureaucracies grow, they may do so in ways that specifically discourage more jobs in the private sector. My father urged his children to be "professionals," rather than corporate employees. He had worked for railroad companies from the Wabash to the Norfolk & Southern. His office was in the Pan Am Building on Park Avenue, which we would call "Daddy's building." But he did not own it and he did not own much of the railroad. When the ringing landline phone would interrupt us at home during the dinner hour, he would flare his nostrils and blurt, "Tell them I'm not here." That worked until one day my little sister answered the phone, turned to my dad, and said in a loud six-year-old voice, "Daddy, are you home?" The steam emerging from Dad's ears resembled the photos of steam locomotives he framed on the wall. My father thought that if his children grew up to become lawyers and doctors, they would escape dinnertime interruptions and a boss's call to arms. He could not, of course, foresee the cell phone, telemarketers, or HMOs turning physicians into mere wage slaves. Still, I can recall my father's frequent refrain, "If you're a professional, you can always hang out a shingle of your own." Sure enough, my brother's name is on the letterhead of a California law firm. I doubt that the offices in downtown San Diego and Los Angeles have wooden shingles but I can find his name on the directory in the lobby.

Before one hangs up a lawyer's shingle, of course, one needs to pass a bar exam and receive a license to practice. We expect that of attorneys and we demand it of cardiac surgeons and airline pilots. Incumbent lawyers and surgeons are pleased to put up obstacles that keep out competitors and help maintain high fees. But what other jobs should require government approval and the expenses that come with preparing for exams and filing for those licenses? How about people who cut hair? Or sell wrestling tickets? Or set DVR machines? In fact, we have a licensing epidemic in the United States, a result of government bureaucracies conspiring with incumbent practitioners. This epidemic robs people of the ability to get work, especially the younger and less experienced. For every "profession," there is a trade association and a state agency working to develop and shape the shackles that block others from competing. Venice's guilds are back, but instead of flying under the flag of the Serene Republic, they fly under the flag of protecting the public. In 1900 just over 4 percent of the labor force worked in professional occupations, but by midcentury states had passed more than twelve hundred state occupational licensing statutes for over seventy-five occupations from physicians to embalmers. About one-third of occupations now require a government license or certificate, including 15 percent of the jobs held by high school dropouts.[30] Arizona demands that hair stylists take sixteen hundred hours of classroom instruction, at an approved cosmetology school. The schools are not cheap, and it can cost $10,000 to $15,000 to fulfill the sixteen-hundred-hour requirement. But here is the shocker. In Phoenix an aspiring policeman attends training school for just six hundred hours! Apparently it is almost three times more dangerous to wield a Revlon blow-dryer than a .40 caliber Glock. Do not try to arrange flowers in Louisiana without a license. And if you do apply for a flower arranging permit, study hard. A higher proportion of applicants pass the Louisiana bar exam than pass the picky flower-arranging exam, which includes a hands-on design test.[31] How ironic: in New Orleans, you can stumble down Bourbon Street flanked by lewd signs for dirty dancing and X-rated T-shirt shops, but put down those petunias unless you have a license to beautify!

Who is damaged by all these seemingly silly, but shrewd regulations? First of all, young job seekers, who must scrounge around and save up substantial sums of money just to start studying to take a job. The licensing epidemic especially hurts women, who are less likely to be represented among the incumbent class. One study showed that excessive licensing burdens for funeral directors reduce the number of female funeral directors by 18 to 24 percent.[32] Second, consumers who pay more for services because of dampened competition. Third, consumers who cannot afford higher prices and therefore take it upon themselves to recklessly cut their own hair or arrange their own tulips. But there are far more serious examples, including "do-it-yourself root canal."[33] A careful study showed that in states with the most burdensome licensing requirements for electricians, more homeowners try to do the job themselves, mismatching wires and, in some cases, killing themselves.[34] The absurdist comedian Steven Wright had a more droll take on such episodes: "I installed a skylight in my apartment. The people who live above me are furious."

LOOKING BACKWARD IS NOT AN ECONOMIC POLICY

Progress can be wonderful, but it can be painful. If you visit Williamsburg, Virginia, you can spend time with the farrier and the candlemaker. They have much free time, because they were replaced by automakers and lightbulb factories, respectively. But trying to stand in the way of innovation in order to protect incumbent job holders does not work out very well. Innovations sometimes literally push aside the old order. Cows did not care much for railroads in the 1880s. Those steel grills on the front of locomotives are called "cowcatchers" and would turn a live steer into instant dinner. That's pretty much the story of economic progress, which Joseph Schumpeter called "creative destruction."

There is often a lot of blood left on the ground. But it has largely been worth the price. Back in the 1880s when Edward Bellamy put forth his socialist utopian *Looking Backward*, life expectancy was about forty-five years of age. Today it's about eighty.

Would you want to go back to the good old days when your great-great-grandfather with a toothache would have his teeth yanked out by a barber who had no better anesthesia than the stuff he might have rinsed his combs in? I vote for modern dentistry. We should be very worried about government policies that protect those with an interest in the status quo, whether barbers waving combs or wild cattle. Consider two recent headline stories. In 2014 the state of New Jersey banned Tesla Motors from selling the world's highest-rated automobile (as ranked by *Consumer Reports* that year) because Tesla had not signed contracts with local, independent dealerships. The original prohibition was clearly a way to fatten wallets of esteemed local campaign contributors (New Jersey's governor Chris Christie reversed the ban in 2015). But how esteemed are those local car dealers? According to a December 2013 Gallup poll, surveying the honesty and ethics of twenty-two different professions, car dealers do *not* rank last. They narrowly beat out congressmen and lobbyists, but lose to everyone else including auto mechanics and lawyers. So why should New Jersey consumers be forced to sit in the waiting room of a middleman dealer and be fenced off from dealing directly with Tesla? Since Tesla's buyers earn much more than the median income, don't they have less need for government "protection"?

Second, taxicab drivers and some taxi commissioners have declared war on Uber and Lyft, companies that allow customers to deploy swift and nifty software to call for cars and pay with previously approved credit cards. Unlike city cabbies, Uber drivers are instantly rated by their customers and if the driver fails to average a 4.7 score on a scale of 1 to 5, Uber tears up his contract. No surprise, then, that Uber drivers often provide bottles of water, courteous service, and pleasant conversation. Would city cabdrivers be willing to subject their licenses to such a rigorous review process? Is the customer better off in a clean, technologically equipped vehicle? To help protect Uber drivers, they get to rank the passengers, weeding out bad patrons. In San Francisco, a city supervisor complained that cabdrivers were "losing about $15 per shift or even more" because more Uber cars were on the roads. Here's another way to look at it: San Francisco residents and tourists are finding the city a more convenient place to live, work, and visit.

INCUMBENTS AND AT-RISK CHILDREN

Too often incumbents want to "look backward" and protect the status quo even against waves of change. A few years ago seven thousand teachers marched in Chicago to protest school closings because the school-age population had shrunk by 145,000 during a decade's time. In Chicago, the black population alone—adults and children—dropped from 1 million in 2000 to 887,608 in 2010. Yes, a shuttered school is a sad thing, but when a population falls because people choose to move into the suburbs, a school district cannot fill those empty classroom chairs with test-crash dummies. The prudent path is clear: send the remaining students to the best nearby schools and pack them with extra resources from the financial savings.

Obstinate school bureaucrats can block children from better ways of learning. I am sorry to report that, in my own professional experience, charter school and private school officials are much more willing to entertain new ideas than the conventional public school bureaucrats who govern almost 90 percent of elementary and secondary education. I have become deeply involved in math education, as the inventor of a patented matrix called the Math Arrow, which hangs in many school classrooms as a poster and is the basis for iPad apps like Kyle Counts.[35] Both the Math Arrow and the apps have won applause from leading education and technology reviewers and from teachers in the classroom. Martin Cooper, the inventor of the cell phone, calls the matrix "ingenious," and a study at Brigham Young University showed that it raises test scores. But when my colleagues and I have tried to make appointments with curriculum supervisors, we noticed that the charter and private school bureaucrats were far more willing to test a new idea than their public school counterparts. In one glaring example, a Success Academy charter school on Lenox Avenue in Harlem (twenty-eight hundred miles from my home) almost immediately introduced the Math Arrow into its kindergarten classroom. In contrast, my local public school officials, who work in an office four blocks from my home, ignored numerous requests just to hold an introductory meeting! Often public bureaucrats do not have sufficient incentives to upgrade their behavior or performance.

Of course, it is wrong to claim that all new ideas are worthy or that all progress is good. Nor is it true that new ideas and new industries create only good and never inflict pain. A free market is not a pain-free market. Good economic policies create losers; but the winners either are more plentiful in numbers or create large enough overall gains to compensate the losers.[36]

Looking backward to prop up old jobs and old buildings is not a strategy for success. It is the desperate flinch of entrenched interests. Jerry Seinfeld recently performed a funny routine teasing the US Post Office, noting that we should not be surprised when a business cannot compete when it is based on a 1630s model of licking, walking, and random pennies. Seinfeld advises, "If you really want to be helpful to us, just open the letters, read them, and e-mail us what it says."

What is worse for a polity? When millions of individuals who are able to work decide not to? Or when those who would like to work are told by bureaucrats to stay home and wait for a check that's in the mail?

CHAPTER 5

Patriotism, Immigration, and Grit in the Era of the Selfie

Here's a joke. Go ahead and laugh, before we get to serious matters of patriotism, immigration, and grit:

Two New Jersey hunters are in the woods when one of them falls to the ground. He doesn't seem to be breathing, his eyes rolled back in his head. The other guy whips out his cell phone and calls 911. He gasps: "My friend is dead! What can I do?" The operator says: "Calm down. I can help. First, let's make sure he's dead." There is silence. Then a shot is heard. Back on the phone the guy says, "Okay, now what?"

If you laughed hard, you may be German. If you didn't laugh at all, you may be Canadian. A study by psychologist Richard Wiseman collected forty thousand jokes and 2 million opinions from around the world to declare this hunting tale "the world's funniest joke."[1] The study clearly showed that Germans laughed most often. This is a controversial finding, not because we doubt German humor—Nietzsche, the man who came up with the idea of the *Übermensch*, went crazy after hugging a horse in the street and spent the rest of his life prancing naked in his own autoerotic Dionysian rite.[2] Now, that's funny. Wiseman's finding is controversial because it is politically incorrect to assert that a people possess a "national character" or personality. Critics of "national character" claim that such discussions simply breed or reflect stereotypes that can dehumanize individuals and turn anthropology and political science into an extended Don Rickles stand-up routine: "I saw this black guy chasing two Irishmen into a bar . . . "

Many of us find ethnic jokes embarrassing and the nastiest ones downright detestable. But our sensitivities do not mean that we are wrong to perceive differences in attitudes and behavior. My German-born neighbor who lives down the street is prompt. To him, "fashionably late" means "on time." My father and his father also liked to be early. We were always the first family to check in at an airport, sometimes arriving before the plane had even left its previous destination. The motto on the Buchholz family crest should have been "Hurry up and wait." Amy Chua's book *Battle Hymn of the Tiger Mother* reached bestseller lists in 2011 with scary tales of threatening to burn her daughter's stuffed animals in retaliation for a poor piano practice session. Chua's "mommy dearest" stories were rather gothic, but serious social psychologists do find that Asian families tend to use shaming as a way to encourage modesty and to develop self-discipline and responsibility.[3] The results of shaming later show up in adult behavior. For example, Asian Americans are more likely than non-Hispanic white Americans or African Americans to feel suspicious when people laugh in their presence and are more likely to avoid a place after having made an embarrassing impression.[4] But whites are more likely to avoid the dance floor, fearing that they will look ridiculous. This is why Billy Crystal got a big laugh in *When Harry Met Sally* when his character explains dating: "You meet someone, you have the safe lunch. . . . You go dancing, *you do the white man's overbite*."[5]

Cultural norms, whether homegrown or carried to a country by immigrants, do differ from place to place and people to people. Of course, we must be careful about unfounded biases, but in this chapter I will argue *that if a nation wants to survive the gale forces of a swiftly changing economy, it had better convey to its children and to its immigrants a sense of its national character and the rituals and stories that can hold it together.* Societies that do not do this die. They leave behind only a clanking cask of skeletal bones and we know little about them. About sixty thousand years ago, several *Homo sapiens* families walked out of Africa, forming many tribes, societies, and eventually countries. But we really know much only about those that left behind a common creed, a language, founding myths, and a culture. We know just about nothing about the Neanderthals who came before them. We also know very little about the Harappans who lived several thousand years ago in what is now Pakistan and western India. The reason we do not know much is that their scribes apparently had little interest in writing down their myths, literature, or scientific thoughts; their technological advancements in metallurgy; or their use of decimals.[6] In contrast, we know much about ancient Greeks, Egyptians, and Jews, the "people of the book." But without their book—packed with customs, commands, and stories—Jews would not have survived five thousand years. They would have been long forgotten, like some isolated Neanderthal clan but without the jutting foreheads. There is no guarantee that even the most robust culture will survive epochs and millennia. The odds are brutally long.

In 1817 the editor of the *London Examiner* heard that the head of an ancient statue of Pharaoh Rameses II would be shipped to the British Museum. He staged a poetry competition, daring Percy Bysshe Shelley and his friend, a doggerel-loving stockbroker named Horace Smith, to quickly pen a sonnet about the old tyrant. Shelley won the competition with a poem called "Ozymandias" (a Greek corruption of part of Rameses's name). The poem has lasted and has been lauded for two hundred years, so far. In one of the final episodes of the hit television show *Breaking Bad*, the protagonist recites "Ozymandias." But the theme of the sonnet is that glory will certainly fade away even for a powerful, arrogant king. Shelley writes of a traveler from an antique land who comes across in the desert "two vast and trunkless legs of stone." On a pedestal, these words appear:

"MY NAME IS OZYMANDIAS, KING OF KINGS
LOOK ON MY WORKS, YE MIGHTY AND DESPAIR!"
NOTHING BESIDE REMAINS. ROUND THE DECAY
OF THAT COLOSSAL WRECK, BOUNDLESS AND BARE
THE LONE AND LEVEL SANDS STRETCH FAR AWAY.

If even a mighty pharaoh and his formidable civilization crumble to sand, surrounded by nothing in a vast desert, what long-term hope does the United States or any other modern nation have? Let's take another poem, even more famous than "Ozymandias" and written just a few years before in 1814. A young attorney named Francis Scott

Key is aboard a British ship in Baltimore harbor, trying to negotiate the release of hostages. The bombing of Fort McHenry begins, and the Royal Navy fires rockets and over fifteen hundred cannonballs across the harbor. Francis Scott Key writes a poem. The penultimate line we know so well is not a declaration but a *question*: "Oh, say does that star-spangled banner yet wave?" Key understood that the answer might be "No!" The United States had declared independence just thirty-eight years before. Countries could die. He knew that the Republic of Belgium lasted just 325 days in 1790. The Republic of Genoa made it through 211 days in 1814. Young countries and old countries could disappear. The Star-Spangled Banner does still wave today. But you can look pretty hard and yet not find any tattered banners of the Harappans or the Minoans. Back to Ozymandias and an irony. The pharaoh had a son who ruled in 1200 BC. In 1896 an archaeologist dug up a ten-foot block of black granite, inscribed with reports of the son's victorious battles. It also includes an inscription from the great leader. He declares, "Israel is laid waste; its seed is gone." He was wrong. The people who had a shared book outlasted the king who had soldiers, fortunes, and monuments that scattered when the sirocco winds blew across the Sahara.

So where is hope to be found for rich nations today who must wonder how long they will last? The answer is in a national character and culture and in those shared stories that can bind us together despite the centrifugal force of globalization that flings us apart.[7]

WHO'S THE STRANGER AND HOW DO WE TREAT HIM?

In an earlier chapter, we looked at William Hamilton's formula that gauges our willingness to sacrifice for others. Our bodies have evolved so they can identify family. While everyone knows that wolves have a keen sense of scent, so do we when it comes to relatives. Blindfolded, a man can identify his sibling by scent but not a half-sibling. We would dive into swirling waters to save a close family member. As for a stranger, well, he can get chomped on by a shark. Yet a healthy society requires a willingness to take risks and accept losses for others: to fight in battle, pay hefty taxes, or forgo stealing a hundred-dollar bill even if you know you will not be caught. But it is awfully hard to persuade people to sacrifice by appealing only to their reason. On D-Day in 1944, Dwight Eisenhower would not have had a chance of coaxing Army Rangers to climb the hundred-meter-high vertical cliffs of Pointe du Hoc against a storm of Nazi machine-gun fire if he had to supply them with an airtight syllogism churned out by an Aristotelian logician.

Modern nations cannot survive unless people identify some alternative way that binds them together, other than blood and scent. In olden days, the church in the town square could play that role, especially when just one religion dominated a people. Just as Jesus is said to have sacrificed himself for mankind's sins, a medieval priest could call on his flock to sacrifice for each other. The eighteenth-century hymn "Soldiers of Christ, Arise" follows the teachings of the Apostle Paul and tells good men to "put your armour on," to fight the devil's schemes.[8] Paul speaks of helmets, breastplates, and swords. Those who would not fight were deemed pagans. Shared religion could substitute for blood and scent. The very word *religion* comes from the Latin verb *religare* "to bind." The root of sacrifice, *sacer*, means holy. But where does this leave us today, in a country where fewer than 20 percent attend a church service each week? Even more worrisome, an additional 20 percent of the population apparently lies about

attending a weekly worship service!⁹ The attendance numbers are
much lower for most of Europe, for example, less than 10 percent
in Germany, France, and Scandinavia.¹⁰ If a nation no longer em-
braces holiness from God and no longer cares about the church
in the town square, it must look elsewhere to bind itself together,
namely in its history, character, culture, and stories.

TURNING CROWDS INTO GROUPS AND NATIONS: A QUICK WASHINGTON TOUR

The word *we* has a little magic attached to it and makes us feel
better. A neat experiment showed that when people see the word
we paired up with a made-up word like *xeh*, they feel more positive about the meaningless *xeh*.¹¹ Even if we are introverts and
loners, we have all experienced moments when a crowd of strangers transforms into a "we" group and feels some connection or affection. On July 4, 2015, I was standing on a lawn in Georgetown
with a few thousand strangers watching as fireworks launched
from the Lincoln Memorial Reflecting Pool soared over a back-
ground view of the Kennedy Center for the Performing Arts and
the Watergate Hotel. All of us in the crowd would follow the path
of the rocket and simultaneously await the "reveal," that moment
when the explosion of color morphed into the shape of a sunburst,
a flag, or a sparkling willow tree. When the rocketeers surprised
us with the unmistakable image of a happy face, we all "oohed"
and smiled together, sometimes making eye contact with each
other. John Adams was awfully smart when he urged that Independence Day should be celebrated with fireworks. On July 3,
1776, he wrote to his wife, Abigail, that it should be celebrated
with "Pomp and Parade, with Shews, Games, Sports, Guns, Bells,

Bonfires and Illuminations from one End of this Continent to the other from this Time forward forever more."[12] On the website of the Massachusetts Historical Society, you can see Adams's handwritten letter and feel yourself in that moment when the United States was newborn and so fragile and hopeful.

Each of the three institutions that provided the backdrop to the fireworks display that day—the Lincoln Memorial, Kennedy Center, and Watergate Hotel—has brought strangers together (and divided them) at different times in US history. They are just piles of brick, marble, and mortar and those raw materials could have been used instead to build a strip mall or a sewage plant. Nonetheless, these structures are now imbued with symbolism and therefore help form the infrastructure for America's soul. Let us start with the Lincoln Memorial. It is not an explicitly religious site, and yet it plays that role to millions of visitors. The epitaph above the statue of the seated Lincoln calls the building a *Temple*, not a memorial:

IN THIS TEMPLE
AS IN THE HEARTS OF THE PEOPLE
FOR WHOM HE SAVED THE UNION
THE MEMORY OF ABRAHAM LINCOLN
IS ENSHRINED FOREVER.

In 1963 the Lincoln Memorial was the place, of course, where 250,000 people gathered to hear Martin Luther King declare "I Have a Dream" and sing together "We Shall Overcome." On a May morning in 1970 at 4:15, President Richard Nixon slipped out of the White House without telling his chief of staff and showed up unannounced at the Lincoln statue to speak quietly to Vietnam War protesters who held a vigil there. It is a reverential place for Americans regardless of their personal political views.

If you stand at the base of the Lincoln Memorial and look to the west, you will see the home of Robert E. Lee looming over Arlington National Cemetery and the 400,000 crosses, Stars of David, crescents (and even a few Wiccan pentacles) marking the grave sites of Americans who died in battle from the Civil War to the latest death in Arabia or Afghanistan.

The Kennedy Center for the Performing Arts hosts opera, symphony, plays, and dance. It opened in 1971 with Leonard Bernstein's premiere of his musical-theater piece entitled *Mass*. This is telling. The musical work includes Latin passages from the Roman Catholic Mass, but also English lyrics by pop star Paul Simon and Stephen Schwartz (later the composer of *Wicked*). Bernstein was not particularly religious, and according to his biographers, he violated at least a few of the Ten Commandments. In *Mass* discordant choir members rebel against God and hurl sacramental wine and bread to the floor. But after the choir members fall to the floor, a flute solo resurrects the choir, which somehow regains its faith. The areligious Bernstein ultimately finds harmony and grace in ritual. Bernstein's handwritten notes from when he was composing *Mass* contain the following passage: "Some religion necessary to every man—belief in something greater than random/systematic biological existence."[13] The Kennedy Center is an areligious institution. And yet whenever an audience cheers, applauds, or laughs together, it helps to form a community. A shared culture can do this.

We know the Watergate Hotel from the clumsy break-in at the Democratic National Committee headquarters in 1972 and the cover-up by the Nixon White House. The scandal divided the country just as the Vietnam War was already wrenching it apart. But as evidence against Richard Nixon piled up, the American people began to coalesce in a shared view that the president must

resign. On August 7, 1974, leading Republican senators Barry
Goldwater and Hugh Scott marched into the Oval Office to tell
him that he must leave. Even his staunchest allies had moved
to form a front against him. When Vice President Gerald Ford
was sworn in as president on August 9, he spoke these powerful
words: "My fellow Americans, our long national nightmare is
over." Note the word *our*. Even a scandal like Watergate, a shared
nightmare, can help tie a country together. Ford continued, "Our
Constitution works; our great Republic is a government of laws
and not of men. Here the people rule. But there is a higher Power,
by whatever name we honor Him." In Ford's speech the Constitution serves as America's eternal document, like the "book" that
ancient Jews would depend on to guide them through internal
crises and external attacks.

Shared experiences can also come from less momentous
spheres, including sports. At Arlington National Cemetery rests
the remains of Joe Louis, who dominated boxing from 1937 to
1949 and is often ranked as the greatest heavyweight champion of
all time, despite Muhammad Ali's colorful rants. In 1936, though,
Louis was knocked out by Max Schmeling, a darling of Hitler
and poster boy for Aryan superiority. In 1938 nearly every American and every German wanted to tune into the radio broadcast
or attend the rematch at Yankee Stadium, alongside seventy thousand other fans. A few weeks before, Louis traveled to the White
House. President Franklin Roosevelt said, "Lean over, Joe, so I can
feel your muscles. . . . Joe, we need muscles like yours to beat Germany." Beat Germany? An ominous choice of words. Remember,
this fight took place three and a half years *before* the United States
entered World War II and a year before the Nazis invaded Poland.
But the pressure was on. Here's how the fight went: Louis charges
Schmeling and in the first two minutes lands a dozen devastating

blows to the head. Schmeling's knees buckle. Louis hits him with a sharp right cross and Schmeling collapses to the canvas. He rolls and rises, only to be knocked down again and to stagger onto his feet once more. Louis fires another right to the jaw and Schmeling crumbles. A white towel of surrender flies into the ring from the German corner, but the referee throws it back. Schmeling does not get up. While, of course, some racist Americans cheered Schmeling, Louis brought millions of Americans together. I was reminded of the power of sports last year, the day after July 4. On July 5, 2015, I was walking through the Baltimore-Washington International Airport when I heard a sudden explosion of cheers. The US soccer team had just kicked the ball past a diving Japanese goalkeeper in the Women's World Cup final match. Strangers, transients passing through an airport slapped each other and felt an emotional and psychological tie. They formed a group and for a split second, as the ball slipped past the Japanese goalie, felt bonded like a fraternity, sorority, 4-H club, or church choir.

WE ARE NUMBER ONE, OR WAIT 'TIL NEXT YEAR

Sometimes bonding requires identifying a common obstacle or foe and a feeling of superiority. That is certainly the case in war or in a World Cup match. Again, it may be politically incorrect to admit that groups and nations need to feel superior ("ethnocentrism") but that is the lesson of history, backed up by modern psychological testing. The Jews called themselves the "chosen people," not the "also-rans." Many Rastafarians, encouraged by Marcus Garvey, believe that Jah (God) has chosen black people as physically and spiritually superior. People feel better when their group succeeds. Psychologists use the acronym BIRG to describe the tendency for people to "bask in the reflected glory" of their group. After a winning football game, more college students will wear sweatshirts and scarves celebrating their team.[14] School songs will often blend battle cries with religious references and declarations of superiority, even in the pursuit of a mere six-point touchdown. I can still recite a fight song from my high school, Toms River High School South, which does all three.

> Ashes to ashes and dust to dust,
> We hate to beat you but if we must we must.
> 'Cause east is east and west is west
> But we're from South and South is best!

Somehow along the Jersey Shore, the Anglican *Book of Common Prayer* ("ashes to ashes") got roped into a tautological geography lesson ("east is east"). Nonetheless, we cheerfully shouted the fight song. And we truly believed that our high school was better than its rivals (it really was!).

Groups like high schools, sororities, fraternities, symphonies, and nations could take a more modest route and simply assert their positive traits without trumpeting greatness or asserting superiority compared with others. But they usually do not take the humble path. Why? Because group identity must boost self-esteem even in bad times. When a team loses a match or a country loses a battle, morale and solidarity fray. Team members and fans feel less attached and are less likely to don team shirts and hold heads high. Defeat serves up the true test of a group's sustainability. *If the group is going to live on, members must be convinced that the defeat is temporary.* It is easy to feel good about one's team or one's country after a massive victory, but every country and every team loses or suffers embarrassment from time to time. That is a promise that history does not renege on. In March 1942 Japanese military forces pummeled American and Filipino soldiers who tried to defend the Philippines from rockets, bombs, and torpedoes. President Franklin Roosevelt ordered the proud and haughty General Douglas MacArthur to abandon his post on the island fortress of Corregidor, leaving behind ninety thousand soldiers who lacked the supplies to combat the Japanese offensive. Many were captured and then forced into the infamous Bataan death march, which killed thousands. Avoiding gunfire, mines, and violent waves, MacArthur and his family traveled over five hundred miles on a small PT boat. MacArthur told the boat commander, "You have taken me out of the jaws of death." But after making it to Melbourne, Australia, MacArthur uttered his famous phrase, "I shall return." His soldiers and the American people believed his pledge. Two and a half years later, MacArthur waded ashore to the Philippine Island of Leyte to fulfill his promise. When the Americans captured Manila, he declared, "I'm a little late, but we finally came." In the next chapter we will see how Alexander the Great used his superior reputation to rally his troops back from defeat.

Asserting superiority (or exceptionalism) allows people to feel that any loss is a temporary setback. "We Shall Overcome" implies a setback but also promises a subsequent triumph. Jewish historians joke that their entire history—pockmarked with killings from Haman to Hadrian to Hitler—can be summed up as "They tried to kill us; we survived; let's eat."

In the boxing realm, neither Joe Louis nor Muhammad Ali would have been considered the "Greatest" had Louis not fought back from his defeat by Schmeling and if Ali had not avenged his 1971 loss to Joe Frazier. Boxing historians consistently rank Louis and Ali above Rocky Marciano, the "Brockton Blockbuster," who dominated heavyweight boxing in the late 1940s and 1950s and retired with forty-nine victories, including forty-three knockouts and not a single loss. But critics gripe that Marciano did not face great competitors on his way to forty-nine straight victories. I would contend that if Marciano had lost and then avenged one brutal slugfest, he would be ranked higher today.

Nearly every group, regardless of the category of endeavor, will assert some real or imagined superiority: Japanese assembly-line workers are better team players; the Seattle Seahawks have a swifter running game; or the New York Philharmonic understands Mahler better than the Philadelphia Orchestra. Abigail Adams must have longed for America when she wrote to her sister from London in 1786 that English birds could not compete with American fowl: "Do you know that European Birds have not half the melody of ours, nor is their fruit half so sweet, or their flowers half so Fragrant, or their Manners half so pure, or their people half So virtuous. But keep this to yourself."[15] Abigail Adams really did think that American birds sang better. No doubt, Keats was tone-deaf in 1819 when he wrote an "Ode to a Nightingale" and in 1961, when Nat King Cole warbled that "a nightingale sang in Berkeley Square," he should have appended the adverb "badly." This all seems ridiculous, but it is often necessary, particularly in stressful times.

How does a group respond when faced with undeniable proof that it is not as good as another group? Let's say that English and American birds have a double-blind sing-off, in which both judges and birds are blindfolded. What would Abigail Adams do if the English birds won? Most likely, she would rationalize the result and suggest some other measure of superiority or provide an excuse for the Americans' failure. Perhaps the American birds are too deep in original thought to sing a silly song by rote memory, or too devoted to their freedom to warble on command. I knew a college professor who, when seeing a twelve-year-old genius score A's on college finals, comforted herself by saying, "Well, at least I have a normal social life." In 1858 Nathaniel Hawthorne traveled to Florence and toured the Uffizi Gallery, which displays works of Michelangelo, Leonardo, and Raphael. Hawthorne marveled at the Italians' "genuine love of painting and sculpture." But Hawthorne could not simply acknowledge their masterpiece achievements on canvas and in marble. He had to blot them with ink or bile. So in his diaries he contends that Italians produce monumental art precisely because they are moral dwarfs: the Italians are "capable of every social crime, and to have formed a fine and hard enamel over their characters. Perhaps it is because such tastes are artificial, the product of cultivation, and . . . imply a great remove from natural simplicity."[16] In other words, Italian masters paint better because they are dishonest and not blinded by simple truths. We are superior because we are not as handy with a paintbrush.

Like Hawthorne, people will often disparage other groups as more primitive or less bound by moral rules. The Chinese consider the rest of the world barbarians. The ancient Greeks came up with the word *barbarian* because it sounded like the gibberish spoken by non-Greeks. We convince ourselves that other cultures appear to have looser rules of dress, looser standards of hygiene, and looser women. And they will eat anything! Some Brits still call the French "frogs." The French have the decency not to ask what is in the dish called spotted dick; the English refer to syphilis as "the French disease" and the French call it "the Italian disease." Foreigners smell bad, and if they use too much soap or cologne, they smell worse. Crazed mullahs in Iran declare that Christians are really monkeys and pigs in disguise. In *Planet of the Apes*, the apes sneer at the scent of Charlton Heston until he barks back, "Get your stinking paws off me, you damned dirty ape!"

If a nation does not have a culture that binds people together, we all begin to look at each other as "damned dirty apes." Military leaders since Thucydides know that they cannot elicit sacrifice and risk taking unless they can turn platoons into brotherhoods. Henry V's rallying cry at Agincourt, "We few, we happy few, we . . . band of brothers," inspired a puny assembly of English forces to trounce the heavily armored knights of France. Henry promises that "he to-day that sheds his blood with me/Shall be my brother; be he never so vile." Of course, these words are really Shakespeare's, not the historical king's. But scroll ahead three hundred years and you come to a real soldier and a real poet, a young lad named Rupert Brooke, who was called by W. B. Yeats "the handsomest young man in England." In his 1914 poem "The Soldier," Brooke writes, "If I should die, think only this of me:/That there's some corner of a foreign field/That is forever England." The soldier's death sanctifies the land, whether or not the soldier believes in God. An unbreakable trinity forms among the soldier, the land, and his people in England. Let's add a coda to this poem. Brooke's poetry was lauded by Winston Churchill, who was serving as first lord of the admiralty during the Great War. Brooke joined the Royal Navy in 1914 and sailed toward Greece to join the Battle of Gallipoli (which I'll discuss in chapter 7). He contracted an infection along the way and died on a ship in the Aegean Sea. He was buried in an olive grove on the island of Skyros, Greece, on April 23, 1915. At 11 that evening a six-foot-deep rectangle of earth became, by his logic and his sacrifice, a part of England.

CHOOSE PATRIOTISM OR NARCISSISM

Pollyanna types might say that groups and nations should just be modest and surrender any drive to feel superior. But that, too, poses a serious risk. Certainly, the untouchables in India did not benefit by accepting their inferior status. These so-called polluted people were barred even from wearing sandals in front of higher-caste members, much less sharing cups, tables, or burial grounds with them. At the other end of the spectrum, hypersuperiority can stir trouble, or even genocide, as the Nazis taught us. But the lesson from the Nazis and Japanese fascists in World War II is to beware of claims of conquest based on blood-lines. The patriotism of the American Revolution was based not on blood but in fact on principles of liberty and the dilution of pure bloodlines (with the exception of slaves, of course). The Constitution's system of checks and balances gives a clear signal that no man, and no single institution, has the ultimate claim on truth and power. We see this in the papers of James Madison, in Gerald Ford's first words as president, and even in comic movies. In one monologue in the movie *Stripes*, Bill Murray's louche character encapsulates the principles above, namely that (1) America's greatness is not based on a pedigree and (2) a belief in greatness means that Americans can climb back from defeats:

> Cut it out! . . . We're all very different people. We're not Watusi. We're not Spartans. We're Americans, with a capital 'A,' huh? You know what that means? Do ya? That means that our forefathers were kicked out of every decent country in the world. We are the wretched refuse. We're the underdog. We're mutts! . . . We're soldiers, but we're Amer-

ican soldiers! We've been kickin' ass for 200 years! We're 10 and 1! . . . All we have to do is to be the great American fighting soldier that is inside each one of us. Now do what I do, and say what I say. And make me proud.[17]

Most individuals harbor a natural wish to feel superior. Sigmund Freud thought we even puffed up the reputations of our ancestors, calling it the "family romance" fallacy. The nineteenth-century British economist and social philosopher Nassau William Senior lamented the unstoppable "desire for distinction . . . that comes with us from the cradle and never leaves us till we go into the grave."[18] Sometimes the quest for individual superiority can hurt others. Economists like Robert H. Frank of Cornell contend that we are engaged in a fruitless competition, not just to keep up with the Joneses but to trample them, which leads to envy and despair.[19] The desire for superiority shows up in spheres far beyond economics, business, and sports. What is sibling rivalry but the urge to show Mother or Father that I am better than my brother or sister? The old cry from the bicycle-riding kid, "Look, Ma, no hands!" is another way of shouting, "The other kids need to hold on, but I'm better!"

Here is the danger I see when we forbid or trample on a group's or a nation's natural wish to feel superior: individuals will turn the drive toward superiority inward and turn more narcissistic. In the United States, patriotism has fallen as narcissism has risen. The public school day used to begin not just with the Pledge of Allegiance but with "My Country, 'Tis of Thee" or "America the Beautiful." In many schools, those songs have been dropped in favor of slogans taped to the walls to build self-esteem, announcing "EVERYBODY IS A STAR!" In my garage are stacks of trophies won by my daughters for playing soccer and softball. Please note,

I did not say they have trophies for *winning*, simply for playing. They probably amassed more trophies than my grandpa Bobby, who boxed, played center on his basketball team, and won the New York City tennis championship. Poor Grandpa should have waited until the 2000s, instead of competing in Calvin Coolidge's day. In the comic movie *Meet the Fockers*, Robert De Niro's character mocks Ben Stiller's: "I didn't know they made ninth-place ribbons."

We have diminished the esteem of the country and instead focused on the self-esteem of the individual. Some preschools have replaced the lyrics of "Frère Jacques" with the words "I am special, I am special, look at me." There are at least three things wrong with this switch. First, teachers have lost the chance to teach a bit of a foreign language. Second, they have replaced "brother" with "I," losing warm fraternal feelings. Third, they have turned toddlers into egotists. Not every finger-painted smudge by a four-year-old deserves to be ogled or stuck to the refrigerator by a magnet made in art class. *The best way to develop self-esteem is to do something worthy of esteem.* Imagine Henry V's speech at Agincourt if he could not pledge his life to the "band of brothers," but instead could refer only to a bunch of "special" youngsters.

In the 1960s Hasbro came up with the idea of G.I. Joe, defying the marketing geniuses who said that boys would not play with dolls. Hasbro showed that if you put a toy grenade or sword in the hands of a doll, the boys will happily stage battle scenes. I cannot locate the talking G.I. Joe that I carried to elementary school, but I can easily recall the urgent lines he would shout when I tugged on the dog tag chain: "Enemy planes! Hit the deck!" and "Medic, medic, get that stretcher out here!" Though the G.I. Joe brand is quite valuable and recent movies called *G.I. Joe: The Rise of Cobra* and *G.I. Joe: Retaliation* have sold nearly

$700 million of tickets at the box office, I doubt that the term "G.I. Joe" would take off if it were coined today. "G.I." stands for "government issue." "Joe" was a just a generic folksy name, like "buddy" or "fella." Here's a test: gather a bunch of seventy-year-old men around a table, point to one with a smile, and say, "He's a regular Joe." The chosen chum will likely smile back and accept the compliment. Try the same tactic with a twenty-year-old and you will hear "Red Alert" alarms and talking G.I. Joes will scream "Battle stations!" No twentysomething wants to be called a "regular Joe." In the 1950s a young man who stepped out of line would be slapped on the head by his father, teacher, or coach and asked in a biting tone, "What do you think you are—special?!" A study of nearly 800,000 books published between 1960 and 2008 showed that recent writers typed individualistic words and phrases like "standout," "I come first," and "I have my own style" about 20 percent more often, and 42 percent more often among novelists.[20] Perhaps Americans should perceive our liberty, not our individual selves, as very special.

People raised in the era of the selfie who design their own computer avatars often feel too special for generic titles. Kids and adults often craft for themselves an online world that is downright pre-Copernican—it all revolves around them: their fun, their hobbies, their circle of friends. Some will even sacrifice friends in order to stay in the center of their own solar system. A survey of fifteen hundred adult women showed that one in four had tagged on Facebook an unflattering photo of a friend (presumably to make themselves appear more attractive). If the friend asked them to remove the ugly photo, 20 percent refused.[21]

Jean Twenge, a psychologist at San Diego State University, studied surveys conducted among college students over the past sixty years. In the 1950s only 12 percent of teens agreed with the statement "I am an important person." By the 1980s 80 percent ticked that box.[22] More young people than ever before agree with this staggering boast: "If I were on the *Titanic*, I would deserve to be on the first lifeboat." No doubt, young narcissists would imagine themselves swanning through the first-class salons alongside the Astors rather than trapped in steerage with the unwashed masses, who looked nothing like Leonardo DiCaprio.

WHAT IS THE AMERICAN CHARACTER?

If we can excuse the drive to feel superior, what should Americans feel superior about? We certainly should not claim mastery of everything and we should not deny our faults. Ben Franklin touted the symbol of the turkey above the bald eagle because the turkey is "tho' a little vain & silly, a Bird of Courage, and would not hesitate to attack a Grenadier of the British Guards who should presume to invade his Farm Yard with a red Coat on." In contrast, Franklin thought the bald eagle was a "bad moral Character," a coward in the face of sparrows and a thief who steals food from the hardworking fish hawk.[23] We could, of course, cite great victories and displays of courage, for instance, Bunker Hill and the Battle of the Bulge. We could speak of displays of magnanimity, including the Marshall Plan or technological achievements such as landing a man on the moon or low-flow flush toilets. But these are notable events and accomplishments, not characteristics of a people. When patriots speak of "American exceptionalism," I would nominate three elements to define our national character, elements that we can list under the memorable acronym GMC. They are Grit, Mobility, and Confidence. As the preceding chapters described, each of these elements has been eroding. Americans appear to work less and try less hard (*grit*). They are stuck in place literally and figuratively (*mobility*); young people are less willing to take a chance and move across state or county lines to take a job. A lack of grit and mobility bespeaks a faltering *confidence*. In 2015, despite a low (official) unemployment rate just above 5 percent, over two-thirds of Americans told pollsters that the United States was headed in the "wrong direction." The three characteristics—Grit, Mobility, and Confidence—must be resuscitated, or the body politic may die. Other nations might exalt other characteristics and more highly rank, for example, thriftiness, kindness, or a passion for artisanal foods. These may all be noble and admirable. But GMC made America. If Americans cannot rediscover these characteristics in their land today, how can immigrants possibly locate them when they arrive by plane, truck, and ship?

WHATEVER HAPPENED TO GRIT?

In addition to a legitimate court system and a dependable currency, a cohesive country needs a population that displays *grit*. Grit is not simply the title on a John Wayne movie poster. It's a specific, measurable psychological trait, indicating perseverance, doggedness, and stick-to-itiveness. People with grit fight to attain long-term goals despite obstacles. They blame others less and take responsibility more. Individuals who show grit are more likely to get a job, pay for a house, and raise successful children. Individuals who lack grit struggle to finish school and cannot keep up with credit card debt. So far, studies of grit have focused on individuals. One widely read study by Angela Lee Duckworth, of the University of Pennsylvania, showed that among new West Point cadets, those who score higher on the grit scale are more likely to survive the fearsome "Beast Barracks," the grueling first-year training that forces cadets to carry forty-five-pound rucksacks while running, climbing, and marching to the beat of somebody else's drummer.[24] Grit better predicts West Point success than measures of IQ, SATs, push-up scores, or even self-discipline. (Of course, we must be careful not to put perseverance on too high a pedestal. Persevering in the face of literally insurmountable odds or infinite costs could be reckless or stupid. A plebe should not stick it out at West Point, if he is better suited by temperament and talent to play the oboe at Juilliard, for example.)

Grit is a national characteristic, not just an individual trait. Countries with grittier populations are less likely play the "blame game" and less likely to go on reckless national spending sprees that bankrupt future generations. Grittier nations extol a degree of self-reliance. A 2013 Cambridge University study explored the psychological concept called "locus of control." Someone with a low sense of internal control believes that the outside world determines his fate, as if he is a billiard ball suddenly knocked around by other balls and a cue stick. So, "What's the point of trying if I'm powerless?" The Cambridge study concluded that individuals with a low sense of internal control generally expect the government to solve their problems, since they consider themselves feckless.[25] A lack of grit shows up in the growing bureaucracies and debt obligations discussed in chapters 3 and 4. Other countries may have closed the *grit gap* with the United States, leaving Americans more vulnerable in a competitive global economy.

Historically, Americans have been known for gutsiness. The lyrics of the World War I song "Over There" point to a specifically American characteristic:

Johnnie, get your gun
Johnnie show the Hun you're a son of a gun
Hoist the flag and let her fly, Yankee Doodle do or die
Pack your little kit, *show your grit*, do your bit . . .
Make your mother proud of you and the old Red White and
Blue.

In an earlier day American companies and individuals boasted of their perseverance. The Avis car rental company admitted it was "Number 2," but claimed, "We try harder." In a memorable advertisement for brokerage house E. F. Hutton, actor John Houseman intoned, "We make money the old-fashioned way—we *earn* it." European nations used to sneer at America's unceasing work ethic. Contrast the plucky American way of thinking to the high-brow British approach. At prestigious Balliol College, Oxford, the semiofficial motto is "*effortless* superiority."

Once upon a time Americans didn't mind sweat and grit but rising incomes in the twentieth century brought a cushier life. In 1900 41 percent toiled on farms.[26] By 2000 only 1.9 percent worked in agriculture and that work is much more likely to involve navigating a GPS-enabled John Deere tractor than shoveling hay and manure with a handheld pitchfork. In the twenty-first century we, understandably, expect more rewards for less toil. Let's go back to the old Sears catalog, as we did in chapter 2. To buy a refrigerator in 1949, a typical worker had to put in 4.5 *weeks* of labor (before taxes). Today, a much better Sears refrigerator requires about 2.5 *days* of work. A worker in 1949 labored for 13.5 hours to afford a toaster. Today, a better toaster costs about 1 hour of work. Of course, these are marvelous developments! But such progress inevitably depletes our need to believe in perseverance. In popular culture and the world of self-help, *The 8-Minute Abs Workout* complements *The 4-Hour Workweek*. A few years ago, Dell Computer's popular ad campaign highlighted a slacker who says, "Dude, you got a Dell," in a laid-back surfer tone, suggesting the Dell laptop was bestowed upon the recipient, not earned.

The short-term, quick-getaway attitude shows up in the corporate boardroom, too, which sends a discouraging message all the way down to the bottom rungs of the corporate ladder. Executives often gear themselves for short-run success, not a long-run battle for market share. Corporations will beef up quarterly earnings just as an executive's stock shares vest, giving him a short-term surge of wealth. No surprise, then, that firms often ignore long-term challenges. Corporations are spending fewer and fewer R&D dollars in the United States, and the United States educates just 4 percent of the world's engineers.

Former Hewlett-Packard CEO Mark Hurd is a former competitive tennis player and an even more competitive executive. When he took over the company in 2006, he immediately slashed salaries, chopped the number of jobs by 10 percent, and set the office lights to shut off automatically at 6 p.m. every day. Wall Street loved the cost-cutting story and pushed up the price of HP shares. But in addition to cutting the office electricity bill, Hurd slashed R&D spending from 9 percent of revenues down to just 2 percent. The demoralized HP engineers and scientists applied for only one-third as many patents. Why did HP sit paralyzed and dumb as Apple triumphed with the iPad? Because HP's R&D for personal computers had slumped to just seven-tenths of 1 percent of revenues.[27] It's sad to think that Wall Street applauded this vision of the future.

A TOUGHER TIME FOR IMMIGRANTS

If native-born Americans appear less patriotic, more narcissistic, and more devoted to short-term gains than building a
long-lasting country, how can we expect more of immigrants?
Immigration has become a divisive issue in most wealthy nations, whether legal immigration through the help of crafty lawyers or illegal migration through bribes to "coyotes" who sneak
human beings over fences, across barricades, and in the trunks
of cars. Not far from my home, near the Marine Base Camp
Pendleton, is an immigration checkpoint. Guards stand in the
middle of the eight-lane interstate 5 to Los Angeles, staring into
car windows and deciding when to pop open a trunk latch or
uncover the tarp over the back of a pickup truck. Yellow road
signs display the silhouette of a man, woman, and child holding
hands running away across a field. The sign has no caption but
presumably means, "Don't run over the fleeing illegals." Though
this book is not devoted to the thorny issue of immigration,
immigrants can contribute to the shattering of rich nations—
unless they are invited, urged, and even mandated to adopt their
new country as their own.

In 1950 nearly 80 percent of foreign-born residents chose to
salute the American flag and become US citizens. Since 2000
only half of eligible immigrants have bothered (compared with
89 percent in Canada and 82 percent in Sweden), reports the
National Academy of Sciences.[28] We can admire them for coming
to the United States for jobs. Nonetheless, a vital nation is more
than a long lineup of unrelated workers sticking their cards into
the boss's punch clock.

It is easy to be nostalgic about the old immigration waves of
the nineteenth and early twentieth centuries: the Norwegians

who settled in Minnesota and brought horrible tasting lute-fisk; the Italians who brought spaghetti to Philadelphia and Joe DiMaggio to the Yankees; the Chinese who built railroad tracks and concocted a stew to suit simple American tastes and called it chow mein; and the Dutch, who had names like Roosevelt. Of course, every child learns that these groups all faced discrimination, from the "NO IRISH NEED APPLY" signs to the racist hotels that invited the highly paid Al Jolson and Bert Williams to entertain onstage, but might have snuck them out through servants' entrances after the show. In the 1840s the Know Nothing movement tried to block Catholics from arriving on US shores. Even earlier in our history, Ben Franklin showed his bias. Although Franklin formed one of the first abolitionist movements on behalf of slaves and donated money to a synagogue in Philadelphia, he was severely biased against Protestant Germans. He called them "Palatine Boors" and said they would never adopt the English language or "acquire our Complexion." Franklin had an odd view of complexion, even insisting that Swedes were swarthy.[29] Clearly, he did not foresee a never-ending road tour of screaming blondes in Abba's *Mamma Mia*.

These earlier waves of immigrants faced enormous pressure to learn the "American way." Much of that pressure was internal. The American-born children of immigrants before the 1960s seldom learned the language of their immigrant parents. Many were ashamed that their parents spoke English with an accent. I am not suggesting that they were right to be ashamed. They were wrong. Yet it bespoke an overwhelming desire to embrace their country. The son of Irish parents, George M. Cohan claimed that he was born on the Fourth of July and even inserted his claim in his song "Yankee Doodle Boy." The grandson of slaves, Louis Armstrong pulled the same patriotic stunt (he was off by a month). Sports stadiums were packed with blue-collar immigrants cheering heroes with "all-American" names like Bronco Nagurski, Babe Zaharias, Hank Greenberg, and Phil Rizzuto. In the opening of Neil Simon's play *Brighton Beach Memoirs* the teen-aged protagonist is throwing a baseball against the wall of a small house in Brooklyn, in a neighborhood "inhabited mostly by Jews, Irish, and Germans." He laments his own ethnicity: "How am I ever going to play for the Yankees with a name like Eugene Morris Jerome? You have to be a Joe . . . or a Tony . . . or a Frankie . . . All the best Yankees are Italian . . . My mother makes spaghetti with ketchup, what chance do I have?"[30] The point here is that Eugene wants to be better at *America's* national pastime, baseball.

There are more serious examples. In the National Portrait Gallery in Washington hangs a colorful painting called *Shimomura Crossing the Delaware.* Roger Shimomura did not cross the frigid Delaware with George Washington on Christmas night 1776 and he is not found in the iconic 1851 oil painting by the German-born artist Emanuel Leutze. Shimomura's cartoonish version, in the style of a woodblock print, depicts Washington's colonial troops as samurai warriors in kimonos. Shimomura, who was taken with his family from their home in Seattle during World War II and forced to relocate to an Idaho internment camp, makes the following point: even though we were not literally fighting with George Washington, we, too, are Americans and entitled to claim him and his daring as our own. This was poignantly true of the second-generation Japanese who fought with the mighty and highly decorated 442nd Regimental Combat Team. Most of the young soldiers faced down Nazi machine-gun fire and tank shells in Italy and France, while their parents lived in internment camps back in the United States. The fourteen thousand Nisei soldiers earned nearly ten thousand Purple Hearts.

War is hell. Trenches and tanks do, however, help integrate disparate people. Eighteen percent of the US soldiers in World War I were foreign born, compared with about 15 percent of the population.[31] Italian Americans made up 12 percent of the army.[32] Today, 4.8 percent of active military personnel are foreign born and 11 percent are of Hispanic descent.[33] Dozens of war movies have been made, featuring a mix of ethnicities forced into the same trench, submarine, or platoon. In one well-told story from 1917 a staff sergeant calls the tongue-twister roll at Camp Meade in Maryland and not a single man recognizes his own name. Then the sergeant sneezes and ten recruits step forward. In a sequel to Neil Simon's *Brighton Beach Memoirs*, entitled *Biloxi Blues*, the character goes off to basic training in Mississippi, where he finally learns the diversity of the country. First he confronts the southern climate: "Man it's hot. It's like Africa hot. Tarzan couldn't take this kind of hot." Then he meets his bunkmates: Roy Selridge, a smelly guy from Schenectady who has "cavities in nineteen out of thirty-two teeth"; Joseph Wykowski, who has a "permanent erection"; and Arnold Epstein, an intellectual with intestinal gas. A motley crew, but they could not be more American. And if you can imagine them fighting side by side, you can see the truth behind Herman Melville's line, "You can not spill a drop of American blood without spilling the blood of the whole world."[34] The US government used words, music, and art to encourage this sentiment. If I had to nominate the two most famous illustrations of America's founding I would choose Emanuel Leutze's painting *Washington Crossing the Delaware* and Howard Chandler Christy's *Scene of the Signing of the Declaration of Independence* in Philadelphia. Christy, who began his career by illustrating scenes of Teddy Roosevelt on San Juan Hill, was commissioned by New York Congressman Sol Bloom to paint the founding fathers, all white Protestants, except for one Catholic. But in 1919, soon after World War I, Christy painted a more diverse portrait for the US Treasury's Victory bonds, which now hangs in the Museum of Modern Art. It is called *Americans All!* and features an elegant woman in a low-cut yellow gown clutching the American flag in one hand and raising up high a laurel wreath in the other. Under the wreath is an "Honor Roll" of names, and the names sound as if they were plucked randomly at the docks of Ellis Island: "DuBois, Smith, O'Brien, Cejka, Hauke, Pappandrikopolous, Adrassi, Villotto . . . Gonzales."

The phrase "melting pot" comes from a play that predates *Biloxi Blues* by about seventy years. Israel Zangwill's 1908 smash-hit drama *The Melting Pot* brings David, a Russian Jew, and Vera, a Russian Orthodox Christian, together in love under the gaze of the Statue of Liberty.[35] David tells Vera to listen to the "bubbling," as "Celt and Latin, Slav and Teuton, Greek and Syrian—black and yellow" unite and "look forward!" Sociologists debate whether the melting pot is an appropriate metaphor and many suggest a "salad bowl" or some kind of goulash, where flavors and ingredients never really meld.[36] Regardless of the metaphor one plucks from *The Joy of Cooking*, the challenge to create and rouse an American character has grown more severe and also more urgent. We face here another paradox: while the very richness of a nation makes it more difficult for immigrants to assimilate, it makes it easier for the nation to unravel.

Let's take a look at three factors, *calluses, cacophony,* and *communication.* During the great immigration waves prior to World War II, immigrants had *calluses* on their hands. So did most native-born workers. In 1900 69 percent of the US working population toiled on farms, in forests, and in factories, or crawled down mine shafts.[37] When immigrants arrived, they quickly learned how to put their calloused hands to work, even if they faced discrimination from unions and bosses. My grandpa Sam used to say that when Irish immigrants stepped off the boat in Manhattan, they were offered a choice: "A hook or a club?" meaning they could haul boxes off ships as a long-shoreman (the hook), or apply for a job as a policeman (the club). The barrier to entry was not physical or economic; it was political. The Irish dominated New York City politics and unions. Nor was the barrier educational. In 1900 fewer than 14 percent of Americans graduated from high school and fewer than 3 percent graduated from college. By the end of the twentieth century, 83 percent graduated from high school and 25 percent from college. These days an immigrant arriving from a country that has not yet gone through the Industrial Revolution, much less the Semiconductor Revolution, is far less likely to find work side by side with a native-born American in the service sector, where literacy, numeracy, and interpersonal skills like salesmanship and marketing are highly prized.

When America was poorer, immigrants created a *cacophony* of noise, as peddlers squawked their wares on the streets speaking their native Italian, Polish, and Cantonese dialects. The unsmiling schoolmarms in Brooklyn and the Bronx, frequently of Irish descent in the early 1900s, had no patience to teach in foreign languages. Even if they wanted to, it would have been impossible. Likewise, the students themselves realized that they would have to learn English in order to get along. Young David Sarnoff, an immigrant from Russia, taught himself English while hawking newspapers next to a streetcar stop; found a job with the Marconi telegraph company; and then helped found RCA and the NBC radio and television networks.[38] If Sarnoff had not bothered to learn English, we might still be staring at Edison's spinning phonograph coils. Today it is easier for immigrants to avoid English, especially because the cacophony has quieted down. In 1910 every language that immigrants spoke was a minority tongue. None had a big enough "market share" to dominate and create a massive, durable enclave (Germans made up a plurality of 18 percent). Princeton sociologist Alejandro Portes has coined the term "segmented assimilation" to describe immigrants who integrate into a single part of American society rather than into the mainstream community. This has become easier because Spanish so dominates among recent immigrants. Mexico alone accounts for 29 percent of immigrants, and the proportion of Spanish-speaking immigrants now reaches about one-half.[39] Portes, a Cuban immigrant himself, worries about "enclaves" where immigrants can be too comfortable with the tongue of their homeland: "You could be born into a Cuban clinic, be employed in a Cuban factory or enterprise, and be buried in a Cuban cemetery."[40] During 2013 the Spanish-language network Univision beat out English-language networks FOX, NBC, CBS, and ABC in prime-time ratings among eighteen- to forty-nine-year olds.[41] Arguably, there is a *lack of diversity* among recent immigrants, and we might be better off with a blaring cacophony among arrivals.

Third, computers are everywhere: in offices, homes, phones, and wristwatches. The price of *communication* has plummeted, leading to the "death of distance." Our grandparents used to cut off phone conversations for fear that the bill from Ma Bell would drain their life savings. Most people today do not even know how much it costs them to call across state or national lines. Even among poor families in 2014, 85 percent owned cell phones and 77 percent used the Internet.[42] Those numbers keep climbing. This is wonderful, though it brings up a first-world problem: why would an immigrant cut off ties to his homeland and dedicate himself to a new place? Like communication costs, transportation costs have plummeted in inflation-adjusted terms over the last century. Because Charles Lindbergh did not auction off his passenger seat in 1927, it is difficult to calculate airline costs over the last ninety years, but since 1978 airfares have dropped about 50 percent. When I travel in the United States, I often ask foreign-born taxi and Uber drivers how often they go back to their homeland. Based on my simple survey, I would say immigrants from Asia and Africa return every two to three years, unless they fled particularly violent places and are frightened to return. A pair of professors at Bergen Community College in New Jersey wrote that many of their students "literally lead a double life, a negotiation between the place of their birth and their adopted home in America."[43] This double life shows up in the most basic life questions: Where should I get married? Where should they bury me when I'm dead? Immigrants a hundred years ago did not flinch. Most could not afford to go back either to visit or to get buried. In the early 1900s immigrant groups often formed jointly funded burial societies named after their village birthplace, because grave sites in American cities were expensive to keep up without sharing costs. Like Dracula, who always carried with him soil from Transylvania as a token of his roots, immigrants in 1900 kept only symbols of their homeland. Most could neither afford nor imagine arranging dual citizenship or dual loyalties. In contrast, in 1996 more than half the Dominicans and Mexicans who died in New York City were flown or shipped home for burial, as were one-third of the Ecuadoreans, according to city death records.[44] With transport and communication costs so relatively low, why not splurge on a final, long ride home?

THE HARDENING OF NATIVES

Because they perceive new immigrants as less devoted to their new country, many native-born American and European citizens have hardened their views. They are not as welcoming because they are not as confident that immigrants will accept and embrace their new country. By appealing to anti-immigrant, Euro-skeptic sentiment, the recently created UK Independence Party quickly became the third largest party in the country and a serious force that worries the Tories.[45] In the United Kingdom and in the United States, over 70 percent of the population would like to slash or better control immigration.[46] Some of this sentiment (especially in Europe) comes from national security fears and intensifies whenever there is a bombing traced to Al Qaeda or other terrorist groups. Baby boomers and their parents are most distressed by high immigration levels, with about 80 percent wanting to reduce immigration to the United Kingdom. As I discussed in chapter 1, the populations of rich nations are getting older and, as they age, people tend to become less open to making new friends or changing their ways. In a *New York Times* feature article, an Arizona college student said that immigration is the "rare, radioactive topic that sparks arguments with her liberal mother and grandmother." A Florida college student said that discussing immigration with older relatives was like "hitting your head against a brick wall."[47] No doubt, her older relatives would like to build a stronger and taller brick wall on the southern border. The article reminds me of a couple I knew when I was a little kid. An Italian family, the Gavonas, lived down the street. At Christmastime, Mr. Gavona, a man in his fifties, would dress as Santa Claus and ride on a fire truck, tossing candy to neighborhood kids. A few times, my brother and I got to ride on the back of the fire truck and help. (I remember being disappointed when on a particularly warm December day, Mr. Gavona pulled off the fake beard so he could breathe better.) Each year when my parents would take a parents-only vacation, my Aunt Kay would stay at our house and watch over us. And each year the doorbell would ring and Mrs.

Gavona would deliver to us a big pan of homemade manicotti, made with ricotta cheese. We would thank her with hugs. But we hated her cooking and after we'd watch her walk away down the path, we would, in an annual ritual, march to the bathroom and flush away the Gavona manicotti. They were good people, the Gavonas. Generous, caring, welcoming to new neighbors in the community. Then something changed. As we got older and as the Gavonas got older, they stopped sharing such kindnesses. We neighborhood kids would play baseball on a vacant lot near their house. When someone hit a home run or if a sharp grounder sliced through some bushes, the ball would roll into their yard. Mrs. Gavona would come out of her house and take the ball. If we trod on their grass to fetch the ball ourselves, Mr. Gavona would yell, "Get off the lawn!" To them we had turned into threatening pests. Meanwhile, we saw them as grumpy, old folks who did not remember what it was like to be young and frisky. "Whatever happened to Santa?" we wondered.

Our relations with the Gavona family match the history of immigration in America. At times, the United States has welcomed immigrants, and all sorts of support groups with names like the North American Civic League and the YMCA have sprung up to help them learn English and learn about democracy. But in more recent years, despite larger numbers of immigrants, many Americans sound more like the later-day Gavonas yelling, "Get off my lawn!" In fact, it is hard to make a case against tighter immigration controls without sounding like a grumpy old man who forgot what it is like to be young, ambitious, and slightly reckless. Instead of "Get off my lawn!" or "Get out of my country!" today's Gavonas should be shouting something about history and culture, such as "Get to the National Archives and learn to read the Declaration of Independence!"

WHATEVER HAPPENED TO YUGOSLAVIA AND THE
HABSBURG GAME SHOW HOST?

A country without a national character, without shared stories and myths, will soon cease to be a nation. Nations face a powerful tendency toward entropy and disorder. Harvard sociologist Robert Putnam, who shot to international fame in 2000 with his book *Bowling Alone*, discovered to his dismay that a more heterogeneous community breeds suspicion and spurs people to withdraw from civic life. In diverse communities, inhabitants tend to "distrust their neighbours, regardless of the colour of their skin, to withdraw even from close friends, to expect the worst . . . to volunteer less, give less to charity."[48] Of all the slogans found on our coins and monuments, perhaps the most difficult motto to live up to may be *E pluribus unum* (out of many, one). I have had the opportunity to visit several of the nations that had made up the country of Yugoslavia from 1918 until it shattered in 1991: Slovenia, Serbia, Croatia, Montenegro, Macedonia, and Bosnia-Herzegovina. Yugoslavians, ripped apart by ancient tribal jealousies, used to joke that Yugoslavia had "eight distinct peoples, six nations, four languages, three religions, two alphabets but just one Yugoslav: Marshal Tito." Following Tito's death in 1980 all began to fall apart. But Yugoslavia was a minor country, an unreliable Cold War pawn played by both the United States and the USSR.

Instead, let's learn some lessons from a major global power that tried *e pluribus unum*, the Habsburg monarchy. As I discussed earlier in this book, the Habsburgs' domain stretched from Amsterdam to Gibraltar to Bohemia and their leadership was capped by the title Holy Roman emperor. Though the Habsburg family emerged from a Swiss castle to rule Austria in 1279, a succession of carefully orchestrated marriages later lured into the family Isabel and Ferdinand's daughter Joan from Spain, along with the sons and daughters of nearly every other ruling family in Europe. If they had not succeeded as monarchs, the Habsburgs would have been the world's greatest gossips and matchmakers.

But did anyone besides blood relatives and in-laws consider themselves Habsburgs? That was the problem. Though Emperor Franz Joseph (who reigned for sixty-eight years starting in 1848) saw himself as a universal force (like the Roman Catholic Church) and even adopted the motto *Virus unitis* (with united forces), he never figured out how to create or instill the *uni* in his subjects. To most of them, he was just another Teuton, albeit one with thousands of cannons in his arsenal. While Franz Joseph was personally popular, the key term here is "personally." His crown was not popular to those who considered themselves Polish, Slovak, Hungarian, Czech, etc. One scholar of the empire, Robert Kann, wrote that the Habsburg monarchy was "composed mainly of torsos of nations," but not the heads or the hearts of the people.

It is hard to cheer for an omnipotent yet remote monarchy. For many the Habsburgs were an abstraction that did not share their faith, history, language, or family ties. How do you rally around a strange abstraction? It reminds me of comedian Robert Klein's observation that his schools in New York did not have a name; they simply had numbers, like PS 406. He'd joke about the school fight song: "Dear 406, we love you!" And "80, your name will rise above . . . 79!" Hardly rah-rah crowd-pleasers.

The Habsburgs struggled with even less success than PS 406. They tried to grant some level of autonomy to various ethnic groups, and article 19 of Austria's constitution ensured that schools would preserve ethnic languages. But what forces would fight entropy, the tendency for the people to break from the center? Without institutions that would celebrate a truly national consciousness, it was just a matter of time before the Habsburgs got swept into history's dustbin.

When World War I broke out in 1914 following the assassination of Franz Joseph's nephew in Serbia, the Habsburgs called upon their troops, who mostly showed up for battle. But they appeared to be fighting for their own homelands, not for the imagined *uni* nation based in Vienna. Battalions of Czech soldiers left Prague for the battlefield singing, "I've got to fight the Russians, but I don't know why." In southern Hungary, in Croatia, and along the Bosnian border, protesters and soldiers rebelled. They were shot, of course.

The Habsburgs lost the war and their crown. What's left of a powerful empire that could not figure out how to create a shared language, shared traditions, and shared values? Just some fading photos of Emperor Franz Joseph displaying a fluffy mustache and muttonchops. Otto von Habsburg, the last surviving child of the last emperor, was born in the family palace in 1912. He died a few years ago at age ninety-nine, but not before seeing his son Karl host a television game show called *Who Is Who?* Indeed.

Unless today's rich nations rediscover and embrace their national characters, they will break apart and the names of those countries will serve only to provide an answer in a trivia game that our great-grandchildren will play.

PART II

LEADING THE CHARGE

Americans have always had a plucky attitude toward authority. In King Arthur's court, Mark Twain's Connecticut Yankee declares, "There is nothing diviner about a king than there is about a tramp."[1] Leaders must earn our respect. Mere fame should bring little admiration, especially in an era where reality television stars command million-dollar paychecks just for showing how they tan their liposuctioned thighs.

In part II of this book we will look at world leaders who were forced to rekindle or reimagine their nations' identity amid bullets flying, jobs disappearing, and empires crumbling. I have not chosen the usual subjects. It would be easier to profile Elizabeth I, Peter the Great, Napoleon, John Adams, Winston Churchill, and the Roosevelt cousins, for example. But bookshelves already bulge with scholarly treatises and pop titles like *Elizabeth I CEO* and *Napoleon on Project Management*. I am not looking to lift up even higher the most powerful and famous characters in the annals of the *Encyclopaedia Britannica* and Wikipedia. Instead I have deployed other criteria.

First, I have chosen innovators. I argue that in business *it is better to make yourself obsolete than to wait for your competitors to do it for you*. Successful political leaders must also understand new trends, even if they feel nostalgia for the past. The leaders profiled here did not sit around and wait. Nor did they stand up in front of the train of progress, hold out a stiff right arm, and scream, "Stop!" In Turkey, Kemal Atatürk flung open the doors to science and toppled the caliph. In Japan, the Meiji leaders risked riling up their own craftsmen by seeking English advice on making silk. Sure, Nagano artisans may have lost face but that was preferable to the Japanese people losing their entire nation. Second, the leaders represent a diversity of time and place, from Alexander in 336 BC Greece to Jose Figueres Ferrer in AD 1948 Costa Rica. This book does not take narrow aim to pinpoint flaws only in the US political economy of 2016; it aims to uncover universal forces so that we may learn from past leaders, regardless of where they lived.

What makes a great leader? In the next chapter, we will see how Alexander picked up his sword and sliced through the legendary Gordian knot when others wasted their time trying to unravel it.

First, a great leader must be brave enough to forcefully kick aside conventional wisdom. In 1980 almost every Republican and Democrat in the United States assumed that the Soviet Union would stick around for decades, if not centuries. The old Cold War strategy was "containment," in which the United States would be happy merely to prevent the further spread of communism. To imagine rolling back communism in Moscow's Kremlin was the perilous pipe dream of fools and reckless cowboys. But in 1977, four years before taking office, Ronald Reagan told a foreign policy expert that his policy toward the Soviets was "simple, and some would say simplistic. It is this: We win and they lose." The expert, who had served at the White House as Henry Kissinger's deputy, admitted he was "flabbergasted."[2]

Second, great leaders must risk reshuffling the social deck, especially when entrenched nobles fight to preserve their special indulgences and prevent the lower castes from competing with them. We will see how the Meiji leaders faced down millions of samurai warriors trained to kill.

Third, great leaders must figure out how to touch the hearts of their people through a shared history, common cultural memes, or a vision of the future. Golda Meir's hands were rough and her calloused feet ached from working in the barren fields. So when she called upon her people to sacrifice, they knew that she too had dodged bullets and stood next to them in the droughts, and she did not rule from a remote palace.

Each of the leaders faced some of the strains we face today: population challenges, debt, bureaucracy, and the entropy of culture. None of them was a saint. None came close. In fact, just about every one of them had the stubborn smudge of gunpowder on his or her hands. But here is the key question. When they exited center stage, whether to retire or to die, did their people answer yes to the following piercing queries: Do you feel more pride in our country today? Do you think our country is more likely to survive the onslaught of disruptive forces, both from within and from across our borders? Today our crises present many traps, barriers, and a blaring chorus of cacophonous nays. Come, let's learn from the yeses of history.

CHAPTER 6

Alexander and the Great Empire

His Mission

- Finding symbols that unify diverse people
- Leading from the front, not the back
- Creating loyalty among non-Greeks by respecting symbols of their past
- Hailing exceptionalism and not feeling guilty for it
- Displaying creativity and mobility in war and in peace

If you stand along the fence of your local elementary school playground and shout "Alexander!" chances are a bunch of boys will snap their heads and look at you from the swing set. If you shout "Alex!" you might also attract an Alexis, Alexia, or Alexandra. Alexander has ranked among the top names in the United States for a number of years and reached number 4 among boys in 2009 (in Greece the name is less popular, ranked 21).[1] How is it possible that the reign of Alexander continues twenty-three hundred years after the Macedonian's death? Now, I suppose that some parents might be commemorating other notable Alexanders, but Alexander Hamilton seldom comes to mind and many young parents might think Steve Jobs created the telephone, not Alexander Graham Bell. In popular culture, the name Alexander the Great appears in TV series and heavy metal music (by Iron Maiden), and is even the name of a barbershop in Tony Hawk's *Pro Skater 4* video game.

The name Alexander means "to protect" or "to ward off," and if you know the history of the real Alexander the Great, you might worry that calling his name even from behind the safety of a playground fence could spark a fierce military charge, led by pointy twenty-foot-long spears and followed by ransacking. Dante places Alexander in the seventh circle of hell, boiling in blood while centaurs aim arrows at him. At the end of this chapter I'll explain why Dante felt so incensed. Other medieval writers admired Alexander.[2]

So if Alexander appears equally at home on television, in video games, on the playground, and in boiling blood, what place does he have in a book focused on the economic and social problems of rich nations? Alexander shows us that many of the challenges we face today are ancient and that some were insurmountable even to one of the most courageous and highly educated men in history. *From Alexander we can learn lessons about the stresses of globalization and multiculturalism, as well as the need to instill grit, mobility, and confidence in the population. He also teaches us that good leaders must identify and then ennoble important cultural sym-*

bols that can bring people together especially in times of chaos. In this chapter I will sketch his fascinating and controversial life, while also discussing the tremors that shake rich nations today. Let us begin with his early days. The most successful business strategy book of our century is entitled *Good to Great.* Alexander's story might be called "Goody Two-shoes to great." He earned his title.

MOMMA'S BOY OR ZEUS'S BOY?

His mother was a sorceress who slept with snakes. His father had just one eye, and it was a roving one that often focused on handsome young men. What makes Alexander great? Merely the fact that he was born of these two eccentrics. His mother was named Olympias and she must have really liked her name, for she concocted stories that she was actually impregnated by a thunderbolt-hurling Zeus, who must have come down from Mount Olympus to mount Olympias nine months before Alexander's birth in 356 BC. Alexander's one-eyed, mortal father, King Philip II, ruled Macedonia and kept six other wives but at least for a few years favored Olympias, who was from Epirus, a region to the west. It would be hard to call King Philip an attentive father, using today's idiom. It was tough to play father while leading cavalry charges in the field and then devising tax systems that covered disparate regions. The king's many hobbies—from heavy drinking and horsemanship to conquests over Illyrian tribes—diverted him from playing father to Alexander. On the day that Alexander was born, Philip received three messengers. The first reported that his favorite general had conquered the Illyrians, giving Macedonia control over its western borders. The second announced that the king's favorite horse had won first prize in an Olympic race. The third declared the king had a new son, Alexander. The king celebrated by ordering his treasurers to mint a new coin—honoring the horse.[3]

With Olympias planting her fanciful visions in his mind, Alexander had no problem developing self-esteem. Roman historians tell us that he grew up to be handsome but not very tall, and that he had a habit of holding his neck at an angle, which some interpreted as haughtiness. His hair was curly and probably tawny, but not nearly as ridiculously bleached Technicolor blond as in the portrayals of him on film by Richard Burton (1956) or Colin Farrell (2004). Plutarch reports that a Greek contemporary said that Alexander smelled nice, with a "pleasant odour exhaled from his skin and that there was a fragrance about . . . all his flesh."[4] Even in Alexander's infancy, Olympias lullabied him with tunes promoting his future kingly glory. But to reign over Macedonia and Greece would never be an easy task. Macedonia was geographically diverse, with mountain herders living in the north and lowland farmers in the south. Though Macedon covered a large swath of land, rivals from Sparta, Thebes, Corinth, and Byzantium stood ready to attack at any moment.

The Greeks disdained the Macedonians as hicks and thugs who could never appreciate democracy or a literate bon mot. When Greeks playwrights wanted to portray a country bumpkin, they would give the yokel a Macedonian dialect.[5] To prepare Alexander for his daunting leadership challenges, Philip found a tutor for him. The tutor was a bandy-legged man with a lisp named Aristotle—which is like getting Albert Einstein to help with your kid's physics homework. Aristotle had studied with Plato but was passed over as dean at the Academy in Athens when Plato stepped down. Aristotle was originally from Macedonia and was comfortable in Philip's court. In legends passed down through the Middle Ages, Philip tells Aristotle, "Take this son of mine away and teach him the poems of Homer!" Aristotle taught Alexander literature, philosophy, science, and medicine. Year later as a battle commander, Alexander nursed his wounded men, using some of Aristotle's medical techniques. Of course the author of *Politics* also taught Alexander about the polity and his views on democracy, ethics, and slavery. Alexander grew fascinated by Homer after Aristotle gave him his own annotated copy of the *Iliad*, which Alexander would carry under his robe into battle. When bivouacked abroad, he would sleep with two items under his pillow: the *Iliad* and a sharpened dagger. Aristotle's political teachings were more than ethereal musings; they had sharp practical points, too. Strolling in the Gardens of Midas, he advised the young man to be a "leader to the Greeks and a despot to the barbarians, to look after the former as after friends and relatives, and to deal with the latter as with beasts or plants."[6] While Alexander would sometimes act ruthlessly, by and large, he was more liberal to foreigners than Aristotle had counseled.

King Philip did Alexander one more favor in his schooling: he required him to learn the art and sciences of wrestling, archery, and warfare. It did not come easy to Alexander, who preferred the flute and lyre to a grappling takedown. Philip sneered at these allegedly feminine pursuits and told his instructors to rough up his effete son and show no leniency. Olympias, who had ties to an orgiastic Dionysian cult, was herself concerned that Alexander was not naturally as macho as other young soldiers, so she arranged for a prostitute named Callixeina to cure her adolescent son.[7] We do not know what the cure was or how well it worked. We know only that Alexander was later known to have both female and male liaisons and to have fathered at least one child, born shortly after his death. Still none of his ancient or modern biographers would call him particularly lusty, randy, or fecund. He could have had his way with innumerable slaves, concubines, and conquered beauties, but he usually passed them by as if they were stone stat-ues, not alluring flesh.[8] His failure to think about siring sons, a successor, or even the fate of his kingdom after his death looms as a major flaw in his reign.

With no leniency in his athletic training and his face ground into the dirt by superior fighters, Alexander eventually learned grit and the skills of a warrior. He came to admire a cranky old tutor named Leonidas, whose idea of breakfast was rousing him at night for a forced march and of supper giving him a light breakfast. Leonidas would also barge into Alexander's bedroom sniffing around for treats that his mother might have snuck in, treats such as candy, not courtesans.[9] Soon Alexander began to show sparks of ingenuity. Hints of Alexander's intellect and un-bounded courage first showed up in a tale of a dark horse, in a story shared with us by Plutarch. In the Louvre today hangs a painting by Charles Le Brun showing Alexander and his steed slicing through the Persian army. (Alexander seems to resemble Le Brun's benefactor, Louis XIV.) One sunny day when Alexan-der was still a boy, a breeder shows up before a crowd offering to sell Philip a beautiful stallion named Bucephalus for an outra-geous sum of thirteen talents (equal today to about a quarter of a million dollars). Philip is intrigued by the man's audacity. When the horse starts snorting, bucking, and proving itself unridable, Philip waves the trader away. Alexander rushes into the scene and confronts the king, telling his father that a man of courage and skill ought to be able to tame that magnificent beast. Philip turns on the boy and scolds:

"Dost thou find fault with thine elders in the belief that thou knowest more than they do or art better able to manage a horse?"

The boy replies, "This horse, at any rate. I could manage better than others have!"

Alexander bets his father that he can tame the beast. Philip laughs and accepts the deal. But Alexander had more than bravado on his side. He had been watching Bucephalus closely and noticed something about the horse's behavior. The stallion appeared to go wild whenever the sun was behind it. However, when the horse was facing the sun, despite the glare, he calmed down. Alexander realized that the horse's oversized body had been casting a large shadow on the ground, and that the mighty Bucephalus was afraid of his own shadow. The boy took the reins and turned Bucephalus's face into the sun. He stroked the horse's muzzle and lips, whispered sweet nothings, and gently turned the horse around. Then with some flair, he threw aside his coat and jumped upon its back. The horse began to buck and the crowd was convinced at any moment the boy would be thrown and trampled. But Alexander held firm and maneuvered the horse to trot, gallop, and then race across the field. When the two returned swiftly and safely, the onlookers cheered and Philip began to weep. Plutarch quotes Philip in a prescient burst of tearful pride: "My son, seek thee out a kingdom equal to thyself— Macedonia has not room for thee"[10] Following his victories in battle, Alexander was memorialized on coins, friezes, and statues, often astride Bucephalus.

LIFE WITH AND WITHOUT FATHER

Unfortunately, as Alexander's relationship with his horse grew closer, his relationship with his father withered. Philip was increasingly drunk, obstreperous, and lecherous. He allowed his court to spread rumors that Olympias was an adulterous witch and that Alexander might be a bastard son. When Alexander was twenty years old, Philip decided to marry a full-blooded Macedonian named Cleopatra, who was the niece of one of his favorite generals and, unlike Olympias, was not known for sleeping with snakes. Cleopatra's family had useful political ties to Caria (now a part of Turkey). An infamous banquet scene finally destroyed the tattered bond between Philip and Alexander. At a feast celebrating Philip's engagement to Cleopatra, the general toasted his king and his niece, wishing them a happy marriage. Then the coup de grâce: with gall and guile, the general wished upon them an heir to the throne who would not be a bastard—like Alexander. Alexander leaped to his feet and angrily hurled his cup at the general. Philip, drunk as ever, stood up and drew his sword, aiming to attack his own son. He stomped toward Alexander, waving his sword aloft. Would Alexander defend himself and kill the king, his father? Luckily for both, the wine won the battle, and Philip tripped to the ground before he could reach the seething Alexander. Alexander shouted, "Look now! The man who is preparing to cross from Europe to Asia can't even make it trying to cross from couch to couch!" Philip probably never heard the mocking line but when he woke up from his stupor, he temporarily banished Alexander. To make things worse, Philip then married off one of his daughters to a young man from Epirus, who was also named Alexander. When Alexander the not-yet-Great returned to the king's court, he was forced to sit with his half-brother-in-law named Alexander and worry whether he would ever have the opportunity to live up to the promises of his crazy mother's Olympian visions.

In 336 BC, Philip drew up plans to invade Persia, aided by his new family ties and their troops. He threw himself a magnificent going-away party, replete with athletic games, musical contests, bouquets, and more banquets. He invited many Greeks to show off his wealth, amiability, and good taste. His architects built a new theater, encircled by gilded statues of the twelve Olympian gods. But visitors were surprised to find a new, thirteenth god among the pantheon of Zeus, Apollo, et al. Who was the new god? It was a statue of Philip himself.[11] Philip strutted into the arena wearing a flowing white robe and surrounded by no one. As if protected by the gods themselves, he shoved his bodyguards aside. Applause and cheers shook the theater. As Alexander kept a wary and jealous eye on his new brother-in-law Alexander, a young court attendant rushed toward the king. Everyone knew the young man. Had Philip forgotten a scroll or called for a last-minute flask of wine? But the boy looked intense and wild-eyed. As Philip's expression turned from hubris to confusion to fear, the young man whipped out a Celtic dagger and drove the blade deep between Philip's ribs and twisted it. He then ran to the gates to jump onto a waiting horse. Finally realizing the treachery, the king's guards tracked the boy and hurled javelins into the air, which landed by piercing his body before he could reach his getaway horse. Meanwhile, Philip's white robe quickly soaked with blood. The king—this thirteenth god—was dead. He had reigned twenty-four years. And now what?

In Macedonia, the king was not usually considered a deity. Moreover, custom did not ensure that his son would inherit the throne. Alexander would have to fight or argue his way onto the throne. As Alexander pursued his father's mantle, many wondered why the young assassin, named Pausanias, had turned on the king. It was a grimy story, but worth hearing to understand the sordidness and perfidy of the court. Just as there were two Alexanders in the royal family, there were two Pausaniases in the court. Both had been favored lovers of Philip. The first lover, the assassin, spread rumors that the second Pausanias was a hermaphrodite, a coward, and a whore. But the second Pausanias was in fact a proud, fierce soldier. To defy the vicious rumors of cowardice, the soldier had sacrificed himself in battle, saving King Philip from a mortal blow. The dead Pausanias was a close friend of Philip's favorite general, Attalus, the uncle of Philip's new bride who uttered the ugly toast at the banquet. To avenge the soldier's death, Attalus arranged a brutal evening for the rumormongering Pausanias. Attalus invited him to a lavish dinner and filled his goblet and his gut with too much wine. Macedonians usually watered down their wine, but Attalus gave the boy the undiluted stuff. Then, with the boy unable to defend himself, Attalus turned him over to his mule drivers, who threw him into the stables and gang-raped him.[12] When he recovered, Pausanias reported the awful crime to Philip, who shared his anger at the barbarism, but refused to punish Attalus. At this point, Pausanias began to sharpen his blade and plan his murderous revenge.

At the time Philip was murdered, he had controlled Macedonia, along with Thessaly, and key city-states of Greece, including Thebes and the snobs in the parlors of Athens. A year before his death he showed diplomatic skill by creating the League of Corinth (or the Hellenic League), whose members pledged not to go to war against each other. Their oath, pieced together in fragments discovered by archaeologists, begins with a charming nod to the gods: "I swear by Zeus, Gaia, Helios, Poseidon, and all the gods and goddesses. I will abide by the common peace and I will neither break the agreement with Philip, nor take up arms on land and sea." The oath contains a key phrase that Alexander would not have missed: "Nor shall I depose the kingship of Philip *or his descendants.*"[13] But would the oath hold? Hollywood folklore says that Samuel Goldwyn once oxymoronically sniffed that "a verbal contract is not worth the paper it's written on."[14] The lawyers in Athens did not think an oath etched in stone was etched in stone. They immediately turned on Macedon and on Alexander. In Athens, Demosthenes, the great orator and unrelenting critic of Philip, declared a holiday and dressed with a garland to celebrate Philip's murder. The Assembly minted a special gold coin in honor of the assassin Pausanias. The Athenians, Thebans, and Thessalians plotted a revolt. The Spartans, who were not members of the League of Corinth, began stropping their swords and mounting horses. Meanwhile, back in Macedon, Philip's generals and courtiers began to point their fingers and blades at Alexander himself. Alexander had the motive and the means to order his father's murder. Many suspected that he was a conspirator, if not the ringleader. Alexander displayed a lean and hungry look 290 years before Cassius gazed on Caesar. It did not help that his mother, Olympias, placed a gold crown on the head of hanging Pausanias, as he was splayed in crucifixion, and then built him a tomb nearby Philip's.[15] One could hear the peals of thunder rumble from Mount Olympus as Alexander and the Greek city-states poised for their next moves.

WHAT WOULD ALEXANDER DO?

Facing a revolt and a possible stranglehold siege by neighboring armies, Alexander rushed into battle. But he knew the battle involved as much diplomacy as weaponry. *His actions teach us that countries under stress must move decisively, but sometimes their fiercest weapons are symbols and gestures.* First, he had to show his fealty to Philip. He gave his father a funeral befitting a thirteenth god, cremating him on a pyre in front of all the Macedonian army. His bones were washed in wine and swaddled in a royal purple robe, before being lowered into a golden chest in a tomb, divinely decorated with hunting scenes and victory medallions. Alexander was, witnesses observed, a worshipful and mournful son. But Alexander could not spend many days with his head bowed. It was too dangerous. He heard that the Athenian blowhard Demosthenes had been sending messages to General Attalus, the man who had insulted Alexander and had thrown Pausanias to the rapists. Attalus was closely tied to noble families in Macedon and tried to incite a coup d'état. Alexander commanded his favorite general to seek out and kill Attalus. When the mission was accomplished, Alexander turned to the treacherous Greek city-states and readied an attack on nearby Thessaly. When the Thessalian army blocked the only road to the city, Alexander ordered his army to build a new path and threatened to wipe out villages. The Thessalians caved in and many joined Alexander's cavalry. He then turned to the north and crossed the Danube to put down rebellions against his reign and then face down the Illyrian tribes to the west. Finally, and most forcefully, he turned to Thebes, the prideful city of Oedipus where citizens believed ancient myths that the city had grown from the teeth of dragons. The Thebans were tired of playing the role of Macedonia's strip mall, a convenient place for Macedonians to pick up tradable goods but not one to respect or admire. Encouraged by rumors that Alexander had been killed in the north, the Thebans attacked a Macedonian garrison. But Alexander was no ghost. His forces launched a blitzkrieg that frightened the Thebans' well-equipped, well-fed army. Their army gave up quickly, but Alexander's troops had something to prove. Under the guise of an order from the League of Corinth, they burned the city to the ground. Demosthenes and the Athenians got the message and dispatched ten ambassadors with a letter of apology and note of congratulations. Alexander still felt a grudge and sent back a demand for Demosthenes himself and several other rebel leaders. Demosthenes gave a speech to the Assembly, citing a fable about a sheep, and the Assembly sent another set of ambassadors to calm down Alexander.[16] The second missive worked, and Athens was spared and humbled. This Alexander was no pampered prince.

WHAT WE LEARN FROM ALEXANDER

Rather than using the remainder of this chapter to document Alexander's triumphs in chronological order, from North Africa to Syria, Persia, and the edges of India, let us set out his methods and lessons that may aid us today. First, I must acknowledge that under our modern understanding of "life, liberty, and the pursuit of happiness" Alexander could be considered a megalomaniacal, enslaving, retrograde pervert. On occasion he burned down villages, took slaves, and put people to death without providing state-appointed legal counsel. The Miranda rights would not have lasted long in his hands. This chapter is not aiming to rescue him from Dante's river of boiling blood, although I will explain why Dante was so tough on him. The purpose is to learn strategy from a great leader, who also had his moments of nobility, kindness, and compassion, as he faced an impossible task of blending disparate peoples, cultures, and economies.

FINDING SYMBOLS THAT UNIFY DIVERSE PEOPLE

In March 2015 the student council at the University of California at Irvine voted to ban the American flag from the campus, charging that it inspired nationalism, symbolized colonialism and imperialism, and triggered hurtful feelings of "racism and xenophobia" among undocumented immigrants and other students.[17] While the council soon overturned its own resolution under pressure from the chancellor, the act does remind us how symbols can both unify and divide. Surely, the original intent of the American flag and the interpretation shared by the overwhelming majority of Americans is that the flag brings far-flung citizens together. The thirteen stripes and fifty stars, of course, represent the *joint* and solemn pledge of the original colonies and of the fifty states. Visitors to the Washington, DC, area line up to snap photos of the Iwo Jima Memorial, the bronze sculpture depicting the five marines and one navy corpsman who climbed to the top of treacherous Mount Suribachi, after days of bombardment, and managed to drive the flagpole into hard and craggy volcanic rock. Not all flags originating in the United States command such acclaim. An overwhelming majority of Americans now believe that the Confederate flag has riled up tensions and bitterness, a view confirmed dramatically when the governor of South Carolina lowered and removed the flag on its state capitol grounds in 2015.

Alexander specifically chose symbols and symbolic words that unified. He called his compatriots and soldiers Companions. This was not a trifling term. He ate with them, slept with them in the fields, and knew thousands by name. The Companions were not the hangers-on party boys from HBO's *Entourage*. Companions (*hetairoi* in Greek) is a Homeric term and young men raised in the courts understood the bond: it conferred both honor and death-defying responsibility. In Homer the Companions rowed oars alongside Odysseus and risked their lives alongside Agamemnon at Troy. When they died, Companions received heroic burials in guarded tombs. Alexander brooded and wept when he lost a Companion, just as Achilles wept for Patroclus. But here was the key to it all: by deeming his men Companions, Alexander pledged that he would be willing to die for them. No one doubted this side of the bargain.

LEADING FROM THE FRONT, NOT THE BACK

When Alexander crossed the Dardanelles to invade Persia in 335 BC, he commanded sixty war boats. He could have hung back in the sixtieth boat or in the middle of the fleet. But instead he grabbed the helm of the first boat, offered a sacrifice to Poseidon, and aimed straight for the very beach where Achilles had made his stand against Hector. Dressed in armor he drove his spear into the ground—much like the men at Iwo Jima—and claimed the land in the name of the Greek gods. In mosaics and paintings of Alexander in battle, he is always in the front, most famously in the mosaic at Pompeii, where he chases down the Persian Darius. This was not propaganda or a matter of supplicant artists genuflecting before their benefactor. Every historical source paints a similar portrait of the man. And if there were any doubters, Alexander would challenge his soldiers: "Come then, let any of you strip and display his wounds. And I will display mine in turn. . . . I have been wounded by the sword hand to hand, shot by arrows and struck by catapult."[18] He forgot the documented cleaver slash to the head. But he was no god, no superhero, and eventually

Alexander limped and faltered from all these battle scars. I might add that Alexander had a penchant for stripping off his clothing, in the interest of maintaining Greek tradition, so they say. After gaining control of Troy, he and his Companions anointed themselves with oil and ran naked around a tombstone dedicated to Achilles.

CREATING LOYALTY AMONG NON-GREEKS BY RESPECTING SYMBOLS OF THEIR PAST

Alexander was not a warrior who came to humiliate villagers and plunder (though occasionally he allowed his soldiers to do so). Even when he conquered a territory, he would show respect to the gods of the villagers by praying at their shrines, or holding games and festivals in their gods' honor. When he chased the Persians from Babylon, women and children greeted him as a liberator and threw flowers at his feet. He did not impose his own gods on the people, however. He commanded his men to arrest looters and then ordered them to restore the Babylonian temples that the Persians had trampled on. After driving the Persians from the Nile in Egypt, Alexander traveled to Memphis, bowed at the pyramids, and then rode to the temple dedicated to the Egyptian god Ptah. Under Egyptian tradition, worshipping Ptah included a specially chosen sacred bull, called the Apis bull. Pilgrims sought blessings from the animal. In the previous century, the Persian king had disgraced the Egyptians by slaughtering the esteemed bull. Alexander reversed this sacrilege by bringing sacrifices to the Temple of Ptah, for which the Egyptians saluted him, some calling him pharaoh. He also established the massive port of Alexandria, later the site of the Library. The Roman historian Josephus writes that Alexander even made a pilgrimage to Jerusalem, where he met with the high priest of the Hebrews and paid homage at the Temple.[19]

Alexander knew that the most far-reaching symbol of his conquests would be indestructible coins. When his troops captured the state mints, the metallurgists began striking coins with his image melded with the image of Greek gods and local luminaries. As merchants traveled with their wares and coins, Alexander's fame spread, from fish markets to brothels. A typical Alexander coin, issued by one of his twenty-six official mints, featured Hercules on one side and on the reverse Zeus seated on a throne. The Hercules image wore a lion's skin, representing the Nemean Lion he killed with his bare hands. Alexander believed that he himself might have been descended from Hercules and sometimes donned a lion's skin for battle. When coins were minted in the east, the figure of Zeus might be seated like a Semitic deity, for instance, Baal. On coins struck in Egypt, Alexander might ride an elephant or wear the horns of the Egyptian god Ammon.

WEST MEETS EAST: ACCULTURATION, ALEXANDER, BUSH, AND OBAMA

Beyond the crises of battle, Alexander faced this thorny question: How to reign over such different cultures? A simpleton would take one of two stark routes: either (1) force all people, whether vassals or allies, to bow down to his language, gods, and culture; or (2) let them scatter in diffuse pluralism and not care whether any unifying themes or forces emerged. We see these debates in nearly every country today, bounded on one side by those who want to prevent any immigration and demand fealty to the past;

and on the other by naïfs who think that a country can hang together even if everyone drifts apart, following the beat of his own drummer, whether reggae, rumba, Ringo, or Gene Krupa. Alexander was no simpleton. He was ambitious and smart and created an innovative but sometimes jittery third path that we can call "balanced hellenization." He brought in his coins and the Greek language, and his engineers designed city streets in straight, classical lines. But he knew he did not have enough Macedonians or Greeks to occupy the known world. So he trained and appointed trusted Egyptians, Indians, and Persians to administer the kingdom. He even adjusted his royal title to fit the geography. For example, when he rode into a Macedonian city he would be called "king," but when in Arabia he was the "suzerain." In Persepolis, he wore the familiar Persian sash and jeweled crown. Then he enlisted tens of thousands of Persians into his army, training them in the same organized manner of fighting as his Macedonian forces. Finally, Alexander himself married wives from a number of different lands so that his tents became a symbol of unity (if you can forgive the polygamy). After capturing the throne of King Darius III (who had managed to escape), he took the king's mother, wife, virgin daughters, and son under his protection and pledged to grant dowries from his own treasury when the daughters reached marrying age. He gave a kiss to the son and jewels to the queen mother, even addressing her as "mother." A man who had the opportunity to butcher and plunder, instead chose to comfortably—but not menacingly—slip on the robe of father and son.

We might take a moment to compare Alexander's welcome in Babylon and his policies with the American and European forces that arrived in Babylon, that is, Iraq in 2003 and Syria in 2015. In 2003 Vice President Dick Cheney gave media interviews stating that the Iraqis would greet Americans as "liberators." His advisers predicted that the Iraqis would throw flowers at their feet. Clearly, Alexander the Great received a warmer welcome than the US Air Force and its allies. Why? Perhaps Alexander's predecessor was deemed more dastardly than Saddam Hussein; or perhaps Alexander's arrival was seen as less heavy-handed than a modern air force's "shock and awe." Second, many military specialists believe that the Department of Defense made a terrible mistake when it disbanded the Iraqi army in May 2003, throwing 250,000 desperate young men into the streets, vulnerable, angry, and susceptible to the enticements of warlords, Al Qaeda, and ISIS. This was called Coalition Provisional Authority (CPA) Order No. 2. One day before, CPA Order No. 1 barred Saddam's Baath Party from all but the most menial government posts.[20] President Bush himself acknowledged the mistake: "The policy had been to keep the [Iraqi] army intact; it didn't happen."[21] President Obama had no better success. In January 2015 he sent hundreds of US soldiers to Syria to recruit and train rebels. The Department of Defense planned to equip five thousand in the first year. But in September 2015 Obama's defense undersecretary sheepishly admitted to Congress that after spending $500 million training Syrians to fight ISIS, just "four or five" were on the ground ready for combat. Not four thousand or five thousand, but only a handful. A few weeks later, on a sleepy Friday afternoon, he quietly scuttled the program.[22] Alexander would have avoided these errors and recruited the best local forces into his own ranks in order to help maintain order. In fact, occasionally Alexander went too far in his idealist push to integrate cultures under one flag. At one point his Macedonian soldiers feared that Alexander was training too many Persian soldiers and they worried that they would be displaced by the newly hired foreigners. When the Macedonians protested, Alexander responded by offering them pensions, pay raises, and vacations.

HAILING EXCEPTIONALISM AND NOT FEELING GUILTY FOR IT

Alexander may have admired other cultures but he felt no guilt when trumpeting his own superiority or that of Greek culture. A man who carries Homer into battle apologizes for neither heroism nor literacy. This is important, for as we learned in chapter 5, a feeling of exceptionalism (or superiority) creates adhesion and cohesion within a group. While chasing his archrival Darius through the sands of Syria, Alexander forges a letter from Darius insulting the Macedonians. When he reads the fake missive to his council, they rise up and demand retaliation. Alexander then sends a letter to needle the soon-to-be-deposed great king. Alexander pens a simple salutation, "King Alexander to Darius," avoiding any title for his foe. Then he accuses Darius of bribing mercenaries, fomenting uprisings among the Greeks, and hiring assassins to kill his father, Philip. Then the boasting begins: "First I defeated in battle your generals and satraps; now I have defeated yourself and the army you led. . . . I have made myself responsible for the survivors of your army who fled to me for refuge . . . they are serving of their own free will under my command." Finally, Alexander offers to give back to Darius his family and his possessions under one condition: "any communication you wish to make with me be addressed to the King of all Asia. Do not write to me as to an equal."[23]

We have learned that feelings of superiority are especially needed to keep groups together in the worst of times, so that members believe that they have a chance to recapture their lost pride or lost terrain. Alexander's troops faced such a moment while fighting in the Hindu Kush. Entering a region known as Sogdiana, the soldiers confronted not the regimented soldiers of Persia, but wild, fearless, horseback-riding guerrilla fighters. An arrow ripped through Alexander's leg, requiring infantrymen to carry him for several days. When Alexander and his men tried to breach a town called Cyropolis (named after King Cyrus II, the Great), they faced thousands of warriors ready for house-by-house combat. As Alexander stood at the base of a city wall, one Sogdian hoisted up and hurled a heavy stone, which smashed down on Alexander's head, knocking him cold. He appeared dead, but later revived, groggy and embarrassed. Soon another band of warriors on horseback, the Scythian tribe from the north, joined the Sogdians, together outnumbering the Macedonians. To make matters worse, the Macedonians ran low on drinkable water and, during a multimonth brutally hot siege with temperatures surpassing 110 degrees, dysentery spread through the Companions, bringing even Alexander to a sickbed and possibly to his deathbed. In retreat, this was his least finest hour in battle. The Sogdians and Scythians massacred thousands of Alexander's Companions. Smelling Macedonian blood, another tribe called the Spitamenes rushed to the scene, unleashing their arrows and catapults. The reign of Alexander could have ended at that moment. But calling upon past glory and relentless determination, Alexander rallied, got out of bed, and led his own swift horsemen on an almost two-hundred-mile trek in three days to the center of the Sogdian city. Alexander had called for reinforcements, but could not be sure how many would arrive. To his relief, he saw twenty-one thousand approaching. The unmistakable pounding hoofbeats of Alexander's cavalry shook the guerrilla warriors, who suspected a massive, unstoppable invasion and turned their horses away, re-treating toward the deserted plains. Alexander had appeared to come back from the dead, in the eyes of his Companions and in the eyes of his enemies. *Each side believed that such a resurrection could take place, because each side had heard of his claim to superiority and his deeds to back it up.*

DISPLAYING CREATIVITY AND MOBILITY IN WAR AND IN PEACE

Contemporary politicians often bemoan "intractable" problems. They shy away from reforming pension programs: "Social Security is the third rail of American politics—touch it and you die." Forty years ago Jimmy Carter called the tax code a "disgrace to the human race," but now it is thousands of pages longer. Congressmen seem content that the ratio of debt to GDP will approach 100 percent in the coming years. The United States has no fresh or potent ideas on how to combat ISIS in Iraq and Syria. (Meanwhile, Vladimir Putin takes advantage of a leadership vacuum and moves from pariah to geopolitical chess master.) Alexander was not intimidated by the status quo and not willing to limit his options to the usual nostrums. From Alexander we get the metaphor of the Gordian knot and real stories of reframing intractable problems in order to create new solutions.

The myth of the Gordian knot predates King Arthur's Excalibur by a thousand years but tells a more instructive tale. In the English, Welsh, or Cornish tale, a magic spell provides that only Arthur can pull the sword Excalibur from a rock and thereby inherit a kingdom. In contrast, Alexander faces a knotted bark on an oxcart, a less royal object, but one that could not be untangled by mere mortals. Alexander must rely on his wits, not a magic spell. So he draws his sword and slices through the knot.[24] That's the legend. But the metaphor is more important than the bark in understanding Alexander's lesson for us. *Alexander shows us that good leaders and strong nations must figure out new solutions when old solutions fail.* King Arthur tried to yank the sword just like everyone else, but he had sorcery on his side. Alexander, however, did not rely on magic. He employed a different method from those who tried laboriously to untangle the knot. The overused cliché in too many business meetings is "thinking outside the box," or even worse, "stepping outside one's comfort zone." (I have become convinced that anyone deploying these phrases should literally be locked inside a box and dropped in a very uncomfortable place, perhaps the queue at the Department of Motor Vehicles on a day when the air-conditioning fails.) Alexander devised innovative answers when the stakes were far more deadly than a twisted piece of bark in an oxcart. For Alexander, mobility required invention.

Off the coastline of Lebanon was Tyre, one of the most powerful of the old Phoenician cities. Tyre's central zone was located on an island half a mile offshore, protected by high stone walls, howling winds, and fierce waves that could crush a landing party that did not know how to navigate the surf. Homer had written of bloodthirsty pirates and kidnappers from Tyre, and Alexander knew that the Tyrian navy was muddling up his trade routes. Convinced that he must take Tyre, Alexander asked his sea captains to plot an invasion. It was too dangerous. The island was impregnable, they told him. Now, Alexander could have asked for, as the frightened sheriff in *Jaws* says, a bigger boat. Or he could have scoured for savvier captains. But instead he gazed at the island and told his men to imagine that it was not an island. Imagine they could march to Tyre with their horses, catapults, and ladders. A fantasy, it seemed. But not to Alexander. He ordered his engineers to build a causeway, a man-made road through the surf to the island. It took months and Alexander helped haul rocks himself. At first, the Tyrians laughed at the folly. Then they took it more seriously, filling a rickety old ship with flammable wood chips, sulfur, and sawdust and launching the flaming wreck into the causeway. Fire erupted, which destroyed some of the road. The Macedonians resumed building and, when they got closer, the Tyrians rained down on them flaming arrows and giant sheets of silicon from the shops of glassblowers. Eventually, Alexander got his battering rams in place and the city fell. But only because Alexander saw a road that no one else could see.

The point here is that Alexander's acclaimed military victories were often preceded by intellectual triumphs. Sometimes though his *intellectual triumphs derived from his study of history*. It turned out that the leader Dionysus had built a causeway in a faraway battle four hundred years before Alexander. In another brawl, with a tribe known as the Triballi, Alexander chased warriors to an island in the middle of the Danube River. Alexander did not have boats to cross the river and did not have engineers to build pontoons or a causeway. This was a smaller skirmish than the siege at Tyre. Scrolling through his knowledge of history, he remembered a trick employed by Xenophon in a battle in Mesopotamia seventy years before. Alexander ordered his men to grab their tent covers and fill them with hay. Then he told them to sew together the edges, basically creating life preservers or small rafts. Though the soldiers doubted that the trick would work and feared they would drown, those who proved to be good seamsters made it across the Danube.

As we look at the stubborn issues facing rich nations today—

pension obligations, low labor participation, etc. —we might want to reframe these issues and show a bit more courage and innovation.

AND HE COULD FAIL, TOO

Alexander's biggest failing—if you forgive the occasional brutal siege of a city—came at his deathbed. How could anyone else hold together the vast lands he had conquered and tried to administer with his balanced hellenization? Where did he hide the instructions for his successor? Was there an heir? No one knew. Granted, he showed some long-term planning, equipping his engineers and scientists with the means to develop new ways of building bridges and better weapons. He nodded toward tomorrow by giving his soldiers time off to go back home and have sex with their wives, thereby ensuring a new generation of soldiers. He even paid back the debts they had amassed when dealing with Arabian loan sharks.

But there should have been more. Perhaps Alexander believed his good press and thought he would live forever. Some small part of his brain did truly believe he carried the blood of Hercules and Zeus. Hubris and vainglory got him in trouble in the end, and explain the mystery of why Dante put him in a boiling stew. Aristotle had a nephew named Callisthenes, who became a close friend of Alexander. Callisthenes was quite literate and became a court historian, a Companion with a sword and a pen. Like Alexander, he revered Homer and Greek literature. But he objected to Alexander's tilt toward Persian customs and Alexander's occasional desire to receive the same deep, servile bows as a Persian leader (*proskynesis*, similar to the Chinese *kowtow*). This was not the Macedonian or Greek way, Callisthenes insisted. Furious that the historian would not bow, Alexander enmeshed Callisthenes in a criminal conspiracy. Soon Alexander's men killed Callisthenes, possibly on a cross. Aristotelians know how to hold a grudge. Aristotle's teachings were preserved in the libraries of Alexandria, Cordoba, and Babylon. In the Middle Ages, Aristotle's teachings made it to northern and central Europe via these routes. Dante worshipped Aristotle, calling him "the Master of those who know," and depicts Socrates and Plato looking up to him.[25] Because Alexander terminated Callisthenes, a direct descendant of the Master, Dante decided to plunge fiendish Alexander into the ring of unforgiveable tyrants.[26]

As for the real Alexander, long before Dante threw him into the bloody river, he died of a fever at age thirty-two. After all the conquests, he went quietly. Here are his last words in answer to the question, who takes over? "*Toi kratistoi*—to the strongest." Upon his death, the "known world" erupted all over again. Now, we should be asking ourselves, which nations will be strong enough, externally and internally, to survive another century?

CHAPTER 7

The Orient Express
Heads West

ATATÜRK

His Mission

- Replacing orthodox religion with science and literacy
- Unveiling women and building the workforce
- Kindling patriotism with a new alphabet
- Turning an ethnic slur into national pride

In Istanbul on the banks of the Bosphorus in a converted warehouse sits the Istanbul Museum of Modern Art, one of my favorite museums. First, it is not large, so you can see much of it in an hour or two. Second, on the walls are colorful paintings by Fikret Mualla of women twirling skirts, children holding balloons, and men strolling with walking sticks. And that is a political and cultural miracle. But for the acts of a man named Atatürk in the 1920s, it might be illegal to put on public display vibrant images of men and women having fun together. Before Atatürk Turkish art was geometrical or calligraphic and had to please the caliph.[1] The interiors of Istanbul's famous mosques offer stunning displays of lines, curves, and Arabic letters. Koranic hadiths and fatwas forbid images of humans engaged in frivolous activity. The sultans had banned displays even of their own images, not just because they might violate the faith, but because the portraits could help murderous plotters carry out their regicidal schemes. Atatürk was not an artist and I do not know whether he ever lifted a paintbrush. But Atatürk did lift the religious barricade set before artists. And that was among the lightest of the obstacles he shoved aside.

Mustafa Kemal Atatürk was born May 19, 1881, in Salonica, Greece. Nearly everything about that sentence is wrong. The man known as Atatürk, meaning "father of Turks," added "Kemal" and "Atatürk" to his birth name years later. He specifically chose May 19 as his birthday since that was the date in 1919 when he stepped off a boat at a Black Sea coastal town called Samsun and launched his campaign for Turkish independence. Salonica was not a city in Greece but a part of the crumbling Ottoman Empire in 1881. Despite all the fakery and folklore, Atatürk was one of the boldest and most direct leaders ever known. Of course, he is not known well in the United States or among younger Europeans today. My daughter's 925-page high school AP textbook on world history assigns just a few sentences to Atatürk, about the same as it allocates to "Evita" Peron—which tells you how much Andrew Lloyd Webber and Madonna can influence serious historians.[2] Atatürk grabbed a moldering empire that straddled Europe and Asia and dragged its culture and character two thousand miles to the northwest so that it would have more in common with a Paris salon than a Babylonian souk. Under the gaze of the sultan, who simultaneously served as caliph, the Ottoman Empire had sought to exalt and protect Islam, not to raise up any individual nation. Nationalism was a pagan totem, a divisive fetish, and a nation's flag was no better than a graven image forbidden by scripture. One hadith puts forth a disturbing image: "He who calls for *Asabiyyh* (nationalism/tribalism) is as if he bit his father's genitals."[3] Atatürk was not concerned about his forefathers or his past. He would be the father of all Turks to come. When he began his quest, women had the same rights as oxen, and clerics were king. In a short period of time, he banished imams to their mosques, invited women to serve in the National Assembly, got Turks to write in an alphabet none of them had ever seen before, erected universities, and spurred Turks to dance to the music of Beethoven and Count Basie. Along the way the Turkish Republic faced all the troubling paradoxes we have discussed thus far: shifting demographics, destabilizing trade, multicultural fractures, and meddling bureaucrats. Atatürk died at age fifty-seven and did not have time to address all these matters. But what he squeezed into his fifty-seven years turned the threadbare remnants of the seven-hundred-year-old Ottoman Empire into a nation.

Atatürk earned the military title general and during his career took up arms against the European conquerors in World War I; against Greek, Bulgarian, and Armenian soldiers; and against Ottoman sultans. He survived shrapnel wounds, a prison sentence, and an assassination attempt. But his toughest challenge was creating and governing a new country. For us, he raises the following question: can a devotion to science and to Western civilization be a sticky enough thing to keep people glued together as a nation? In this chapter I will begin by sketching the contours of the crumbling Ottoman Empire and explaining Atatürk's rise from discontented son of a lowly clerk to father of a new republic. Then we can examine the lasting lessons from his reign as Turkey's first president.

A BOY FROM SALONICA

Alexander the Great thought he was descended from gods on Mount Olympus. Mustafa Atatürk had no such fantasies, although his father, Ali Riza, was a customs clerk for the timber harvested on the slopes of that famous peak. By the time Mustafa was born his mother, Zubeyde, had already given birth to three children, but none of them had survived. It was a house of grieving. A lone surviving son usually gets lavish attention and Atatürk never shied away from a spotlight. Though Salonica (in the region of Macedonia)[4] was controlled by the Ottomans, Muslims were in the minority. Walking through neighborhoods one could smell the wafting aromas of Armenian goulash, Bulgarian *kavarma*, Russian beef Stroganoff, Turkish *guvec*, and Greek *stifado*. If you looked at young Mustafa's face, you would not correctly guess at what table he would feel most comfortable. Blue-eyed and light-haired, the "Father of the Turks" looked more like a Slav. Because Jews outnumbered Muslims in Salonica and because many Jewish families had converted to Islam to escape persecution (they were known as *Dönmes*),[5] some scholars have even speculated that Atatürk might have been of Jewish descent. This seems unlikely, since his father was not originally from the city (his paternal grandfather came from Albania). Salonica was prosperous and busy, but non-Muslims provided the backbone of the economy, raising serious questions about the Ottoman work ethic. Russian farmers plowed fields, Macedonians raised cotton and wool, and Armenians and Greeks fished and worked in restaurants. Jews, who made up nearly one-half of the population of roughly 130,000, loaded and unloaded ships as stevedores. In 1907 Salonica's docks were the third busiest in the empire, handling twice as much cargo as Baghdad or Alexandria. At the turn of the century Salonica was the most important Ottoman commercial center, other than Constantinople (Istanbul), controlling 40 percent of Ottoman trade in raw materials, including tobacco and cotton.[6]

Atatürk watched railroads spur the Salonica economy and reduce the time it took to send goods and people to far-off destinations. Trains sped faster than boats and made overland caravans seem Stone Age. The future military leader also noted that trains could bring enemy soldiers, if they gained control of the tracks. The United States had completed a transcontinental railroad in 1869. Atatürk saw trains as a badge of prosperity and class. He was not so interested in tracks that traveled east to Aleppo. He was more excited by those that could take him to Vienna and beyond. The chic jet-setters of the 1960s were preceded by the privileged passengers of the Orient Express. Europeans in 1900 could board a train in Paris after seeing the opera and sixty-one hours later glide or screech (depending on maintenance) into Constantinople's famous Sirkeci Station for dark Turkish coffee. The cost was the equivalent of sixty-nine dollars, with an additional eighteen dollars for a sleeping car.[7] Agatha Christie, who made the Orient Express far more famous than its owners did, giddily reported: "I am going by it! I am in it! I am actually in the blue coach with the simple legend outside Calais-Istanbul."[8] Sirkeci opened in 1890 near the shadow of Topkapi Palace. If you visit the station today, you can tour the Orient Express museum, which displays special dinner china and other artifacts, including a mannequin wearing the stylish uniform. The Orient Express would become a symbol of Turkey's emerging status as a European nation. As president of the Turkish republic Atatürk funded a railroad-building campaign.

Atatürk did not grow up in a multicultural paradise. There has never been a multicultural paradise anywhere, unless you count Walt Disney's Epcot in Orlando, which opened in 1982. But one hundred years earlier in Salonica many ethnicities managed to get along without killing each other. Employers sometimes complained that hiring Christians, Muslims, and Jews to work together created chaos, not because they hated each other, but because each group would be absent from work on different religious holidays. And since each religion used a different calendar, scheduling for absences was impossible. There was religious equality in one respect: all the lower classes of each ethnicity huddled in fetid slums and the wealthy did not. A snooty English observer reported that while poorer Salonicans exhibited racism and resentment, the upper crust hobnobbed just fine and the "better classes of Greeks and the Moslem officials . . . patronise the Jewish educational establishments." She describes a charity ball for a school, featuring brightly lit trees in a garden, dancing, cigarette smoking, and card playing. The governor general, Dervish Pasha, and his son moved among the dancers, while the "Greek Archbishop made a distinguished figure in his tall cylindrical hat and black robes, seated side by side with the . . . Chief Rabbi, in black and white turban."[9]

A quiet, but confident young Mustafa lived in a pink house. Perhaps this influenced his sense of style, for he was always happy to stand out as the best-dressed figure in a photograph. In some of his most famous adult portraits, he wears white tie and tails and, with his widow's peak, looks remarkably like Bela Lugosi, the Hungarian-born actor who played Dracula in movie classics from the 1930s to the 1950s. He was a proud boy and apparently refused to play leapfrog because he did not want other children to jump over him. Although he sometimes played backgammon at coffeehouses, a classmate who later served as president of the National Assembly recalled that "one could see easily that Mustafa Kemal did not like losing."[10] Atatürk's later rivals might have saved themselves a great deal of frustration had they known of these stories.

TO WHIRL OR WALTZ?

His parents did not always agree with each other, especially on Mustafa's schooling. His mother was a more traditional Muslim and enrolled him in a religious neighborhood school. Mustafa's academic career began by parading with other children through the streets wearing a portion of the Koran strapped to his chest, followed by a ceremony filled with proper prayers. His father was patient and waited a few days. Then he pulled the boy out of the koranic school and enrolled him instead in a nonreligious institution run by a *Dönme* named Semsi Efendi. Unfortunately, the father died a few years later and the mother and son retreated to a farm, where Mustafa first tried a Greek school, then an Albanian tutor, and finally returned to Salonica for a state prep school. None of these succeeded for Mustafa, who looked longingly at the boys at a nearby military school who had shed their baggy oriental trousers for crisp uniforms and parades with swords and rifles: "It was when I entered the military preparatory school and put on its uniform, that a feeling of strength came to me, as if I had become

master of my own identity."[11] Perhaps in joining this environment he could recapture the masculine relationship he lost when
his father died. Mustafa stayed in military dress through high
school and into the war college. As a young man, he cultivated an
image that was noble and even dashing. He was well-liked, quick
at math, and not so quick as a runner. He could, however, dance
and took waltz lessons. Waltzing presented a dilemma for young
Muslim men, who were prohibited from dancing with girls. In
fact, one could encapsulate the battle for Atatürk's loyalties in
the following choice: "Whirl or Waltz?" To whirl was to join in
with the dervishes, enraptured in mystical prayer. To waltz was
to glide toward Vienna and Paris. In one vacation break from
school, Atatürk engaged in both. But his loyalty to the ways of the
West would soon win out.

TO LOSE AN EMPIRE

If Mustafa did not like losing, the Ottoman Empire was no place
for him. By the time Mustafa Kemal Atatürk was born, a con-
sensus of historians tells us that the empire was losing territory,
losing its markets, and losing any sense of hope. During the
1860s and 1870s, Serbia, Bulgaria, Moldavia (present-day Mol-
dova), and Montenegro crept away from Ottoman rule, following parts of modern day Greece a few decades earlier. With the
loss of European regions and the gain of refugees, the empire's
population was becoming more Muslim. Tsar Nicholas I said
that the empire had "fallen into a state of decrepitude," which
inspired the label "sick man of Europe," a tag that ever since has
traveled around Europe like a tour bus, stopping in England in
the 1970s and more recently in Portugal and Greece.[12] We must

admit, though, that the Ottomans had enjoyed a glorious run for half a millennium. In the 1500s, Suleiman the Magnificent marched his armies beyond the Mediterranean, slashed through much of Hungary, and battled at the walls of Vienna. To the east and south, the Ottomans stormed through western Georgia and Armenia, not to mention Baghdad, Cairo, and Somalia. From the Euphrates to the Danube to the Nile, the Ottomans reigned. By controlling Mecca and Medina, Suleiman became God's partner:

> God's might and Muhammad's miracles are my companions. . . . In Baghdad I am the shah, in Byzantine realms the Caesar, and in Egypt the sultan; who sends his fleets to the seas of Europe, the Maghrib and India. I am the sultan who took the crown and throne of Hungary. . . . The voivoda Petru raised his head in revolt, but my horse's hoofs ground him into the dust, and I conquered the land of Moldova.[13]

Even Alexander the Great might have blushed at the braggadocio. The population was to be loyal to the sultan, for he was the protector of all things holy.

Individual nations meant nothing to the sultan. He would not have thought of himself as a "Turk." Until the "Young Turks" rebelled in the late 1800s, the term sounded pejorative, conjuring up the image of a nomadic hick. It was Atatürk who would later exalt this lineal image as a picture of nobility and honor.

Beyond sharp swords and swift boats, the Ottoman economy was built on agriculture and guilds, which did not seamlessly mesh with the Industrial Revolution. As modern machines like steamships and railways arrived from Europe, they were matched and mismatched with more primitive ways. Trains arriving in Ankara were greeted by thousands of camels. While literacy rates rose sharply in England and France in the 1800s so that workers could master new machines like the steam engine, literacy and numeracy in the empire lagged behind. However, it is not true that the Ottoman economy was collapsing or even sinking during the final fifty years under the sultans. I would argue, in fact, that a rise in living standards fractured the empire more than a fall. The economy continued to grow in most of the Ottoman lands, even if growth rates trailed those of England, France, and the United States. As families bought and deployed new tools, from looms to reapers, productivity leaped. In agriculture, exports jumped 45 percent between 1876 and 1908.[14] Exports of silks and carpets also multiplied. From territories in Iraq, trade quadrupled between 1860 and 1900.[15] While the Ottomans racked up debt to pay for the Crimean War in 1853–56, theirs was not a terribly indebted government until it started getting wealthier in the second half of the century.

By then the Ottomans did face a few disadvantages compared with their European rivals. First, there was water. In Europe plentiful streams and rivers spun waterwheels to mill and hammer flour, paper, and textiles. Without as many navigable internal waterways, Ottoman transportation costs did not decline as quickly as those in Europe. Even camels must stop for water once in a while and they cannot carry as much as a riverboat down the Rhine. Consider that today one might take a riverboat cruise from Amsterdam to Bucharest, but few suggest a long camel ride from Ankara to Mugla. Tribal toll takers would also hamper swift transit. Second, as the protector of Islam, the sultan could not as easily countenance business contracts that provided for interest paid on debt. Christian authorities had long figured out how to get around biblical bans on lending money.[16] Only in recent decades have banks developed sophisticated sharia-compliant bonds to ease commerce. Third, the empire covered so much territory and so many battling tribes that government administrators faced an impossible task. Moreover, in times of war—and there were many—it was increasingly difficult to sound a call to arms in the name of a sultan whom few had ever seen in person or in a photograph or drawing.

Sultan Abdülhamid II was neither a monster nor a ninny. He began his reign in 1876 by trying to goose the modernization effort that began with his predecessors Mahmud II and Abdül-mecid I, who presided over a reform movement known as *Tanzimat*, which pushed for modern schools and a more modern military. *Tanzimat* also abolished the slave trade, decriminalized homosexuality, allowed non-Muslims to join the army, and gave non-Muslims equal rights under the law. However, the Ottoman Empire crumbled *despite* rising incomes and despite a de facto expansion of civil rights, culminating in the First Constitutional Era beginning in 1876. Of 115 members of the Chamber of Deputies, forty-six were non-Muslims, including Armenians, Arabs, Jews, and Greeks. Unfortunately, almost as soon as the parliament met, the empire found itself at war with Russia and besieged by the British navy. Moreover, a large part of the Arab population distrusted their new constitutional rights, seeing them as permission for sinful licentiousness. Smugglers of tobacco, opium, and vodka felt they had gained new rights, too. Anticonstitutionalists pointed to transvestite prostitutes smoking hashish and whispered that it was all a Masonic scheme. They called Constantinople the "Byzantine whore." The founder of modern Turkish poetry, Tevfik Fikret, called the city "a widowed virgin of a thousand men."[17] Faced with Russian and English guns, as well as Arab scimitars in the hinterlands, Abdülhamid officially revoked the constitution. Despite the revocation, though, a more liberal spirit began to spread. Even as the sultan ostensibly sneered down from Yidiz Palace in a grumpy, despotic mood the director of a school in Izmir praised the de facto freedom:

> What strikes a Bulgarian when he enters Turkey is, before everything else, the air of freedom that one breathes. Under a theoretically despotic government, one definitely enjoys more freedom than in a constitutional state. . . . One almost does not feel that there is a government. . . . The absence of an irksome police, of crushing taxation, of very heavy civic duties.[18]

Newfound freedoms spurred nationalists of every sort to gather in the twisted alleys of bazaars to dream, and even to plot the breakup of the empire into independent homelands for Arabs, Armenians, Kurds, and Albanians. Turks had the same idea. Why shouldn't Turks shed the crusty patina of an empire spread too thinly across thousands of miles? What good did the empire do for Turks? Besides, it kept losing wars and territory.

Recall our theme from chapter 5 on feelings of superiority. The Industrial Revolution was breeding more trade and more economic upheaval at a time when the Ottoman Empire could not engender a durable, widespread, or passionate feeling of group superiority (except by appealing to religion). When citizens saw that railroad cars were stamped "MADE IN GERMANY" instead of with the sultan's seal (*tughra*), and that mechanical looms came with English-language instructions, spirits sank (even if those rails and looms lifted incomes). When the empire began losing battles and terrain, morale evaporated and it could not be revived. Because few believed that the empire was better than its rivals—in peacetime or in wartime—fewer believed that it would rebound from defeat.

Though he was a loyal and decorated captain in the army, Atatürk agreed with and joined the Young Turks in the 1908 revolution, which restored the 1876 constitution and elections. Andrew Mango, the author of a comprehensive biography on Atatürk, recounts Atatürk's initiation ceremony into a rebel group, which resembles either a college fraternity initiation or a "made man" sequence in a *Godfather* movie: blindfolded recruits would be walked into a house and "take an oath of loyalty with one hand resting on a Koran and another holding a pistol, which was to be used against them if they betrayed their oath . . . candidates for admission wore red cloaks . . . while the rest of the company had their faces covered with a black veil."[19]

Once again, though, a constitutional revolution that created a multiethnic Chamber of Deputies was followed by more fighting. First it was internal, as anti-Constitutionalists incited an army mutiny in Constantinople. At this point, Sultan Abdülhamid slipped onto a train to hide in Salonica (guarded by a friend of Atatürk) and let his brother Mehmed V take charge. His was not a very peaceful reign. In 1911 the Italians declared war to take Tripolitania (now Libya) and a year later the Balkan League (Greece, Montenegro, Serbia, and Bulgaria) attacked, conquered, and created Albania. Macedonia and Crete were gone, too, pushing the empire almost entirely off the map of Europe.

What else could go wrong? Six hundred miles away from Constantinople a skinny little Serb named Gavrilo Princip, who was told he was too small to join the army, showed up in Sarajevo, drew a pistol, and shot Austrian archduke Franz Ferdinand and his wife, igniting a war that would kill sixteen million people. It would also dismantle forever the Ottoman Empire and allow Mustafa Kemal Atatürk to declare the birth of the nation of Turkey.

AND NOW A WAR

In 2014, on the hundredth anniversary of the beginning of World War I, I took my daughters to the Smithsonian's National Museum of American History in Washington, DC. A special exhibition covered almost an entire floor. It was entitled "The Price of Freedom: Americans at War" and provided testimony to and explanations of each important battle and war fought since 1754. One could see a Civil War musket, Andrew Jackson's coat from the Battle of New Orleans, and a Red Cross uniform from World War II. What attention did World War I merit? It got a nook in a dim corner.[20] At first I thought this was a snub, until I noticed that the nook did post the depressing number of soldier and civilian deaths by cannon, mustard gas, and disease. Then I realized that the Smithsonian provided so little space to commemorate World War I because not even the Smithsonian's experts really understand why it was fought! Better to gloss over it than to get stuck in a web of treaties, miscommunications, and long-held grudges among kings who were almost all related to each other, including cousins King George V, Kaiser Wilhelm II, and Tsar Nicholas II. Poor Mehmet V was the outlier, not invited to any summer soirees but invited and, in fact, forced to fight for his throne in the Great War.

I will not be giving away a dramatic ending to tell you that the Ottomans, who joined Germany, lost. In the decades preceding the war, the sultans had created a close relationship with the Germans, who sent advisers to the Ottoman army and to Ottoman universities. The Germans also tried to gin up a hatred of the Allies. Kaiser Wilhelm despised his first cousin, England's King George, and instructed his aides to publicly tear the "mask of Christian peaceableness off of England's face." He told his agents in Turkey and India to "inflame the whole Mohammedan world to wild revolt against this hateful, lying, conscienceless people of shopkeepers."[21] Perhaps Germany's blandishments and money would not have drawn the Ottomans into the war without a third factor: the Ottomans could not resist the chance to bloody their archenemy, Russia, which fought on the side of England. In the previous three hundred years the Ottomans had fought the Russians thirteen times. Ottoman sailors escorted German warships through the Dardanelles and the Sea of Marmara into the Black Sea and even allowed them to fly Turkish flags. When the kaiser's vessels began bombarding Odessa, Russia declared war on the Ottomans. It did not go well for the sultan's soldiers. Amid a snowstorm in a desolate and steep mountain range called Allahuekber ("Allah is great"), eighty thousand Ottoman troops trudged toward the Russians in December 1914. Only ten thousand returned, many of them frostbitten and never able to serve again. On the Egyptian front, eighteen thousand crossed the Sinai Desert and tried to cross the Suez Canal, only to be beaten back by the British. Ottoman losses were three thousand. The Egyptian Muslims did not join them in trying to repulse the Anglo heathens.

A few years earlier during the Italo-Turkish War in Libya, Atatürk tried to organize flighty Arab tribesmen, to plan reconnaissance missions, and generally to keep his sanity in the North African desert. A fellow soldier who knew him as a young man wrote to a friend, "You should see Mustafa Kemal sorting out dry beans" for the chef.[22] Atatürk complained that the Arab sheikhs, while ostensibly on the Ottomans' side, were more interested in stringing out the war and receiving a continuing flow of funds than in actually winning.

GALLIPOLI

In 1915 as the blood flowed freely Atatürk marched into the middle of the red stream. The word *Gallipoli* recalls one of the fiercest campaigns of the war, a debacle for the British Empire and a stunning display of bravery by Atatürk's troops. The British War Council knew that if Britain could command the Dardenelles they could strangle Constantinople and the sultanate. In March they sent battleships and gunboats steaming through the Aegean. Atatürk and his division defended the land on the eastern shore, while Turkish sailors and army soldiers fired on the invading ships, sinking three battleships and disabling one-third of the fleet in a single day, March 18. A new plan. The British, along with Australians and New Zealanders (Anzacs), an infantry brigade from India, Gurkha regiments from Nepal, and Newfoundlanders, would send landing boats to the Gallipoli Peninsula and take it by gun, bayonet, and hand-to-hand combat. The Australian public cheered on its boys and the folks back home displayed colorful battlefield maps and patriotic commemorative ceramics. They could not imagine what would happen. At 6 a.m. on April 25, four thousand Australian troops began boarding boats and then rowing to the beaches, facing ravines and cliffs too sheer to scale. Atatürk rallied his cavalry into position, equipped with machine guns. He ordered them to fire, and the Aussies battled back. By 8 a.m., eight thousand men were ashore and the last arriving Australian troops saw the stumped limbs and lifeless bodies of 650 of their comrades, who had arrived earlier that morning. But then some of the Ottoman troops began to retreat. They had run out of ammunition.

"If you've got no ammunition, you have your bayonets," Atatürk told them.

He later recalled ordering them to "fix their bayonets and lie down. As they did so, the enemy too lay down. We had won time."

But now the trench warfare began. His entire regiment was nearly blown apart. "I don't order you to attack. I order you to die," he said. "By the time we are dead, other units and commanders will have come up to take our place."[23] New troops did show up, and for eight months the Ottomans kept the Brits and Anzacs from snatching more than a toehold. The Allies finally evacuated in January 1916. By then Kaiser Wilhelm had already awarded Atatürk the Iron Cross.

As the Gallipoli plan imploded, covered in blood and human tissue, the master of the plan, General Ian Hamilton, asked in words that would have commanded the attention of Alexander the Great, "Are the High Gods bringing our new Iliad to grief? Whose door will history leave the blame for the helpless, hopeless fix we are left in?"

The Australian government's official description of Atatürk, its former enemy, states that his "superb grasp of strategy and ability to inspire his troops by his reckless bravery in action boosted Turkish morale and proved decisive in thwarting allied plans."[24] For his bravery, Atatürk was awarded the title of pasha and, more important, he earned the fame that would catapult him into the presidency of a new republic.

After the war Atatürk sealed his reputation with the Aussies and Brits by delivering a speech in praise of their heroism and in promise of brotherhood among the countries. The speech is engraved in the Atatürk Memorial at Anzac Parade in Canberra. While there are some doubts about whether the text was spoken word for word, the message is stirring and poignant. Just as the British forces touted and cheered their Johnnies, the Turks could

cheer and honor their Mehmets, those that survived, and those
that died:

> Those heroes that shed their blood and lost their lives . . .
> You are now lying in the soil of a friendly country. There-
> fore rest in peace. There is no difference between the John-
> nies and the Mehmets to us where they lie side by side here
> in this country of ours. . . . You, the mothers who sent their
> sons from faraway countries, wipe away your tears; your
> sons are now lying in our bosom and are in peace. After
> having lost their lives on this land they have become our
> sons as well.[25]

His message reminds one of the Rupert Brooke poem "The
Soldier," which I cited in chapter 5. Brooke died on his way to
fight at Gallipoli. His prescient poem avows that wherever a soldier dies becomes the soil of that soldier's homeland. Atatürk adds
a touching coda. When that soldier dies in a foreign land, he
becomes a son, too, of that faraway place.

Atatürk's bravery on Gallipoli would not save the Ottoman
Empire. For all his passion and persuasion, 300,000 soldiers not
under his command deserted and, under the influence of a hyp-
notic Brit in Arab headdress named T. E. Lawrence, Arab tribes
switched sides and starting bombing Ottoman rail lines. The
Russians continued to advance and the Ottoman government
deported suspect Armenian, Greek, and Assyrian populations,
leaving their fate to genocidal zealots who felt no shame or guilt
in ethnic cleansing and killing perhaps 1.5 million.

To complete the echoes of the *Iliad* and the *Odyssey*, the Ottoman surrender took place on October 30, 1918, aboard a ship
called the *Agamemnon*. You might recall that the story of Aga-

memnon tells of a king whose troops fight a protracted war in the Dardenelles. Then he is killed. It was not a good omen for Sultan Mehmed V.

THE CARVING BEGINS

The old sultan did somewhat better than Agamemnon. Though hounded by Turkish nationalists and humiliated by Allied victors who trampled on Istanbul as if they were shopping at JCPenney for last year's markdowns, the sultan clung to his palace for a few more years. As he looked out he saw strange sights: the French commander General Louis Franchet d'Esperey rode triumphantly into Constantinople on a white horse. The joke was on him, because British general Edmund Allenby had already arrived on his own white horse a day earlier. A British officer scoffed that it was "like having two prima donnas on the stage together and the play went much better if we could keep one in her dressing room."[26] As the old-time vaudevillian Jimmy Durante said, "everybody wants to get into the act." The king of Greece, Alexander, marched toward Ankara and Constantinople with thousands of his troops. He got stopped by a pet monkey. While strolling with his German shepherd Fritz, the king saw the dog suddenly embroiled in a fight with a pet monkey. Perhaps weary of wars, the king tried to play peacekeeper but the monkey bit him in the leg. He contracted a quick infection, called out to his mother in delirium, and died (Fritz was not badly injured). The king's successor took Greece back into war with Turkey, and Churchill remarked that "a quarter of a million persons died of this monkey's bite."[27] And why did the pooch of a Greek king have a German name, Fritz? Ah, yes, those relatives! Alexander's mother was the daughter of Emperor Frederick III of Germany and was Kaiser Wilhelm's sister.

The Allies approached the Ottoman Empire's far-flung provinces (*vilayets*) with a carving knife and a pen.

Today we look at a map of the Middle East or the roster of the United Nations and see distinct names like Syria, Jordan, Iraq, and Israel. But it is hard to imagine that these borders and nations simply did not exist one hundred years ago. Foreign policy commentators today may speak of forcing Israel to go back to the 1967 borders or even suggest that the state is illegitimate, but do they realize that there were no real borders separating any of these countries until after World War I? After the war the British and the French essentially dipped pens in inkwells and began drawing up boundaries and awarding fiefdoms to those tribal leaders who had been most helpful, based on the Sykes-Picot Agreement of 1916. In some cases they imported dominant Arab families from one region and installed them in power in another. Take a look at a map and the border between Jordan and Saudi Arabia. Some geographers explain the bizarre zigzag jutting into Jordan as "Winston's Hiccup." They surmise that as secretary of state of the colonies Churchill must have burped up whiskey and quivered while holding a pen and trying to draw a straighter border line in 1921.[28] The ink was permanent, which is more than one can say for these artificial Middle Eastern borders. Around the same time, Faisal, who was born in Mecca (now Saudi Arabia) and raised in Constantinople was made king of Iraq because he was trusted by the British and rode camel sorties with Lawrence of Arabia. Diaries show how casually British prime minister David Lloyd George and French prime minister Georges Clemenceau could discuss their power over the map and over millions of people:

"Tell me what you want," Clemenceau said to Lloyd George as they strolled in the French embassy in London.

"I want Mosul," the British prime minister replied.

"You shall have it. Anything else?" Clemenceau asked.[29]

Along with carving apart the empire, they resolved that Saudi Arabia should be controlled by the house of Saud, a family that had deep roots in the Arabian Desert and had also helped the British battle the Ottomans. The British agent in charge was actually named William Shakespear. The idea of naming a country after a family sounds like a comedy routine, and in fact, Ali G, the fake hip-hop reporter played by Sacha Baron Cohen, had it almost right when he interviewed a United Nations representative:

Ali G points to a seat marked Jordan: "Ain't it stupid to let one sportsman have his own seat? No matter how powerful he is?"

UN official: "That is not *Michael* Jordan . . . that is the *state* of Jordan."

Ali G: "Innit ridiculous letting one person have the same power as a whole country?"[30]

ATATÜRK TO THE FRONT AGAIN—BUT WHICH ONE?

Atatürk's rise was no accident. He was as shrewd and savvy in public relations as in battle. During the occupation of Constantinople by British, French, and Italians, Atatürk checked into the Pera Palace Hotel, built to host Orient Express passengers. He asked the hotel manager to arrange a meeting with a *London Daily Mail* reporter who had arrived on the *Agamemnon*. Atatürk appeared in a frock coat and fez, "a handsome and virile figure, restrained in his gestures, with a low, deliberate voice," the reporter recalled. Atatürk then explained that he preferred the British to the French and would like a role in reshaping the conquered land. Charles King, who wrote an engaging history of the Pera Palace Hotel, states that Atatürk "met with virtually anyone who would receive him: military officers, cabinet ministers, disgruntled parliamentarians, and on four occasions Sultan Mehmed VI himself."[31]

While the Allies gave a master class on creative cartography, the fighting resumed, as Armenia and Greece tried to pick at the Ottoman corpse. Atatürk and other officers led brigades to fight them off. Once again Atatürk showed great skill but now he was torn. Who was he fighting for? On the surface, he was still fighting for the Ottomans and taking orders, but he was also fighting against the Ottomans on the side of the Turkish nationalists who wanted to toss the sultan from the throne. Word of his Gallipoli heroism spread fast. He was becoming a symbol of Turkish nationalism and created a rival National Assembly and government in Ankara. If the sultan could not defend Constantinople from European dandies gallivanting on white horses, then Constantinople should no longer be the capital. Atatürk wondered, should I fight for the remnants of his Ottoman Empire? Or for a people, the Turks, a name that sounded like an ethnic slur? The answer became clear. He would first defend against new onslaughts from Armenia and Greece and then fight for a new entity he would call Turkey. The term had not been used officially until the armistice agreement on the *Agamemnon*.

How many would die in a civil war between the Ottomans and the nationalists? Who would the Arabs, Serbs, Bulgarians, and others side with? In Smyrna, Muslims outraged by an attempted Greek invasion had already lynched the Greek archbishop. A twenty-three-year-old reporter from the *Toronto Star* named Ernest Hemingway was worried about the capital: "There

is a tight-drawn, electric tension in Constantinople such as people
who live in a city that has never been invaded can[not] imagine."
He reported that "foreigners are nervous . . . and have booked out-
going trains for weeks ahead." He described Atatürk as a "short,
bronze-faced blond Turk with a seasoned army of 300,000 men."
Hemingway confronts Atatürk's man in Constantinople:

"Canada is anxious about the possibility of a massacre of
Christians when Kemal enters Constantinople," I said.[32]

"What have the Christians to fear?" he asked. "They are armed
and the Turks have been disarmed. There will be no massacre."

But in 1922 Sultan Mehmed VI (who took over when his
brother died in 1918) was as worried as Hemingway. He feared
that Atatürk would, in a highly organized way, arrest him, try
him, and hang him for treason, or, alternatively, that marauding
anarchic bandits would climb the gates of Topaki and hang him.
So the sultan did the safe and logical thing. He arranged for British soldiers to kidnap him and shuffle him way. While he took a
walk with his son, soldiers threw them both into an ambulance
and sped to the harbor. A British warship took them to Malta,
from which they sailed up the coast to lovely San Remo on the
Italian Riviera. His five wives the sultan left behind. When the
ruler skipped his usual Friday religious service in Constantinople, the Brits admitted that the royal palace bed was empty and
the National Assembly appointed Mehmed's cousin as caliph, but
denied him the title of sultan. The house of Osman was an empty
house for the first time since 1299.

Around this time the League of Nations administered an exchange of populations between Greece and what was left of the
Ottoman lands. Both Greece and Turkey signed the agreement,
which sent about 1.5 million Orthodox Greeks from Anatolia to
Greece, and 500,000 Muslims in Greece to Turkish lands.

Atatürk took charge and was named president of the Turkish republic. In a metaphorical nod to the story of Oedipus, he had killed off the Ottoman sultan/father and declared himself the new leader and father of his country. His march to reform was faster than any blitzkrieg tactic he learned from the Germans.

BIRTH OF A REPUBLIC: REPLACING RELIGION WITH SCIENCE AND LITERACY

Atatürk grew up wanting to march in military parades waving a sabre. But after he took office in 1923 he mostly ruled Turkey like a man who held out a dove toward its neighbors. Though he had proved that his army could still overwhelm Greece's, he never tried to take back Salonica, his birthplace (now Thessaloniki). Nor did he exploit revolts against Libya's Italian occupiers or political quakes across Arabia as an excuse to send his army marching to swipe oil wells. Imperialism was over. This, I think, is one of the most important accomplishments in political history over the past two hundred years: Atatürk would lead a nation based on patriotism and nationalism—but this nation would not turn into an imperialist conquerer, even of its weaker neighbors. Critics of nationalism assume or make broad claims that such feelings always translate into trampled borders and pillaged neighbors. Certainly, Nazi Germany and fascist Japan did in the 1930s. But is it a force of law, or a choice of men and women? Atatürk proves it is a choice and gives us hope that we can resuscitate fallen morale without letting slip the mad dogs of war.

Atatürk was forty-two years old when he took power. He knew that his biggest challenges were at home. The previous twelve years had been brutal. Everything was "one-third off," but this was not a retail sale: international trade had plummered by one-third and Turkey had one-third fewer people and one-third less land than under the Ottomans. Atatürk was determined to lead a nation of Turks, but the Turks themselves could not follow his logic. They had been taught to be ashamed of their very name. How could he persuade them to show pride and confidence? Newspapers would not help much. Literacy rates were dreadful, about 10 percent for men and less than 5 percent for women. The majority of newspapers in cosmopolitan Constantinople were in foreign languages.[33] Muslims had been slow to accept even the technology of printing. The first Muslim-owned printing press had not arrived until 1727 and it came from a Hungarian. Sephardic Jews and Armenians had been using printing presses in Ottoman cities since 1494 and 1567, respectively.[34]

In prizing handwritten calligraphy over printing, the Muslims denied themselves Shakespeare, Isaac Newton, and Galileo. Of course, Muslim scholars reminded Atatürk of the historical glories of early Islamic math and science, including algebra and camera optics. Some Islamic philosophers even claimed that Einstein's theory of relativity could be derived from the Koran and its use of the word *nur* (light). But Atatürk had no patience for a history lesson or for fanciful religious boosterism. He needed to plunge Turkey into the future, authentic and gritty. To Atatürk, the calendar said 1923, but the overriding mentality still read AD 1299. In fact, even that was wrong. The Ottomans had used a different calendar from the West, the solar-based Rumi calendar, which starts with the year of Muhammad's journey from Mecca to Medina in AD 622. Under this calendar, it was still the year 1339, not 1923. Atatürk had no time to lose in a country where it was almost impossible to tell time. He could not depend on the muezzin's five-times-a-day call to prayer, since the exact time changed from day to day and from place to place depending on the town's longitude and latitude.

In sum, Atatürk faced two disparate but primary tasks:

- First, create a nation that Turks could take pride in.
- Second, push that nation to adopt science and the learning of Western civilization.

Secular schools spread, universities emerged, and Atatürk recruited scientists from England, France, and Germany to lecture. In the 1930s when the Nazis came to power, Turkey invited Jewish scholars and other educated escapees to teach and do research.

Atatürk found himself nearly gored on the horns of the dilemma I discussed in chapter 2. He clearly saw that orthodox Islam and an insular attitude threatened Turkey's economic progress. When he walked past the shelves of bookstores and libraries he had to squint to see any books written in Arabic, for they were far outnumbered by books written in Western languages. But there was another horn of the dilemma: chapter 2 showed us how globalized economies and worldwide trade can disintegrate the traditions and bonds that link citizens together. How could he and Turkey escape the treacherous dilemma? *He had to figure out a way to disband the orthodoxy yet devise or uncover unifying myths, stories, and themes for a new country.*

The republic began with a 101-gun salute. The next shot was a verbal one fired at the caliph. Soon Atatürk dismissed him and disbanded the Islamic courts that had regulated everything from debts to divorce. New courts would enforce a version of the Swiss civil code. The caliph scooted away to Bulgaria on the Orient Express. As the train was about to pull out of the station, the governor of Constantinople slipped him an envelope stuffed with cash and waved good-bye to the caliph and two of his wives. Atatürk was sorry there was not room on the Orient Express for all the clerics. He had a very clear view on religion: it stood in the way of Turkish pride, personal responsibility, and science. "I wish all religions at the bottom of the sea," he explained to an interviewer. "My people are going to learn the principles of democracy, the dictates of truth and the teachings of science."[35] Atatürk did not mind that other people worshipped; he just did not want their worship to blind them to the real hard work of nation building. "Superstition must go," he added. To Atatürk, orthodox Islam was like a toxic cloud that broke down the idea of free will and personal responsibility: "To expect help from the dead is a disgrace for a civilized society."[36] Help yourself, he said.

But Atatürk also knew that religion could drive people in remarkable ways. In the trenches of the war he described his devout soldiers calling upon unearthly inspiration that made them stronger than the enemy and willing to carry out orders that could send them to their death:

> They see only two supernatural outcomes: victory for the faith or martyrdom. Do you know what the second means? It is to go straight to heaven. There, the *houris* [heavenly virgins], God's most beautiful women, will meet them and will satisfy their desires for all eternity.[37]

This raises a profound question for a secular leader: How do I inspire without appealing to holy spirits? An agnostic or atheist army general simply cannot promise virgins in heaven. But he'd better promise something better than a roll in the hay with a wartime prostitute and a vial of arsenic to combat syphilis.[38]

Atatürk also had to be careful about separating religion from the government, without pricking Islamists so sharply that they might declare jihad on the new, fragile state. In a clever rhetorical twist he argued that a more secular, westernized education would ultimately *help* Islamic learning. He asserted that Christian scholars from France and Germany had plumbed more deeply into Islamic theology than even Islamic clerics, who felt forbidden from questioning their elders. Clearly, European institutions were devoting resources to preserving and studying Islamic scripture. Atatürk would have been pleased that in 2014 the University of Birmingham discovered in its collection portions of the Koran that are at least 1,370 years old, possibly written during Muhammad's lifetime.[39]

UNVEILING WOMEN AND BUILDING THE WORKFORCE

In chapter 1 we saw how prosperity can send birthrates plunging, which threatens to shrink a country's workforce. Atatürk was not worried about fertility per se, but he knew that Turkey's workforce suffered from two problems: (1) a shortage of hardworking Turks and (2) a badly educated population of males. He quickly conjured up a solution. He would educate and liberate women, while encouraging them to enter the workforce. In 1923 he did not appear to be a likely booster of women's rights. He had spent his life in the company of boys at schools and men on the battlefields. When Atatürk took the new oath for the presidency of a new Turkey, he was forty-two years old and had just gotten married for the first time. While he got along well with his mother, the "apron strings" had been cut long ago when he took the entrance exam for military training without telling her. She had died a few months before his presidency and when he visited her grave he blamed the former sultan's "secret agents, the spies, the hangmen of tyranny" for the miseries she faced in life. Nonetheless, he would encourage the women of Turkey to climb over the barricades stacked up by sultans, clerics, and tradition. He had been planning this for a long time, and back in 1916 wrote in his diary that Turkey should "be courageous in the matter of women . . . adorn their minds with serious knowledge and science."

Liberating women was bold and smart and had long-term repercussions. Having lost millions of people through the wars, population swaps, and surrendered territory, Turkey needed more bodies in the workplace. A series of reforms banned polygamy, while overriding Islamic law and allowing women to divorce, inherit equally, and attend public schools. The right to vote would follow and in its early years Turkey's National Assembly would have twice as many women serving as Western European parliaments.[40] In urging reform Atatürk turned to women and addressed them separately but as patriots:

To the women: "Win for us the battle of education and you will do yet more for your country than we have been able to do."

To the men: "If henceforward the women do not share in the social life of the nation, we shall never attain to our full development. We shall remain irremediably backward, incapable of treating on equal terms with the civilizations of the West."[41]

At his mother's grave site before he could launch any reforms, he stated: "I am sorry that I lost my mother, but the mother [country] has its freedom and it is developing, and this eases the pain that I feel inside me."[42] A few years ago I attended a meeting of the executive committee of Garanti Bank of Turkey. I was impressed to see a far greater proportion of women than I had ever seen at a US or UK board meeting. Some of them were concerned, though, that Atatürk's reforms could be rolled back by the administration of current president Recep Tayyip Erdoğan, who represents the Islamicist-based Justice and Development Party. Erdoğan has been criticized for tightening controls on the press and removing judges that were known secularists and supporters of Atatürk.[43] Across the southern Turkish border in Syria and Iraq, the situation is far more dire. Female professionals in Turkey know that just a few miles beyond the border, ISIS runs villages.

Encouraging women to become educated and to join the workforce at the highest levels changed Turkey's demographics, pushing down its fertility rate. Women of Turkey's Kurdish minority, who do not usually go to school for as many years, have a fertility rate twice that of other Turks. In Turkey's more prosperous western areas the fertility rate is just 1.5, well below the replacement ratio. Atatürk's reforms, while putting Turkey on the path to greater wealth, may have accelerated the risks for Turkey's demographic survival.

THE HAT

It is hard for us today to appreciate the power of a hat. In Atatürk's era Broadway theater seats had hooks on the back for gentlemen's hats. A 1923 photograph of the opening day of Yankee Stadium shows every man and woman wearing a hat, except one or two that must be dangling a hat from their hands.[44] My father told me of a tradition on the Staten Island Ferry, where on the last day of summer, men would toss their summer straw hats into the harbor. The Bible prescribes head coverings, and religious Jews still follow the commandment. Catholic cardinals and bishops wear skullcaps. Islam teaches that men and women must show appropriate modesty (which may be interpreted as a headscarf, *kaffiyeh*, or even a hijab for women). Around the world, hats were never just about fashion. They defined status, religion, gender, and military rank. The fez, named for the Moroccan city, had been costume de rigueur in Turkey since the early 1800s. It was often worn over a skullcap and it had practical religious purposes beyond its stylish appeal. Lacking a brim, the fez aided men in prayer, for it allowed them to demonstrate their humility before Allah, while also permitting them to touch their foreheads to the floor of the mosque.

To Atatürk the fez showed a different sort of subservience—subservience to old-fashioned "orientalism." Atatürk thought that civilized Westerners looked down on a fez-wearing Turk, who would be taken no more seriously than a "Chinaman" holding a paper umbrella or an African carrying a spear. Once again, he used inventive arguments to bolster his case. He would argue that the fez also hurt the economy: "Skullcaps, fezes, turbans—it all costs money which goes to foreigners."[45] He did not explain why money for homburgs and Panama hats would not also go to foreigners. Nonetheless, he abolished the fez and urged men to wear brimmed Western hats.

WESTERN VICES AND THE VIRTUE OF WESTERN MUSIC

Atatürk's thrust toward westernization carried with it more controversial symbols like prostitution and alcohol. In the latter realm, he had personal experience. He was known to raise a glass or two or three. While some were aghast at the idea of official licensed brothels, Atatürk explained, "Most of the people in our country are, in terms of culture, still quite primitive," and presumably needed their primitive urges taken care of.[46] During the occupation the French had taken control of awarding licenses for Constantinople's brothels and administered weekly medical inspections. They threw aside the idea of *égalité* and set aside the fanciest rooms for high-ranking officers. Most of the clients were sailors and tourists. Under the republic, Turkey set up a new bureaucracy to manage the trade, which flourished amid the jazz-age nightclubs. Occasionally the government would arrest and deport particularly bad characters who straddled the Venn diagram of jazz, liquor, and sex, including one deportee whose job title was officially classified as "pianist/pimp."

Atatürk was not a jazz aficionado but, as I discussed earlier, he preferred the Viennese waltz over the dervish whirl. Violins showed up in Turkish homes. He praised symphonic music and invited famous pianists and composers to tour, including Paul Hindemith from Germany. Choosing Hindemith shows that Atatürk was not simply feigning nostalgia for the dusty classics of Mozart and Bach. Atatürk was not a poser, someone who lines his bookshelves with leather-bound volumes of Goethe and Molière, never to be cracked open. Hindemith was known for bringing to the stage avant-garde composers like Arnold Schoenberg and Anton Webern, who could frustrate audiences who loved hummable melodies and tonal scales. Later the Nazis condemned Hindemith's own modernist compositions as "degenerate," and Joseph Goebbels dismissed him as an "atonal noisemaker."[47] Like Schoenberg, Hindemith tried to reinvent musical composition and saw fluctuations between dissonance and consonance as natural rather than artificial. He developed his own methods of setting out harmonic structures. By endorsing Hindemith, Atatürk proved that Turkey would take Western culture forward, not just bow down to its past.

KINDLING PATRIOTISM WITH A NEW LANGUAGE

Atatürk must have felt a brotherly connection to someone like Hindemith, who was willing to overhaul convention. By the time the composer toured Turkey in the 1930s, Atatürk had already introduced an entirely new alphabet for Turks, which he believed would raise literacy rates. Instead of Arabic script, children would learn the Turkish language with Latin (Western) letters, which would more easily allow for the multiple vowels in the Turkish language. Instead of calling the letters "Latin," he described them as "Turkish" and they became an emblem of patriotism. Atatürk was not content to rely on teachers. He personally toted blackboards around the country, and joined in the nationwide teach-in for Turkish literacy. Literacy rates doubled from 1923 to 1938.[48] There was a problem, however: Turkish had a deficit, a "word gap" with Western languages. While the Turkish dictionary listed forty thousand words, French and German dictionaries listed more than twice that number (English was far higher because of its more mongrel origins). Turkey needed more words and Atatürk would not stand on the sidelines. He placed a blackboard in his dining room and asked guests to submit new words. Partly due to Atatürk's dining room, in the past ninety years Turkish has closed the word gap.

WHAT WAS A TURK? TURNING AN ETHNIC SLUR INTO NATIONAL PRIDE

Women's rights, public secular education, a new alphabet—could these form the foundation of a Turkish people? In addition to shoving aside the Ottomans and carving out a new future, Atatürk realized that Turks needed to feel an emotional tug from the past. Playwrights call it a backstory. Where had the Turks come from before the Ottoman sultans showed up? He worked with historians to develop an "Outline of Turkish History" that tried to show how modern-day Turks descended from noble, nomadic, prehistoric tribesmen. Moreover, these same early Turks had allegedly multiplied and had colonized much of the modern world. There was certainly some mythmaking going on in this backstory exercise. And just as Atatürk embarked on this historical venture that would attempt to instill pride in the very name *Turk*, he got a lucky break from French and Austrian linguists. They informed him that an early form of Turkish was the mother tongue of all languages! This was exquisite timing for Atatürk's backstory. According to the Sun Language Theory, primitive Turks worshipped the sun, whom they called *ag*, and the guttural sound *agh* became the original building block for human speech. It turned out to be pseudoscience, but Atatürk was unstoppable.

Having set out a past and a future and created a new alphabet and a theory of language, he still needed to redefine for the present the very word *Turk*. He used the phrase "a good Turk." A good Turk would be proud, diligent, and confident. The cynic would say it sounded like a Boy Scout pledge. But symbols and words matter. "A good Turk" could be applied to a bricklayer as well as to an artist. A good Turk would learn to play music with discipline and skill or to show up for work on time.[49] Atatürk told his countrymen that the word *Turk* comes from *turka*, meaning strong. In the haunting movie *Midnight Express*, which is rightly despised by anyone affiliated with the Turkish tourist bureau, the imprisoned American spends his day walking clockwise around a large stone wheel along with other inmates, most of them addled or crazed.

One day the American decides to rebel. He begins to walk counterclockwise. The others try to dissuade him or push him in the correct direction. One of them, trying to be helpful, grabs his shirt and says, "A good Turk always walks to the right."[50] The point here is not the direction or the disturbing prison. The point is that even a prisoner thinks that he should aspire to be a "good Turk."

But could this work? Could Western science and a bit of Turkish nationalistic pseudoscience sufficiently bind a nation together? The economy held up well enough that Turkey did not spin into the hyperinflation of Weimar in the 1920s or the crippling Great Depression that spurred fascism in the 1930s. Turkey performed better than the other losers from World War I and avoided fascism, communism, disintegration, and annihilation. Each of those four disasters was a real possibility.

Today Turkey bleeds from its perilous relationship with Kurdish separatists. In October 2015 Turkey suffered the most deadly terrorist attack in its modern history, when suicide bombers linked to ISIS killed ninety-seven people, many of whom had gathered for a pro-Kurdish peace rally. Many Kurds blamed President Erdoğan for not protecting them and for attacking their separatist cause. In an election a few weeks later, Erdoğan's "get-tough" attitude won his party a majority in parliament. While Atatürk did not favor independence for Kurdistan, he did convince many Kurds (and Assyrians) that they, too, were legitimately Turks and entitled to all the privileges of being so. Subgroups like Kurds and Assyrians could fit within his nationalism. He wrote to Kurdish leaders and assured them that they are "true brothers joining hands in . . . sacred unity."[51] Atatürk's concept of Turkishness may not have eliminated a Kurdish desire to separate but it did discourage extremists from taking more violent action and encouraged them to take part in the emerging Turkish economy.

We cannot discuss "Atatürkonomics," because his economic policy was rather eclectic, in other words, confused. An opposition party, the Free Republicans, briefly sprang up to argue for laissez-faire economics. There were periods of free markets and then periods of New Deal–like regulation. During the 1920s and 1930s the economy grew at a healthy pace of nearly 5 percent per year, despite the headwinds of the Great Depression in the 1930s.

A LEGACY

Atatürk was mostly adored by his public and applauded by foreign leaders. Critics called him dictatorial and he often was. Multiparty democracy did not come until well after Atatürk left. He did not acknowledge the plight of Kurds and Armenians. But what individual, commission, or gang would have done better? I was speaking with a Turkish political scientist who told me that Atatürk "moved too fast" with his reforms. He should have spread them out over a long period of time, my friend contended. I am not convinced. If the Turkish republic had begun by forming committees and subcommittees to determine whether women should have equal rights or whether secular science should be taught in classrooms throughout the land, those meetings might still not be adjourned. Atatürk was in many ways an extremist. But an extremist in the pursuit of what? I am reminded of Barry Goldwater's controversial pronouncement that "extremism in the defense of liberty is no vice! And . . . moderation in the pursuit of justice is no virtue." Atatürk was no saint and his motives could be infected by egoism. And yet he managed to drag a defeated, polyglot empire toward Western civilization and to simultaneously restore its pride. And that pride would be based not on the will of heaven, but on the hard work of men—and women.

Atatürk was nervy and optimistic. In 1926 a band of assassins plotted to murder him. The police dragged in one of the hired assassins before Atatürk for questioning. This conspirator did not know that Atatürk was the man standing in front of him. He admitted that he had been hired to shoot Atatürk because the leader had purportedly harmed the country. Atatürk asked, "But how could you kill a person you had never seen? You might have picked the wrong man." The assassin explained that another conspirator was to point out Atatürk before he fired. Atatürk drew his revolver and handed it to the assassin, saying, "Well, I am Mustafa Kemal. Come on, take this revolver and shoot me now."[52] The man collapsed to the ground sobbing.

I hope Atatürk was not too optimistic about the durability of civilized republics. He stated that "Civilization is a fearful fire which consumes those who ignore it."[53] "Fearful fire" sounds more biblical than secular. In fact, around the world today we see radical throwbacks like the Taliban and ISIS conjure up a religious fervor that literally sets cities ablaze. They do this by inflaming young minds with sweaty, reckless rage. There is a danger that Atatürk will be proved wrong: incendiary anticivilization forces may be more powerful or at least more easily motivated than civilized forces. Civilized people go out on a summer night to hear a symphony orchestra play acoustic cannon instruments to accompany the *1812 Overture*. Uncivilized people go out to shoot real cannons.

In 1938 Atatürk became ill and was diagnosed with cirrhosis of the liver. He died soon after. Naturally, his critics grumbled about alcohol. The clock in his bedroom at Dolmabahce Palace is still fixed at 9:05 a.m., the time of his death. This, too, turns out to be a victory, for the old Ottoman clocks would have used the confusing, old-fashioned Ottoman numerals, where "5" was symbolized by a "0." Even in death, Atatürk made things more modern.

Atatürk did not win at everything. His marriage had lasted only two years. But over the years he adopted seven girls and a son. One of his daughters grew up to become the world's first female fighter pilot. Atatürk was a father to his eight children, and to an entire republic.

CHAPTER 8

Can East Meet West?

Their Mission
- Toppling the feudal shogunate
- Terminating the mighty samurai
- Breaking up guilds, promoting mobility and literacy
- Sprinting ahead, while clutching at Old Nippon

It's a cliché to say that Japanese people collaborate more than Americans or Europeans. During Japan's economic glory days of the 1980s, when Toyota, Honda, and Datsun (Nissan) trounced Ford, Chrysler, and General Motors, management experts lauded "quality circles" and even encouraged American assembly-line workers to imitate the Japanese by showing up early each morning to chant company slogans while performing jumping jacks together. Japan could do no wrong. A 1987 book on corporate Japan was subtitled "The Art of Fumble-Free Management."[1] The mania died down in the 1990s, when Japan's soaring economy fell into a twenty-five-year stall. Some social psychologists challenge the idea of a Japanese "collectivist mentality" while others report that Japanese people feel group emotions more than Westerners do.[2] Regardless, when we examine one of the most dramatic transformations in world history—the Meiji Revolution—we see the work of many. In this chapter, we will focus not on one individual but on several extraordinarily brave leaders who figured out how to overthrow a settled regime while facing down 2 million sword-wielding samurai.

HOLD FAST, FALL APART

Midnight. Ryoma slept next to a sword and he knew how to use it. A few feet away on a tatami mat lay his friend, also deadly with a blade. They had blown out the candles and locked the shutters. Ryoma and his friend were young men, still in their twenties, but they were precocious—they'd already amassed enemies. Real enemies, not sports rivals with grudges or jealousies. It was a distinguished list of foes, including some of the most feared samurai in the country. On this night maybe Ryoma and his comrade should have stayed awake like sentries, but when you're on the run the adrenaline crash eventually catches up and forces your eyes to close. That was a mistake late on this night in 1866 at the Teradaya Inn, outside Kyoto.[3]

About twenty samurai were circling the inn, gauging the possible escape routes, in case the ambush went wrong. A young maidservant named Oryo knew Ryoma and his bodyguard friend. When they had arrived she noticed the jittery and weary look in their dark eyes. After they settled in for the evening, she soaked in a hot bath. She tilted her head back, when suddenly she heard a door flung open. From the corner of her eye she saw the glint of spears in the candlelight. She couldn't get to the hook that held her robe, so she ran up the back stairs, stark naked, and burst into Ryoma's room to warn him. Ryoma and his friend jumped up, threw a blanket around Oryo, and sent her back down the hidden stairs. They hauled up their loose-fitting trousers and grabbed their swords, but Ryoma grabbed something else, too. A Smith & Wesson pistol. If this was going to be a wild west duel, then Ryoma would come fully loaded. America had stirred up all this craziness, he thought.

Ryoma and his friend crouched in the corner, listening to the intruders rush up the stairs and duck into the room next door. Then the attacking samurai stormed into Ryoma's room, swords slashing. Ryoma ducked behind a piece of furniture and began firing the revolver. Six bullets. They all hit. Six men dropped. But the samurai kept coming. Ryoma tried to reload but the swords were getting closer. One young warrior leaped at him and a blade slashed Ryoma's left hand. He dropped the ammo. Ryoma and his guard swung their swords and knocked a few spears out of the attackers' hands. But how many more attackers would show up? They were outnumbered and trapped. Except for a window. They grabbed the ledge and rappelled down into an empty courtyard. The courtyard had no exit to the street, though. Staying a few steps ahead of the attackers, they climbed back into the building through a first-floor window and hacked their way through the paper doors (*shoji*) that separated room from room. One of the bedrooms was not empty and a young couple were startled to see two sweaty, fleeing samurai rushing past their futon. Finally, they slit their way to an exit and tore across the road, leaving behind cutout figures of themselves and their swords in the paper screens. The attackers would not forget. They would come back for Ryoma. Would he be ready for them next time?

The true and tense daring of Sakamoto Ryoma has inspired seven television shows, six novels, five films, numerous video games, several long-haired action figures, and artistic flourishes atop coffee lattes. But Ryoma sliced his way into Japan's history books not because of his katana blade but because of his heroic and shrewd political action. A survey by Japan's leading television network showed that Japanese people rank Ryoma as the world's most influential historical figure, just edging out Napoleon. Walt Disney comes in at number 40 and Shakespeare shows up at number 87, easily beaten by Freddie Mercury of Queen at number 52.[4] Matthew Perry comes in last. Not the actor from *Friends*, but the American commodore who steamed into Tokyo harbor in 1853. These two characters, Ryoma and Perry, sparked a revolution in Japan's government and culture that made Japan more open, less feudal, and more free. Japan turned away from a quiet, homogeneous culture of small villages and rice paddies and moved toward raucous cities built on smelting steel and dependent on foreign traders. In this chapter we will examine the Meiji Revolution and the collapse of the Tokugawa shogun regime. There are few examples in history of a society specifically choosing to upend its entire traditional order, a choice made without a cataclysmic civil war or a bloody revolution in which ruling families are summarily shot (as in Russia in 1917) or their heads are marched out on spikes (as in France in 1789).

The scene above, Ryoma's escape from the Teradaya Inn, sets forth two key themes to discuss: First the role of samurai and the bitter split among them. Second, the Smith & Wesson. The Japanese revolution would not have taken place but for the wild west American revolver and its rifle cousins. Let's find out how and why it matters to us today.

FEUDALISM UNDER THE SHOGUNATE: THE SWORD
CUTS BOTH WAYS

The Tokugawa family had ruled Japan since 1603. Yes, a parade
of emperors technically outranked the shogun, but the emperors
were like jewels on the handle of the long blade, glimmering
but useless. The Tokugawa shogun sat atop an elaborate feudal
structure that stretched across Japan's four major islands. While
a shogun feigned loyalty to the emperor, he had the power to
prohibit the emperor from leaving Kyoto without permission.
This prevented the emperor from building up an independent
constituency of knights or even from complaining too loudly of
his treatment. In 1900 a popular song in the United States was
titled "She's Only a Bird in a Gilded Cage." It could have been
a Japanese song describing the life of an emperor: luxurious yet
trapped.

Let's take a few moments to set out the feudal classes beneath the Tokugawa shogun, starting with the 270 regional
daimyo, feudal lords who presided over the agricultural output
(chiefly rice) of their fiefdoms. The daimyo could impose their
own specific laws and taxes, but were then compelled to send
"presents" to the shogun, a cut of the revenues. To keep the
daimyo from conspiring against him and to slyly drain daimyo
resources, the shogun forced the daimyo to spend alternate years
in Edo (as Louis XIV forced his nobles to live at Versailles),
requiring them to expend money to maintain several homes.
Even more severely, the shogun forced the daimyo's wives and
children to live in Edo, effectively as hostages, during those
periods when the daimyo stayed in their home regions (*han*).
The daimyo, who were the highest-ranking samurai, enjoyed
an income of approximately fifty thousand bushels of rice.[5]

Confucian thinking prized hierarchies and an orderly class structure (as Elizabethan society in England embraced a "Great Chain of Being" that set forth a social structure from angels to kings to common workers and beasts). In Japan, beneath the great lords/daimyo was the main body of samurai, who served as government officials and honored soldiers. With their families, they numbered around 2 million, in a population of 30 million. The government paid a stipend to each samurai to keep his loyalty. Lower-ranking samurai included peasants who fought only in times of war. The most interesting and in some ways most pathetic among the lower-ranking samurai were the ronin. They had no master or lord. They were vagrants, for their masters had died or dismissed them, leaving them adrift. The word *ronin* means "wave man," as if they were pushed around by the seas. If a samurai's master died prematurely, the samurai was expected to commit ritual suicide (seppuku), for he must have been at fault. If the ronin did not kill himself, he might escape and wander in disgrace. We'll return to Sakamoto Ryoma later in this chapter and see how he chose to turn from honored samurai to ronin.

Nonsamurai commoners also adhered to a rank, starting with village heads and descending down to farmers and artisans, who might shape and sharpen the samurai swords. Let us skip one tier and go to the very bottom for a moment. There languished the filthy beggars (*hinin*), as well as the *eta*, a caste of untouchables, who handled the dead, disposed of human waste, and served as executioners.[6] Census takers did not even bother to count these people, since they were classified as animals and forced to live apart like lepers. In 1871 the government officially abolished the terms *eta* and *hinin*, though the stigma remained.

WHO KILLED THE SAMURAI? REVENGE OF THE LOWLY MERCHANTS

We skipped over one lowly caste in order to dive to the mucky bottom of the social barrel: the merchants (*chonin*). Their role is crucial to understanding why the Tokugawa regime crumbled. The samurai sneered at the moneygrubbing merchants, who lacked honor and had no formal code of behavior. Nor could the merchants defend themselves against physical attack. Only samurai were permitted to carry swords. In the late 1500s the great general Hideyoshi forced farmers to turn in their weapons. The merchants were not untouchables; instead they were deemed parasites and lived in the shadows of more polite society.

The tremendous status gap between samurai and merchants helped implode the Tokugawa regime. In short, the samurai grew deep in debt to the merchants. Since the merchants were not just social inferiors but social pariahs, this humiliated the samurai. *The very idea that a bottom rung of the status ladder could clobber a high rung undermined the legitimacy of the society.*

At the denouement of the original *King Kong* movie, starring Fay Wray and a twenty-two-inch-high rubber doll covered in rabbit fur, the leading man muses, "It was Beauty killed the beast." The fearsome samurai did not fall off of a skyscraper or paw at airplanes but in the second half of the 1800s they were killed off by something we consider beautiful and good: peace and prosperity. In an echo of the Spartans, the code of the samurai (later named *Bushido*, the way of the warrior) emphasized self-discipline, self-sacrifice, bravery, and contempt for those who strive to acquire material possessions. The samurai were soldiers standing ready either to rush in and slice open the bellies of their opponents or, failing their mission, slice open their own bellies. They were a standing army. But here is the problem: all they were doing was standing around, and eventually lolling about. It was not their fault. What is a samurai to do when there are no enemies, when the shogunate succeeds at tamping down internal warfare and blocking foreigners from its ports? At the same time, peaceful towns and countrysides permit merchants to transport goods and create a more commercial culture, in which the merchants' wealth inevitably climbs. Eventually the merchants appear less like parasites, and more like the people who can successfully get rice, *zoris*, and silk kimonos to show up in urban centers and in remote villages. Unfortunately for the samurai, their culture would not countenance joining the merchants in their own game. As a result, the samurai were revered but unemployed. They were lethal, and they had too much time on their hands. Their plight recalls the discussion in chapter 4 of Marienthal, Austria, where a shuttered factory threw men into a state of depression. The samurai felt the same way. "They may be called the samurai, but it is hard to keep up the samurai spirit," a contemporary reported: "They lose their self-respect, and the samurai spirit is constantly on a downward trend, as if pushing a cart downhill."[7]

THE SAMURAI DEBT AND DEATH SPIRAL

The downhill cart began careening out of control when the samurai and even the daimyo began to borrow from the merchants in order to keep up appearances. Because the shogun began displaying ostentatious wealth, the daimyo were forced to display their own lavish costumes and jewels while visiting the shogun in Edo and while back in their home fiefdoms. Where would they get the money? They shipped more rice and other farm goods through the merchants, who became even more powerful and even more despised. The samurai also needed to flash their nineteenth-century version of bling: silks, gleaming swords, etc. The Tokugawa economy was improving and everyone needed to flaunt his riches. The pressure showed up even at the kitchen table. Take this simple example: in earlier days of the regime, a guest at dinner would typically bring his own food and the host would serve cold soup. By 1816, as a witness described it, "people are so extravagant in their consumption of sake and food, and their pastries contain all sorts of delicacies" that a host could not get away with cold soup anymore: "For example the price of an elegant meal for one person is anywhere from two to three bags (*hyo*) to four to five bags of rice . . . nowadays even those lowly people who live in insignificant town houses and back alleys refuse to eat cold soup."[8] Notice how the observer converts the price of a meal into rice. Rice was the medium of exchange. But the Tokugawa economy soon grew more sophisticated and required cash and credit, managed by the bankers and brokers who ran the rice storehouses and markets in Kyoto and Osaka. The aristocrats and samurai were tempted, of course, to spurn the merchants or chop off their heads. One daimyo earned 300,000 bushels of rice per year but buried himself in debt equal to fifty to sixty *years* of crop yields.[9] *Overleverage* was not a term invented in the 2008 US real estate market. The samurai might simply refuse to pay debts, steal the goods, or murder the merchant.[10] But even dead merchants could retaliate, because the surviving merchants would soon hear of the deeds and cut off credit to the deadbeat daimyo or dishonorable samurai. The merchants switched from being an annoying pebble in the samurai's shoe to a shoelace binding ever more tightly.[11]

The Tokugawa regime did not fall because everything went wrong. It did not generally suffer from vanishing incomes, collapsing trade routes, ill health, or warlike conditions. Quite the opposite. The Tokugawa regime fell because it could not justify the reigning social order in the face of *rising* incomes, expanding trade, longer life spans, and relative *peace*. Now and then peasant farmers would rebel against a corrupt local official or pummel a merchant who foreclosed on loans after a crop failure, but these were exceptions.

Nor was the tax system a plague on wealth. Instead it prodded farmers to expand their businesses. Here's how it worked: Once farmers had paid a certain annual tax based on an old census and historical yields of the land, they paid a very small tax if they could figure out how to grow more rice, soybeans, wheat, etc. This drove farmers to adopt new technologies including better fertilizers and plows. The tax rate on the additional output shrank toward zero. With more abundant crops, cities could expand since fewer farmers were needed to grow grain. In Osaka a thriving cotton-textile industry emerged. Literacy rates jumped up until nearly half the men could read (but only about 15 percent of women).[12] The merchants, though deemed vulgar and crass, ignited an artistic outburst in the cities, funding and patronizing artists and playwrights. The woodblock prints that inspired Edgar Degas and Édouard Manet often depicted urban life in the 1800s, including erotic women, sumo wrestlers, and kabuki actors. These prints are called *ukiyo-e*, which translates as "floating world." It denotes the ephemeral world of pleasure found in the cities. But I would suggest a second meaning. It shows that the formerly rigid social structure of the Tokugawa Era was starting to break apart and the barriers between castes were beginning to shift, mix, and ultimately float out to sea like jetsam and flotsam.

I have thus far neglected one other crucial force in the fall of the house of Tokugawa. From across the seas, Japanese patriots could see flickering lights. As the lights got closer, Japanese sentries could make out a flag: the Star-Spangled Banner. It was not a pretty sight to them. The new floating world would bring much danger.

HOW THE WEST WAS WON AND THE SHOGUN LOST

The Japanese had seen big-nosed, round-eyed Westerners two hundred years before. In 1542, a half century before Shakespeare wrote *The Tempest*, howling gales blew Portuguese explorers off course, smashing their ship onto the rocks of Kyushu. The Japanese, holding spears, warily watched the strange men. After a while the sailors apparently got hungry, for they took out an odd tool that was long and metallic and aimed it at the sky. Then they shot a duck. When the duck fell, the Japanese put down their spears. Summarizing the next several hundred years in two sentences: First, foreign merchants began trading for Japanese pottery, lacquerware, copper, and silver, and eventually paraded Christian missionaries down their gangplanks. Second, when the Tokugawa regime took hold in the 1600s, the shogun grew increasingly annoyed by the missionaries and felt exploited by the traders, so he pulled up the metaphorical drawbridge, persecuted the missionaries and their converts, and closed Japan to foreign traders for the next two hundred years. In *Moby-Dick*, Herman Melville calls Japan a "double-bolted land." The Japanese isolated themselves (except for Dejima, a privileged Dutch trading post on a man-made island in Nagasaki Bay). They occasionally got wind of new intellectual currents. In 1720 the government lifted a ban on Western books as long as the books reported on medicine, military affairs, and geography. The Japanese were shocked and dismayed to learn that their medical texts, which were based on those of Chinese doctors, were inferior to the anatomical explorations of Europeans.

In 1853, when US commodore Matthew Perry sailed into Edo Bay, the Japanese faced a force they could not easily repel. He was sent by President Millard Fillmore, Secretary of State Daniel Webster, and the US Congress. When journalist Horace Greeley famously advised, "Go West, young man," he was referring to places like Oregon and California. By 1850 those territories were under control. The White House turned to Perry and told him to, essentially, "go *really* West." He did, sailing four ships under a coal-fired black cloud, on a mission to pry open Japan for trade, just as Britain had successfully opened up China. In addition, the Americans wanted a safe harbor so that whaling ships could restock their supplies (whaling was the fifth largest industry in the United States). The Japanese had never seen such naval power before. Like the sixteenth-century islanders who were shocked by Portuguese firearms, the Japanese elites felt simultaneously awed, repulsed, and paralyzed. Perry left behind a letter from Fillmore and returned six months later, this time with seven steaming ships and gifts, including a toy train set. The Japanese had never seen a real train or even a toy version. They soon realized how far ahead the barbarians had surged. They established an "Institute for the Investigation of Barbarian Books." What did the institute study? Not the things we might associate with the word *barbarian* such as battle-axes, plunder, and Attila the Hun. Instead the institute's researchers studied trains, trolleys, and rickshaws. Most Japanese had never seen a wheel because the Tokugawa banned the device, fearing that it could enable rebels to roll cannons to Edo. How could the Japanese of 1853—people without wheels and steam engines—compete militarily or commercially? That was the practical question. And here is the lacerating philosophical question that forced the Japanese to rethink and upend their social structure and economy: "How could the barbarians who smelled bad and were covered with body hair outthink the sons and daughters of a divine emperor?" Looking into the barrels of wide-bore Western guns and cannons and confronted by superior Western technology, the Japanese realized that they had misunderstood their place in the world. But what about the relative ranks within Japan? Wasn't it possible that the Japanese leaders had misunderstood the place of each caste? Why couldn't an untouchable rise up or a samurai fall down? And if a samurai fell down in society, must he then fall down on his sword?

For a few years, the Tokugawa regime tried to stave off these questions and gave only minor concessions to the Americans, sometimes with comical results. The Japanese government shunted the first American consul, Townsend Harris, to Shimoda, an isolated port that had just been destroyed by a tsunami. No Americans visited Harris for fourteen months to deliver supplies and the Japanese sold him roosters that were too tough to chew and required him to live in an old temple, which apparently was godforsaken though infested with rats.[13] Despite losing so much weight that he said he looked as if a vice-consul had been sliced out of him, Harris proved an effective diplomat. He eventually got the shogun's signature on a treaty that became a blueprint for Russian, Dutch, French, and English delegations. It opened more ports, shaved tariffs, and dampened the opium trade. Americans who broke Japanese law would be tried in American courts. Many samurai, including Sakamoto Ryoma, grew furious. One prominent daimyo, the former lord of Mito, was disgusted merely by seeing the Americans steaming into Edo Bay and firing guns in salute, in addition to conducting surveys without permission: "this was the greatest disgrace we have suffered since the dawn of our history."[14] To retaliate for the shogun's concessions, a band of ronin tracked down and killed Harris's interpreter.[15]

Japan faced a dilemma. Option one: open up to the West and learn its technology but lose face. Option two: try to repel the Westerners. The shogun faced with this momentous choice was only twenty-nine years old. He was also sickly and had no heir. But he made a choice: he signed the Harris Treaty of Amity and Commerce because he knew he would lose a humiliating naval war against the United States. Knowing that he was on shaky ground with samurai, who felt degraded, he tried to recruit the largely ceremonial emperor to support the decision by proposing marriage to the emperor's sister.

Many of the daimyo opposed the treaty and refused to accept the end of isolation. They blamed the shogun and, sensing weakness in Edo, pushed for the end of the Tokugawa reign. They, too, appealed to the emperor and marched under the slogan *sonno joi*, "Restore the Emperor, Expel the Barbarians."

TOPPLING THE FEUDAL SHOGUNATE: RYOMA'S MARCH OF REBELLION

The Satsuma, Choshu, and Tosa domains began rebelling both against the Westerners and against the timorous shogun in Edo. Samurai from Satsuma killed a British visitor who was traveling to Yokohama. The United States and the British retaliated by bombing feudal forts. The daimyo in Choshu unleashed their own gunboats to fire on Western boats using American Civil War rifles. But then came the most infuriating insult of all: the shogun allowed the listing, smoldering Western ships to be repaired in Japanese boatyards. Traitorous! thought the samurai.

Now we come back to Sakamoto Ryoma, a few years before our opening tale when the shogun's troops stormed the Teradaya Inn on a mission to kill him. He was a master swordsman and living in the Tosa daimyo where about two hundred samurai shouted the *sonno joi* battle cry. They called themselves *shishi*, men of high purpose. Ryoma joined the enraged group, which schemed to overthrow or assassinate a regional leader. But Ryoma thought the focus should be on the shogun in Edo, not his local surrogate. Ryoma left his master and became a ronin, a rootless renegade trained to kill. His first assassination target was one of the shogun's highest-ranking military and policy advisers, named Katsu Kaishu. At the time, Ryoma was hardly a theorist. He said he had been born a poor potato farmer and had no scholarly interests. As a child he'd been bullied in school, perhaps because he looked weak, perhaps because his father was a lower-rank samurai who sold sake. Like many kids who were abused on the playground, he wanted to learn how to defend himself. So he took up swordsmanship and mortal combat. The kids stopped bullying him. But as an adult, he resented the bullying of the shogun and of the foreign invaders.

When he confronted his target, Katsu, Ryoma's physical skills were fearsome. But when he began to speak with Katsu about Japan's future, he realized that his own intellectual insights were those of a child. He must learn more. Katsu explained that merely destroying the shogunate was not enough. Nor was expelling the barbarians. Japan must learn the ways of the barbarians, the weapons and technology that propelled their navy to dominate the seas. Instead of an assassination target, Katsu turned into a master teacher for Ryoma. Katsu taught him about military strategy, corporate structures, and the US Bill of Rights. Ryoma soon realized that he must transcend *sonno joi*. Japan's goal should be harvesting the knowledge of the foreigners, not slaughtering them. While sailing on a Japanese warship, he composed his Eight Point Plan for a new Japan that would end the shogun's reign, bolster the emperor, create a bicameral legislature, and establish a modern navy. All of these things would come to pass. Some were more urgent than others. A new navy could not wait for politics. Ryoma founded a private navy (a precursor to Mitsubishi). His navy's first mission: attack the shogun's forces. To this day, Ryoma is known as the Father of the Imperial Japanese Navy.

Ryoma, the rootless ronin, realized he could do none of what he sought to accomplish alone or even in concert with Katsu. He needed to recruit daimyo. Unfortunately, the daimyo were now arguing among themselves and engaging in armed skirmishes. Choshu and Satsuma were longtime rivals. Yet each felt aggrieved by the shogun's mandates and his willingness to allow belligerent foreign vessels to be repaired in Edo shipyards. Calling on his skills of persuasion rather than his sword, Ryoma brokered a military alliance between the Choshu and Satsuma. Tokugawa leaders learned of Ryoma's negotiations and slapped a target on his back, sending its loyal hitmen in pursuit. Ryoma's negotiations with the two rebellious daimyo were tiring and dangerous, of course. It was amid these talks that Ryoma and his guard hoped to rest at the Teradaya Inn, only to be awakened by the shogun's murderous but unsuccessful band of assassins. Remember in our telling of the Teradaya story that Ryoma picked up a Smith & Wesson. How ironic—an original leader of the "expel the barbarian" movement escaped with his life by firing a barbarian weapon at his countrymen, who were defending the invasion of the barbarians. It does, however, make sense, for Ryoma's political strategy called for drawing from the foreigners their best tools, which on that evening included drawing a pistol on fellow samurai.

Ryoma took command of a warship and helped lead Choshu's peasant militia to rout the shogun's navy near Shimonoseki. Satsuma was preparing its own attacks. Japan was about to plunge into its own civil war, within a few years of the US Civil War. Then Satsuma and Choshu hatched a clever and nervy plan. They basically abducted the emperor and proclaimed that they had restored imperial rule. Suddenly, these mutineers looked like the real patriots. Ryoma's Eight Point Plan was funneled to the shogun, who had watched his men get slaughtered. The shogun, whose family had ruled for two and a half centuries, picked up Ryoma's plan and proclaimed it his own. He stepped down in November 1867, announcing that he had "put his prerogatives at the Emperor's disposal." The emperor was in charge. He was fourteen years old.

A few weeks after Ryoma's stunning masterstroke, he stopped over at a Kyoto inn with a friend and his bodyguard, a former sumo wrestler. Again a band of commandos broke into their room. Again Ryoma grabbed his sword, but he could not find an escape route. He was assassinated, along with the sumo wrestler and his friend. Later, the former leader of the deposed shogun's special police force was eventually executed for the crime, but real proof was elusive. The motive was not: Ryoma, through his sword, his cunning, and especially his diplomacy, had destroyed the shogunate.

Today politicians compete almost comically to sidle up to Ryoma's memory. A few years ago Japan's former justice minister bolted from the ruling LDP party because he "wanted to play the role of Sakamoto Ryoma," while a competing party leader retorted that his group was already "playing the Ryoma role." The land minister then admitted that he was "extremely displeased," because he was a greater fan of Ryoma.[16] Everybody seems to be a fan, and when the government minted Ryoma's stern but noble visage on a thousand-yen coin, collectors immediately bid up the price by many times its stated value.

MEIJI RESTORATION OR MEIJI REVOLUTION?

The emperor's name was Mutsuhito but they called him Meiji (the enlightened one). He did not know how to wield a sword, fire a gun, or ride a horse. The shogunate was gone but what would come next? Could this rigid society operate without Confucian order and a caste system enforced by bayonets and by shame? A movie from the early 1980s called *Eijanaika* reenacts the frenzy of confusion, depicting farmers, prostitutes, pimps, and former samurai riotously singing in the streets, in the brothels, and in the beer halls. They are not cheering new democratic rights and a bicameral legislature. They are cheering the lifting of the feudal barricades. In one scene women dance wildly, lifting up their kimonos and flashing their bottoms at the police. The title of the film translates as "Why Not?" The future was wide open—for better or for worse.

I disagree with those history books that refer to the Meiji *Restoration*. Highlighting the term *restoration* was campaign hype from the rabble-rousers who wanted to gather public support for the emperor. In truth, the emperor had not been in control since the twelfth century. Meiji was not a leader in hiding or a Hamlet waiting to retake the throne from a vicious usurper. After the shogunate disintegrated, the emperor was more the marionette than the puppet master. He was on the throne to witness a revolution, not to direct a restoration. The Meiji Revolution dissolved the feudal barriers; embraced a constitution to protect the people; glorified Western civilization; dismissed the samurai and replaced them with a conscripted army. The new government unveiled a Charter Oath, which promised open discussion and to end the "evil practices of the past." All of this was achieved with far less bloodshed than the French and American revolutions, or the Russian revolution to come. I submit that historians do not generally call the Meiji period a revolution because the count of battlefield corpses was too low.[17] Japan should get credit for achieving so much on the backs of so few bodies.

The Meiji Revolution allows us to ask the following questions that are crucially relevant today: *Can a country stage a revolution while simultaneously (1) maintaining a sense of patriotism and (2) overhauling nearly everything? How can a country hold itself together while acknowledging that a huge swath of the population (the 2 million samurai) had for years been idle, unproductive, and demoralized?* Before we answer these timely questions we need to discuss what the young emperor saw at the revolution that was conducted in his name.

We will not spend much time on the emperor himself. For those who want to know more, Professor Donald Keene of Columbia penned a masterful and thick tome. Quite briefly, the emperor did not have a normal childhood. He was born in a small, plain house away from the palace because custom held that the birth process was "polluting." He was raised by his father's consort, not his birth mother. His own mother did not die in childbirth but, since she was a concubine, she was destined to serve the baby by calling him "your royal highness," not "my son." When Mutsuhito grew up, he visited his father's consort but "never set foot across the threshold of his real mother's house."[18] This quotation comes from Mutsuhito's doctor, who was a German.[19] That is the real point. The imperial throne discarded the Chinese-trained doctors and chose instead a Western physician.

WESTWARD HO: THE IWAKURA MISSION

When Meiji came to power the slogan *sonno joi* was also discarded and replaced with *bummei kaika* (civilization and enlightenment). The Charter Oath, which stemmed in part from Ryoma's Eight Point Plan, urged the people to abandon "absurd customs" and to replace them with "accepted practices of the world." A mania for Western ways broke out. The symptoms were sometimes cosmetic, sometimes much deeper. Former samurai chopped off their topknot hairstyle and adopted a Western mane, styled by a barber. A popular song blared, "If you slap a barbered head, it sounds back 'civilization and enlightenment.'" Married women and former nobles stopped shaving their eyebrows and blackening their teeth. Toothbrushes came into style. Since Westerners ate beef, Buddhist priests were told to eat beef. The government began to discourage infanticide and abortion, which were common during the Tokugawa Era.

An official named Iwakura decided that the government needed more firsthand experience in the ways of the West. So he took a cruise on a spanking new, 363-foot-long, coal-fired ship that cost over $1 million to construct. It was almost as wide as the original Princess Love Boat and provided thirty first-class and sixteen second-class cabins. The name of the ship was telling, the SS *America*. It was built in Brooklyn. Along with forty-eight officials and scholars, Iwakura led a two-year mission to San Francisco,

Washington, DC, England, France, and ports throughout Europe, followed by a return journey to Egypt, India, and China. In Washington he handed a letter to Ulysses S. Grant signed by the emperor and prime minister pledging that Japan will "reform and improve" so it can "stand upon a similar footing with the most enlightened nations."[20] It must have been a remarkable sight—the Japanese, fluent in English, significantly shorter than their American hosts, walking into meetings dressed in top hats and tails, while the Americans dressed more casually.[21] An earlier Japanese visitor to the US Capitol had remarked that congressmen "shouted loudly to each other," and dressed like workers in "our fish market."[22]

In Victorian London the delegation visited the Crystal Palace and Madame Tussaud's wax museum. They ogled the world's first subway system and their designated historian noted that "[t]rains run beneath the street of our hotel, so we can hear their thunderous rumbling." Describing the railways, the historian reported that passengers "boarding the trains cluster like bees, while those alighting scatter in all directions like ants."[23] The Japanese learned their lessons well. A century later, Tokyo subways would be famous for employing *oshiya* (pushers) to jam passengers onto cars during rush hours. The visitors also inspected carpet factories, dye works, and steel and cotton mills. The Japanese were trying to figure out how to modernize but also how to prevent being swallowed up by their more advanced trading partners. One prominent official asked a professor at the University of Glasgow, "Tell me, Professor Rankine, how do we in Japan set up a factory to make guns?" The professor replied that Japan should instead set up a college to train young men as engineers.[24]

Not all discussions were laudatory. At a meeting in Washington, DC, with US secretary of state Hamilton Fish, the Japanese testily debated religious freedom. The Japanese vice ambassador was offended and called the discussion "intolerable." But then he changed his mind and upon returning home stated that "[foreigners will always] regard us as a barbaric nation" unless Japan abolished rules against Christians and others.[25]

The Iwakura mission was a very successful venture and the Japanese returned inspired to reinvent their economy and reorder their social priorities. Within a few years a sister ship of the SS *America* came along. The new one was called the SS *Japan*, and Mark Twain called it "the perfect palace of a ship."[26]

Today on Japan's ten-thousand-yen note is a picture of a prolific intellectual named Fukuzawa Yukichi. If Ryoma was the sword that sliced through the reins of the Tokugawa rulers, Fukuzawa was the pen that spread new learning throughout the country. He too was born of low-ranking samurai stock. He traveled to the West even before the Iwakura mission and came back to write a book called *Seiyo Jijo* (Things Western), establish a university, and launch a newspaper. His book *An Illustrated Course in Physics* became a standard text in schools. He argued that a woman should have equal rights in family property and should be educated, especially in matters of law and finance: "it will be like providing the women of civilized society with a pocket dagger for self-protection."[27] Most important, though, Fukuzawa encouraged an independent spirit. He believed that while money can buy schools and factories, civilization cannot be bought. It must be earned: "unless we can instill in people a spirit of independence, the outward manifestation of a civilization become merely vain appendages" to a country.[28] Sounding like a combination of Adam Smith, Milton Friedman, and Ronald Reagan, he criticized government bureaucrats for intervening in everything from commerce to literature and treating common people like "mere parasites." He pointed out that in his travels to the West, he found that "not a single invention in commerce or industry was created by the government. All worthy inventions were the products of great minds. . . . The steam engine was invented by James Watt and the railway was the brainchild of Robert and John Stevens." At first the Meiji government ignored much of Fukuzawa's economic advice and took over shipbuilders as well as silk and cotton textile factories. The government issued bonds to pay for them. However, by the end of the 1870s, the bills started piling up and the government careened into a U-turn, selling those businesses to private investors and subcontracting work to them.

Let us be clear about Japan's Herculean efforts to learn the ways of the West: the vital motive was to strengthen the Japanese country, not simply to ape the democratic precepts of Thomas Jefferson and Edmund Burke. The slogan *bummei kaika* could be accompanied by *fukoku kyohei*, meaning "rich country, strong army." Ultimately, Japan was more interested in advancing its economy, its finances, and its military might than in winning applause from moral philosophers. Its leaders were bigger fans of John D. Rockefeller and Andrew Carnegie than of Ralph Waldo Emerson. Japan's central challenge was to harvest the West's know-how, blend it with the traditional heritage of Japan, and create a stronger, freer country. Could it be done? It sounded impossible for a nation that for two hundred years had been hiding behind thin paper screens, fat sumo wrestlers, and deadly samurai swords.

TERMINATING THE MIGHTY SAMURAI: WHO PULLED THE MARIONETTE'S STRINGS?

Iwakura and about a hundred other wise men (a few not-so-wise men snuck in, too) took charge from behind the throne. While surely some may have been motivated by avarice, arrogance, and a desire to avenge past slights, in sum their pronouncements and the results of their decisions demonstrate a remarkable devotion to the future of their people. Many were young and most came from the lower and middle classes of samurai. The Charter Oath provided scaffolding for their emerging democracy, but it was a shaky apparatus. At the start of the revolution, the government had no power to tax in the form of money and, besides, the nation had no standard currency. The shogun was used to collecting bushels of rice. The daimyo had title to most of the land, and 2 million samurai expected their regular stipend. A full-fledged constitution (based on the German model) did not come along until 1889. Since the Charter Oath insisted that "the high and the low shall all unite in carrying out" affairs, one thing was certain: the feudal structure must be blown up. The Meiji leaders were fearless. A former radical named Kido Koin, who helped draft the Charter Oath, traveled across the country to persuade powerful daimyo to surrender their land titles to the emperor in exchange for bonds and for a voice in the new government. Kido succeeded and the daimyo moved to residences in Tokyo and told their loyal soldiers to report to the emperor's commanders.

The biggest challenge came next: What to do with 2 million samurai?

The samurai were proud and restless and they were sitting next to swords that had gone rusty during roughly two hundred years of peace. What was their place in this new world of steamships, railroads, and education for women? The new leaders, in the name of the emperor, began by proclaiming that the caste system was over. Japanese citizens could now pursue any job they wanted. The low-caste people who had spent their lives hauling human waste would be given equal rights to study medicine and law. The truly heroic, literally death-defying decision came next: the samurai were terminated. The government sliced their hereditary stipend in half (and soon converted it into a bond). A society has only three goods to distribute: power, wealth, and prestige. The Meiji leaders had ripped all three from the samurai. The samurai were now called *shizoku*, an empty title that carried no special rights and only the sadness of prestige evaporating into the mist. In 1876 the government banned *shizoku* from wearing swords, though some tried to skirt the rules by carrying the swords in their hands (the ploy did not work).[29] As the new rules were announced, Kido said that the samurai considered him "an extremely dangerous person. Those who never held a grudge against me became angry with me, and all the anger of the world was centered on me. . . . I was prepared to die for the cause."[30]

Raging samurai began to rebel and organize an attack on Tokyo and on individuals like Iwakura and Kido. But the new leaders had made another brave and smart move. After abolishing the samurai class, they announced that they would form a new imperial army made up of commoners. The army would be ready to take on a samurai revolt or even an invasion from foreigners. One of the army leaders pointed out that Peter the Great had built warships in Saint Petersburg and commanded a standing army of several million. In response, he wrote, "we must now have a well-trained army . . . officers and soldiers . . . manufacture and store weapons."[31] Before the new army could think about facing Russia, it had to confront twenty thousand raging samurai in Satsuma. The new imperial army crushed the rebels and, in samurai fashion, the rebel leader Saigo Takamori committed seppuku.[32] Often called "the last samurai," the highly principled Saigo had led the fighting against the Tokugawas but resented the humbling of the samurai. His remaining followers, the last of the breed, raised up their blades and rushed into the deadly aim of the emperor's army of commoners. Samurai would be resurrected in myths, movies, and books, but never again on a real battlefield. Twelve years later, in a display of magnanimity and a bow to their shared history, the Emperor Meiji pardoned Saigo posthumously, in the same year that the constitution was enacted.

The samurai rebellion was a life-and-death matter, but the Meiji leaders bravely decided to overhaul their feudal system. And they took the risk of angering a well-armed constituency. Today's leaders in the United States and elsewhere who are too sheepish to reform entitlement programs or revisit government programs because there are too many beneficiaries and too many bureaucrats at risk should consider the samurai example. Perhaps it could give them some courage. The Meiji leaders showed great patriotism in making tough, and somewhat thankless, choices.

BREAKING UP GUILDS, PROMOTING MOBILITY AND LITERACY: THE MEIJI ECONOMY UNLEASHED

Earlier in this chapter I pointed out that the Tokugawa economy was not a failure, nor was it perched on a precipice waiting to collapse. Although it was chiefly agricultural, it did not rest on slavery, as did the American South. The tax system even incentivized peasant farmers to invest in their fields and grow more crops. But Meiji Japan needed an industrial revolution, too. To achieve this, it needed mobility. I mean not only trains and ships to deliver goods, but a greater mobility for people to move geographically, occupationally, and spiritually. Breaking apart the caste system was a vital first step, for it freed people to change occupations and to travel across regions to accept new work.

Some of the ex-samurai put down their swords and picked up hoes, hammers, and rivets. Others left the farm for the cities. The new regime abolished road tariffs and tolls, creating a more fluid internal market. Less than twenty years after Commodore Perry had unveiled his gift of a quarter-size toy locomotive with a passenger car and 370 yards of track, which elicited ogles, Japan cut the ribbon on a real train connecting Tokyo to Yokohama. The government sacked the guilds, which had prevented young people from taking up new trades and had driven up prices. Here again, we see an extraordinary instance of reformers defying powerful, well-organized clans. Today's congressmen who complain they are stymied by special interests should take note, as should public-choice theorists. Because productivity during the Meiji era jumped even faster than during the Tokugawa era, Japan imported less food. This was not a sign of hunger but a sign that the Japanese had figured out how to grow more food with fewer peasants toiling in the fields.

Agricultural success freed up more resources, which entrepreneurs then poured into industry.[33] Japan moved from exporting raw goods like rice to exporting fine, finished textiles. Japan's prosperity was built in part on the hard work of a worm. The silkworm led Japan to become the greatest exporter of silk. Factories rose up and in the first decade of the Meiji regime, the number of cotton spindles multiplied. A British negotiator on cotton tariffs later compared the mills of Manchester and Osaka and concluded that Japan's advantage came not from exploiting "cheap labour and lengthy working hours," but instead because "Osaka has carried into practice the value and the economies of mass production."[34] A noted economist focusing on Japan called its ascendance "astonishing."[35] Cotton output jumped almost threefold in 1889 and over tenfold in the 1890s. Wages climbed in order to attract workers and kept rising into the twentieth century.[36] Supporting Fukuzawa's earlier arguments on entrepreneurship, a new and fascinating study by Carnegie Mellon researchers using precise company-by-company data reveals that the companies that boomed the most had received no government funding or assistance.[37] With more businesses succeeding, firms sold stock to the public and the number of shareholders jumped from 108,000 in 1886 to 684,000 in 1898. The number of entrepreneurs grew, and they were not generally from the elite families. Roughly three-quarters came from families that had earlier been classified as commoners.[38] Most important, the public was getting smarter and more educated. The Charter Oath pledged that there would be not "one family in the whole land, or one member of a family ignorant and illiterate." By 1900 just about all Japanese children, including the girls, attended school. Meanwhile, the government built universities and sent talented students to study abroad, channeling business students to the United States, science scholars to Germany, lawyers to France, and maritime students to Britain.

SPRINTING FORWARD WHILE CLUTCHING AT OLD NIPPON

So now the cotton spindles were twirling faster than England's, boys and girls were learning the hard sciences, and government officials were walking around in top hats and tails. There had to be a backlash.

In accord with our earlier findings, Japan's higher standard of living soon brought a lower fertility rate and a bigger bureaucracy. But the backlash was more spiritual and cultural. Who and what had the Japanese become? Americans? Germans? Poseurs? Wannabes? The Japanese isles had once prided themselves on a spirit of unity and order. Was there room for rugged individualists, the nouveau riche, and the dead souls of the samurai? What about long-held traditions, good and bad? Could the Japanese sit comfortably among the leading nations of the world and defend their discriminatory, often infantilized view of women? How could Meiji preserve a uniquely Japanese character and hold his country together while still encouraging his people to borrow from the West? Few doubted that Japan needed to learn better ways to grow cotton, faster ways to run machines, more durable methods to build homes that could withstand tsunamis, and more advanced Western medicines that could defeat disease. But were those trains speeding from Tokyo to Kyoto in the shadow of Mount Fuji racing away with Japan's soul? The most famous Meiji-era novelist, Natsume Soseki, wrote a haunting novel called *Kokoro* about the loneliness of people crowded together on streetcars in cities made of cement: "You see," says an old man, "loneliness is the price we have to pay for being born in this modern age, so full of freedom, independence, and our own egotistical selves."[39]

Around this time, Giacomo Puccini composed *Madama Butterfly*, a poignant tale of the risks in giving up traditions and joining the fleeting ways of the West. Though Puccini was Italian, the tale stems from real stories that Japanese told to missionaries. After a few melodic notes cribbed from "The Star-Spangled Banner," a young American navy lieutenant named Benjamin Franklin Pinkerton arrives to take fifteen-year-old Cio-Cio-San, a former geisha girl, as his bride. He also takes a 999-year lease on a house that overlooks Nagasaki harbor. The lease can be canceled on a month's notice. This is the Japanese way. The marriage can be canceled on a month's notice. This, too, is the Japanese way, he suggests. In act 1 Benjamin Franklin Pinkerton warns that he will "play with the butterfly even if doing so will damage its wings."[40] Cio-Cio-San willingly gives up her Buddhist faith and converts to Christianity, but then her husband sails back to the United States. She waits three years, dutifully raising their son, awaiting the lieutenant's return. Then a cannon blast. She sings the soaring aria "Un bel di" (One beautiful day), climaxing on a heartrending "*l'aspetto*" (I will wait for him). His ship, the *Abraham Lincoln*, is in the harbor. She decorates her home, "everywhere must be full of flowers," and dons her wedding dress. But the lieutenant has not come for a second wedding night. He has come to take away his child, who will be raised by his American wife. In one of the most excruciating scenes in opera, Cio-Cio-San places a blindfold on her young son, puts an American flag in his small hand, and then picks up a dagger and stabs herself. She had surrendered all Japanese traditions but one—a noble death: "To die with honor, when one can no longer live with honor."

The government debated ways to avoid turning the entire country into a population of lonely streetcar riders and Cio-Cio-Sans. It went back in time to revive the Shinto religion and Japan's mythological roots. In the centuries before Meiji, Shinto priests had been elbowed aside by Buddhists and Confucians. But the Shinto stories provided a more uplifting, singularly Japanese philosophy than the others, which were grafted from China. An eighth-century-AD text called *Kojiki* describes Japan's mythical formation thousands of years ago. On a floating bridge to heaven the male god Izanagi and female goddess Izanami hoist up a "jewel-spear of Heaven" and then plunge it into the sea and stir. When Izanagi lifts the spear aloft, four drops of crystallized salt fall back into the sea, forming the lands of Japan. Therefore, according to the story, Japan is the result of a divine act. The government began exalting Shinto and a pantheon of deities led by the Sun Goddess. It established an office of Shinto affairs and a Ministry of Rites. Who was the Sun Goddess's son? The emperor Meiji. So now the slender, young man had three mothers: his birth mother, his father's consort, and the goddess of the sun. It was a big burden and few Japanese really believed that he was divine—until his navy clobbered the Russians in 1905. At that point the idea of divine imperial rule sounded plausible.

The Meiji leaders made four tough choices: First, to keep up with higher standards of living, they pried open their country to trade. Second, they faced down those who benefited from castes, guilds, and other barriers to social mobility. Third, they cut off the samurai, fearsome foes who had long stopped contributing to economic and social progress. Finally, they realized that money and genetics were not enough; they would have to promote some unifying, uniquely Japanese spirit in order to keep the four islands united.

When Meiji died in 1912 of diabetes and gastroenteritis, proving that he was human after all, Japan was far more prosperous and slightly more confused than it had been before he came to power. The barricades of the castes had come down; and now young men and women needed to navigate between the *Wa* and the *Yo*, between the Japanese tradition and Western styles. We still see that struggle in Tokyo today, in the young man who worships his ancestors at a shrine, but then slips on Beats headphones and rolls back to the street on his skateboard, uttering a hip-hop-inflected "yo."

CHAPTER 9

Two Audacious Leaders
and No Excuses

DON PEPE AND GOLDA

The year 1848 saw revolutionaries storm royal barricades in Germany, Italy, France, Hungary, Sri Lanka, and elsewhere, while Karl Marx and Friedrich Engels published their fiery *Communist Manifesto*. In contrast, for 1948 a time line in the *World History Encyclopedia* aimed at schoolchildren cites two important events: first, a man named Peter Goldmar invented the long-playing record. The second was even less important, a meeting of the World Council of Churches.[1] For us, though, 1948 teaches many lessons. In this chapter we will look at two individuals who had virtually nothing in common with each other—except that both ascended to power while their countries convulsed with radical change. Furthermore, each confronted common excuses that ordinary politicians give for their country's failings.

Our first example is Jose Maria Figueres Ferrer from Costa Rica, known as Don Pepe. He battled a corrupt government and launched a revolution that brought long-lasting peace and democracy forty years before neighboring leaders in Central America did so. He could easily have reached into the rusty bucket of bad excuses and said, "This neighborhood is too corrupt to expect us to do better than Nicaragua and Panama." We will see that Don Pepe got his hands dirty in the process of gaining power and could even be accused of taking part in terrorist acts. Does this invalidate his later deeds? A second excuse available: "Costa Ricans can't take pride in a country whose modern founder fired bullets and lobbed bombs." Don Pepe shows us that a country can be full of pride and patriotism, even if its founders were less than saintly.

Golda Meir came to Palestine to plant vineyards and gardens. She found heavy rocks, drought, and chauvinistic men of all religions. Quite often, we hear of countries blessed by extraordinary natural resources—oil in Venezuela, gold in Ethiopia, copper in Haiti. Palestine had none. Golda joked that the only natural resource was sand. As an early leader of the Zionists and as prime minister of Israel, she could have also dipped into the rusty bucket of excuses and said, "We have no natural resources." But she kept planting and recruited others to do so, and within a few decades the land she settled was exporting fruits and vegetables throughout the world. In recent years, that sand that Golda joked about has been turned into silicon and Israel's own "Silicon Wadi" launches more tech start-ups per capita than any other region in the world.

Come read about Don Pepe and Golda Meir, who arguably made 1948 far more remarkable than the guy who invented the long-playing record.

DON PEPE: WHAT MAKES A MONSTER AND WHAT MAKES A MAN?

His Mission

- Abolishing a corrupt army
- Creating a durable democracy
- Making the children of black immigrants citizens and bringing women into the voting booth
- Walking away from power, rather than clinging to it

He had slender shoulders and a nose that drooped down his face. He was short, dark, and balding, not exactly leading man material. An FBI agent said he looked like the owner of a mom-and-pop candy store. But on this day in 1971, Don Pepe was not toting a Snickers bar. He was clutching a submachine gun and playing the role of hero. Just moments after a plane had taken off from Miami, a band of Nicaraguan terrorists burst into the cockpit and pulled guns on the pilots, demanding to land in Havana. When a passenger tried to resist, they shot him. The pilots convinced the hijackers that they must refuel in San José, Costa Rica. Don Pepe, serving his second term as president (the first was in the 1950s), rushed to the tarmac alongside the police. He grabbed a submachine gun in his unshaking hands, stared down the terrorists, and joined the police in firing at the engines and flattening the tires. "I saw that inside the plane, one of them [the hijackers] was pointing a gun at a stewardess," he said. "At that very moment I ordered tear gas to fill the plane."[2] The bullets killed two of the hijackers and wounded one other. All the passengers survived.

Why was he so nimble with a submachine gun, this man who

turned Costa Rica into Latin America's most stable democracy, the only one in Central America until the 1990s? Few of his fans, especially the pacifists, remembered his roots. Don Pepe launched his political career by himself blowing up buildings and scaring civilians. So what moral standing did he have to attack terrorists? A lawyer might invoke the "clean hands" doctrine. A literature professor might bring up that pesky spot that Lady Macbeth could not rub off her hands. For us Don Pepe brings up the following question: can a country rebuild its pride, its democracy, and its economy, even if its leader himself once took up arms in a way that could be described as terrorism?

A PROUD GRADUATE OF THE PUBLIC LIBRARY

Though Jose Maria Figueres Ferrer did not exactly come from noble blood, his father was an immigrant doctor from the Catalan region of Spain, putting the family in a pretty high class from the start. His mother was a teacher and also from Spain. Costa Rica was downright primitive in 1906 when Don Pepe was born and did not improve much for the next fifty years. Dirt roads, flies, no toilets, naked children, and water rationing for peasants. Jose Maria was a smart boy, excelled at math and physics, and even took a correspondence course from a school in Scranton, Pennsylvania. He must have liked what he read about the United States in correspondence school, because a few years later he hopped onto a boat and, against his father's instructions, enrolled at MIT to study engineering and hydroelectricity, while working on the side as a translator for a tea company. He soon dropped out of MIT but then created his own curriculum by hanging out at the Boston Public Library and reading engineering texts, as well as Cervantes, Martí, and Kant. Despite Don Pepe's dropout status, today MIT claims him as its son.[3] He would disagree. He said that his alma mater was not MIT, but BPL.

LOVE, THEN WAR

He returned to Costa Rica in 1928 and a few years later settled on a farm about a seven-hour horseback ride from San José. He became a successful farmer of coffee beans, hemp, and agava cactus, from which he extracted the cabuya fiber and turned it into rope and gunnysacks. Apparently, the MIT engineering training did come in handy. In 1940 an odd couple was formed. A twenty-two-year-old Presbyterian girl from Montgomery, Alabama, with a fitting name, Henrietta Boggs, and little knowledge of Spanish came to dinner while visiting her aunt in San José. Don Pepe was invited, too. The aunt was convinced of two things: first, that the young couple would marry, and second, that Don Pepe would become president. Henrietta explained that her aunt made wacky predictions about lots of thing—hurricanes, droughts—but the predictions never came true. Except her forecasts for Don Pepe. The aunt just knew, Henrietta recalled, because "the curve of the back of his head was just as beautiful as a Greek statue, and that proved he was going to be President."[4] Henrietta soon accepted Don Pepe's marriage proposal and expected that she would begin an exotic but charming, old-world life on a plantation, married to a suave Latin, albeit one with a magnificently curved skull. It did not turn out that way.

Don Pepe was restless. When World War II broke out, Nazi U-boats sped across the Atlantic to drop off spies and to attack ships in the Gulf of Mexico and the western Atlantic. Most Americans today have no idea that German submarines infiltrated waters from the entrance of the Panama Canal to Long Island Sound. On July 30, 1942, a U-boat blew up the *Robert E. Lee* with 406 passengers aboard, just forty-five miles from the mouth of the Mississippi.[5] A few weeks earlier a U-boat known as U-161 snuck into the harbor of Puerto Limón, Costa Rica's largest port. The Kriegsmarine commander looked through his periscope and spied dockworkers unloading freight from the steamship *San Pablo*. He directed his men to fire two torpedoes directly into the side of the *San Pablo*. The ship exploded and fire ripped through the dock. The attack killed twenty-three Costa Rican civilians, along with a sailor.[6] During that year in the Gulf of Mexico, twenty U-boats sank over seventy ships in a mission the Nazis called "Operation Drumbeat," or "Second Happy Time."

When the *San Pablo* exploded, so did Costa Rica. On July 4, twenty thousand Costa Ricans rushed to a public square to hear President Rafael Calderón's response to the German treachery. He did not show up. Protests turned into riots and speakers condemned Calderón for not protecting them from the Axis forces. Mobs stoned buildings and then looters took advantage and broke into 123 shops owned by Germans, Italians, and some Spaniards. A man threw a bicycle into a German-owned camera shop, as looters swiped everything from the shelves.[7] Police arrested one hundred Germans and Italians, mostly from families that had immigrated to Costa Rica generations earlier to run sugar, coffee, and banana plantations. (In the 1930s Germany was purchasing 40 percent of the country's valuable coffee crop.) Four days after the attack on Pearl Harbor, at the behest of Franklin Roosevelt's administration, Costa Rica had already begun constructing an internment camp in the capital for suspicious foreigners and immigrant families. The newspaper *La*

Tribuna called it a "campo de concentración," with capacity to house four hundred people.[8]

ON THE RUN AND RUNNING GUNS

It was a confusing time in the capital. Calderón, the target of many protests, said that the demonstrations "greatly pleased him." Presumably he was referring to the attack on German-owned businesses, not the marchers denouncing his leadership. Don Pepe, whose shopkeeper friends lost their livelihoods in the riots, bought time on a local radio station and began blasting Calderón for incompetence and for allowing looters to destroy civilian property. After Don Pepe harangued for too long, the police broke down the studio doors, flipped off the microphone, and dragged him to a prison. The government accused him of treason and giving away military secrets to the Nazis. Henrietta visited him in prison, and described her bloodied, dirty husband as too weak to hold himself up by the bars in the prison cell. But suddenly Don Pepe was a national hero and the government could not "disappear" him. Instead Calderón exiled him to El Salvador, from which he made his way to Guatemala and then Mexico. Henrietta came along for the treacherous ride, carrying her toddler daughter and young son. During the next two years in exile, they ate badly and consorted with renegades and guerrilla fighters in the mountains: "What in the world am I doing here?" Henrietta asked, "I should be back in Birmingham working for a newspaper, going to the country club and just living a normal life of a Southern woman. Instead, here I was wandering through the mountains, scared out of my head, being shot at." She survived and in 2011 at age ninety-three wrote a charming memoir of these harrowing years.[9]

Don Pepe plotted to return, even if it meant carrying a belt of machine-gun bullets under his poncho. He smuggled weapons back to Costa Rica, sneaked out for late-night meetings, and even dragged Henrietta along as a decoy while ducking out to pick up shipments of rifles. He said that "you can't make chocolate (rebellion) without cacao (weapons)."[10] Meanwhile in San José, Calderón formed a bizarre and unwieldy coalition including the Communist Party, fascist police thugs, the Catholic archbishop, and some feudal lords of the coffee plantations.[11] In 1944 Don Pepe returned from exile and was permitted to form the Social Democratic Party, which gave him a platform from which to accuse Calderón and his successor, Teodoro Picado, of embezzlement.

At this time, all of Central America was inflamed and rebels of all stripes shared rifles and formed battalions that resembled the cast of *The Dirty Dozen*, including twenty-one-year-old Fidel Castro, who was pegged by the others as more of an egotist than a communist. Journalists called them the "Caribbean League." During an attempted invasion of the Dominican Republic, secretly backed by Cuba's president, Castro was arrested aboard a navy vessel, but jumped overboard and swam away.[12] Don Pepe trained with a ragtag group of ex–World War II soldiers and in 1945 and 1946 schemed with some landowners and student revolutionaries to overthrow the Calderón/Picardo government. His soldiers practiced at his farm, called La Lucha Sin Fin (The Struggle without End). One of his allies, a former president, called Don Pepe the "war chieftain" and "loco." Their tactics would include terrorism.

In the 1948 presidential election, Calderón ran for another term but lost narrowly. Street violence broke out, the building housing the ballots burned down, and his party annulled the election. Looters charged into the streets again. Don Pepe began his march to the capital, which had been shut down by a strike.[13] Along the way his troops captured the cities of Cartago and Puerto Limón. They were relentless. Their opponents included Calderón's army and the "mariachis," a ludicrous mix of fascist and communist-leaning banana pickers from the lowlands who wore blankets over their shoulders to keep themselves warm in the hills. Two thousand people, most of them civilians, died during the forty-day civil war, which ended when Calderón stepped aside. Don Pepe took power as the leader of the "Founding Junta of the Second Republic of Costa Rica." If he did not have blood on his hands, he certainly had gunpowder smudged on them. What would he do next, this hemp-farming, guerrilla-fighting, arms-smuggling rabble-rouser? And no matter what he did, could Costa Ricans feel proud about a government won by the ammo belt of a machine gun?

REFORMATION IN THREE ACTS

At the time Don Pepe took power in 1948, future Latin American leaders seemed to be getting fitted for camouflage (à la Fidel Castro) or called themselves generalissimo and dressed more like a doorman in front of the Plaza Hotel than a democratic leader. Don Pepe was done with epaulets, epithets, and guns. His first act as leader was to abolish the army. He symbolically knocked over a wall at Bellavista Fort and turned the keys over to the minister of education to establish a museum. Ever since that day, Costa Ricans have proudly quoted Don Pepe and boasted that they have more teachers than soldiers. When he announced to a crowd that he was abolishing the army (which was actually a small force),

Henrietta asked the minister of public works why the audience was not applauding. He replied that they thought her husband must be crazy, since other Latin American leaders relied on the army to keep them alive. Don Pepe's move was not motivated solely by charity. He knew that a standing army could just as easily murder him in a coup d'état as support him. By liquidating the army, he probably made his own position more secure. Still, his other reforms were just as striking. In his eighteen months as leader he gave citizenship to the children of black immigrants, enabled women to vote, guaranteed public education, outlawed the Communist Party, and put forth a constitution that was written in plain language. Then, most impressively of all, he escorted a properly elected president into the presidential mansion and returned home to his farm.

WALKING AWAY FROM POWER, RATHER THAN CLINGING TO IT

To walk away from absolute power—that is a test that has been passed only by remarkably confident leaders, starting with Cincinnatus. Cincinnatus was the Roman farmer-statesman who was plowing his field in 458 BC when panicked senators chased him down to ask whether he would take charge of the republic. Rome was losing key battles to rival tribes on horseback. The senate offered him the title "Dictator." Cincinnatus accepted the title, personally charged Rome's enemies on the battlefield alongside infantry soldiers, and won. Then he disbanded his army and gave up his crown. For fifteen days he had been dictator. He could have stayed for decades. About twenty years later, the senators chased him down again. Cincinnatus became dictator again, defeated a coup, and returned to his farm. George Washington twice gave up ultimate power, once after winning the Revolutionary War and again after resigning his presidency. Lord Byron eulogized Washington as "the Cincinnatus of the West," and the American poet Philip Freneau composed this rhapsodic rhyme in Washington's honor: "Thus, He, whom Rome's proud legions sway'd/Return'd, and sought the sylvan shade."[14] They might have written a similar ode to the narrow-shouldered Don Pepe.

Here are the key questions: Were Don Pepe's reforms merely a shrewd and temporary strategy to enable his power grab and allow him and his allies to survive their time in the presidential mansion? Or were they intended to permanently imprint a stable democracy on Costa Rican's national culture? The evidence strongly points toward the latter. From the 1950s to the 1990s, Costa Rica was located in a very hazardous neighborhood. In the 1950s Nicaragua tried to invade Costa Rica. Thirty years later Sandinistas carrying Soviet Kalashnikov AK-47s took over Nicaragua and emblazoned the assault rifle in their artistic murals.[15] El Salvadorans were plagued by death squads on one side and ruthless friends of Fidel Castro on the other. Manuel Noriega ran Panama like his own franchised drug dealership. In the decades following Don Pepe's reforms, Costa Ricans had numerous legitimate reasons to rearm the military. But they passionately believed that Don Pepe had put them on a path that they should not veer from, despite dangers on either side of the narrow landscape. To this day, Costa Rica spends proportionately far less on security than most of the other countries on the continent. In less than ten years after Don Pepe took power, Costa Rica's education spending climbed from about 3 percent of the budget to about 20 percent.[16] When he rolled out a new cultural initiative, he asked, "Why tractors without violins?"

When I was a teenager I sent an op-ed to the *New York Times* entitled "Your Terrorist or Our Freedom Fighter?" (I never heard from the *Times*, but they really should have published it.) The essay argued that you cannot confidently identify someone as a terrorist or freedom fighter until *after* the questionable individual takes power. What do they do then? Do they build hospitals and schools? Or do they buy more tanks and machine guns? Do they try to institutionalize peace, or do they spread warfare internally and externally? Don Pepe, George Washington, and Mustafa Atatürk said he was a man of honor. But we could not believe it until after the bombs had stopped exploding. We had to wait and listen to hear whether the next loud blasts came from laying the bricks for schools, hospitals, and symphony halls. In the case of Don Pepe, yes, he had gunpowder on his hands when he took power. But in 1998 his proud constituents unveiled a bronze statue near the Bellavista Fort—the fort at which he knocked down a wall in 1948. In the statue, Don Pepe wears plain clothes. And his hands look pretty clean.

THE LEADER WORE SENSIBLE SHOES: GOLDA MEIR

Her Mission

- Sweating and working the land
- Embracing technology, but keeping emotional ties
- Creating a more mobile nation
- Defying chauvinistic men

She could have had a comfortable life in Milwaukee. She had a best friend, was valedictorian of her school, and in 1909 as an eleven-year-old organized a fund-raiser to buy books for poor immigrants kids. Richard Nixon would later joke with Golda Meir that though Milwaukee lost the Braves baseball club it was lucky to have had her and, Nixon added, "as a matter of fact, the Braves could use you as a pinch-hitter right now."[17] Golda Meir was no pinch-hitter lounging around in a clubhouse sauna until some late inning when the team was down and needed a hit. She slogged through just about every pitch and every risky play in Israel's early history—the drought that sent farmers begging for drops of water; the gunshot that killed the driver sitting next to her; the British soldiers who blocked bedraggled Holocaust survivors from getting off ships and instead forced them back to detainment camps. She had the bags under her eyes to prove what she had seen, and when she was sworn in as prime minister in 1969, she already looked remarkably like the exhausted Lyndon Johnson who had just stepped down from the White House, give or take a foot and a half in height.

ATTITUDE, NOT LATITUDE

This section is not focused on the controversies of Israel's numerous battles or its tense relations with Palestinians today. Instead, Golda Meir's life gives us an opportunity to examine the following oft-told excuse for a country's woes: *"We do not have natural resources."* Golda frequently scoffed at the problem and admitted that it was hard to forgive Moses for dragging the Jews forty years in the desert only to bring them to the one place in the Middle East without oil. But these were laugh lines, not leadership strategies. She was gritty, undaunted, and unstoppable, as long as she got a meager four hours of sleep and a pack of Chesterfield cigarettes. It is common for laypeople, historians, and even professional economists to get hung up on natural-resource worries. When I was a kid I would flip through atlases and feel a little envious that the USSR had not only more land than the United States, but also more gold and even bauxite. I didn't know what bauxite was, but it must have been a good thing if Rand McNally put it on the map. Economics textbooks speak of "factor endowment," implying that the stuff buried under the ground may dictate economic growth. Jared Diamond's best-selling books direct us to ecological explanations for the rise and fall of nations: Eurasia was blessed with docile horses, but Africa got stuck with bucking zebras. Alpacas marched around Chile, but the Andes were too tough to climb so the Aztecs were denied lush wool and strong pack animals. When Europeans colonized the Americas, the Caribbean looked far more promising than the North American landmass, with Cuba's and Barbados's per capita GDP at least 50 percent higher than the American colonies'.[18] Voltaire could not understand why France and England bothered to clash with Indians in the 1750s. Canada was just a country "inhabited by barbarians, bears and beavers," and in *Candide* Voltaire sneers that Europeans were battling in a "beautiful war" over "a few acres of snow."[19] Some experts seem to look at countries as if they are model homes and care only about "location, location, location," as if that determines economic health: "Australia is too far away!" "Look, Venezuela has oil!" Yet Australia is clearly a much wealthier place than corrupt Venezuela, even though it's a twelve-hour flight away—after changing planes at LAX—and it was settled by exiled criminals. What matters most to an economy? *Attitude, not latitude.*

Golda Meir and the founders of Israel had the attitude to work hard and did not care very much what was under the ground or what was growing in the sand and rocks when they began. Mark Twain had been to Palestine and described a despondent wasteland:

> Of all the lands there are for dismal scenery, I think Palestine must be the prince. The hills are barren, they are dull of color, they are unpicturesque in shape. The valleys are unsightly deserts fringed with a feeble vegetation that has an expression about it of being sorrowful and despondent. The Dead Sea and the Sea of Galilee sleep in the midst of a vast stretch of hill and plain wherein the eye rests upon no pleasant tint, no striking object, no soft picture dreaming in a purple haze or mottled with the shadows of the clouds. Every outline is harsh, every feature is distinct, there is no perspective—distance works no enchantment here. It is a hopeless, dreary, heart-broken land.[20]

GROWING UP: POPCORN, HOT DOGS, AND COSSACKS

Golda had seen even rougher, less hopeful settings. She was born in Pinsk, Russia (now Belarus), at a time when Jews were either corralled into special precincts of fetid villages or huddled from pogroms perpetrated by the tsar's soldiers and their marauding accomplices. When Golda was a little girl walking with a friend, a drunk peasant grabbed their heads and banged them together, saying, "That's what we'll do with the Jews." She recalled that her father's only weapon to protect his family was just a few planks nailed together. Moshe Mabovitch was a carpenter and by all accounts not a terribly successful one. The cupboards were bare and dinner consisted of a few spoonfuls of porridge. After a short and miserable stay in Kiev, Moshe did pull off one wonderful achievement: he figured out how to escape Russia and how to bring Golda, her mother, and her sisters to Milwaukee. Traveling was dangerous, of course, and required a visa. Merely the process of applying for a visa could stir up extortion (as if the family had anything to give) or kidnapping, especially for girls. When they arrived in Milwaukee, they were not alone. Hundreds of thousands of other immigrants lived nearby, including Russians, Poles, Germans, and Italians. The luxuries were slim, although the Schlitz Brewing Company apparently provided free steam baths. The immigrants learned American songs and cheered at patriotic parades, seemingly in a competition to see which ethnic group could come off as more Yankee than the next. Golda's synagogue held special services on Thanksgiving, even though the Bible does not does mark the fourth Thursday in November as a particularly sacred day. Naturally, some scars of Russia remained. Golda remembered applauding on the sidelines of a Labor Day parade. "The brass bands, the floats, the smell of popcorn and hotdogs—symbolized American freedom," she wrote. But when the police rode by on horses, her little sister began to "tremble and cry, 'It's the Cossacks! The Cossacks are coming!' The America that I knew was a place that a man could ride a horse to protect marching workers: the Russia I knew was a place that men on horses butchered."[21] Her sister was sobbing so loudly she had to be taken home and put to bed. Golda stayed.

Golda was headstrong and her mother griped that she was always talking. Her mother called her the *kochlefl*, the spoon that stirs the pot. Sometimes she stirred too much, as did her sister Sheyna, who was nine years older and spoke as if Karl Marx and Friedrich Engels were whispering in her ears. Utopian socialism did not make much sense to Golda's parents. Even more disturbing to the parents' old-world ways, Golda and Sheyna demanded an education. Golda had to lodge her own personal protest just to get permission to attend high school. Her father wanted her to wear frilly dresses and tried to calm her down, confiding that "men don't like smart girls," and her parents suggested she work in a hat shop or maybe go to secretarial school.[22] When she found out that her parents had already picked out an old man for her to marry (in his "early thirties," Golda recalled), she erupted at the "Pinsk on the Milwaukee River" attitude and followed her rebellious sister to Denver.

It is not clear why Sheyna thought Denver would be the next hot spot for socialist dreamers, but the clean Rocky Mountain air helped her symptoms of tuberculosis and Golda found the social climate more progressive than her parents' small clapboard dwelling. She listened in as Sheyna's friends debated Lenin and Trotsky and discussed the early Zionists who followed the ideas of Theodor Herzl. Golda's mother described Sheyna's boyfriend from Denver as a "lunatic with grand ideas and not a cent in his pocket." She would not have thought more of Golda's boyfriend Morris Meyerson, who was a sign painter when he found work and the rest of the time a sensitive, underemployed admirer of Byron and Wordsworth. Golda told her best friend in Milwaukee, "He isn't very handsome but he has a beautiful soul!" Morris made a romantic marriage proposal and sixteen-year-old Golda thought about accepting. But she had a different life plan from the one Morris proposed. He pictured the two of them alone and cozy together as a Victrola played a Brahms lullaby. She pictured them in Palestine digging trenches by day and sleeping in the barracks of a kibbutz at night, while fellow kibbutzniks stared down at them from their bunks. After some time Golda accepted his offer of marriage, but laid down one irrevocable condition: he would have to move with her to Palestine. Their marriage, which lasted until his death in 1951, never made much sense to anyone, including their children.

ESCAPING TO A BARREN PLACE

Zionists had been escaping Russia and Europe for the Holy Land for years, and Golda was ready to dirty her boots and help them. It took a long time to get there. In New York, she and Morris boarded a former cruise liner that had been turned into a US Navy transport ship during World War I. In the spirit of a famous heroine, it bore the name SS *Pocahontas* and its infamous and calamitous one-month voyage to Naples sounds like a Mafia pot-boiler. According to a contemporaneous *New York Times* report, the ship collided with a dock in Boston; two days later the engine room was flooded and a sailor who was accused of starting a fire on another ship was placed in irons.[23] The next day a fire broke out at a generator and the electricians were placed in irons. The engineer was told to "remain in his cabin by the ship's doctor, as he was suffering from nervous strain." His body was later found overboard, his hands tied to a large pipe so he couldn't swim. That same day a crewman was found with two hundred pieces of stolen silver; this was followed by the boiler mate being put in irons, along with the first and fourth engineers. By the time the ship made it to Naples, eight feet of water flooded the lower decks, and presumably Golda and Morris Meyerson were convinced that Palestine would be safer and more comfortable. When they teetered off the ship in Naples, they discovered that the Arab boatmen who controlled the transportation to the port of Haifa would not allow any Jews to sail. Golda and Morris had to sail to Alexandria, Egypt, and then find a way to get to Palestine by jeep, train, or camel.

When they finally climbed off the Palestinian Railway at the Tel Aviv station, they stepped into ankle-deep sand. They saw just about nothing. Tel Aviv was a few paved streets, the smell of donkeys, open latrines, blowing dust, and a mayor who rode around on a white horse.[24] Golda saw one tree. They had no running water and shared an outhouse with forty other people. And yet this offered more privacy than the kibbutz they would try to join. I use the verb *try* because they were rejected at first. The kibbutz men thought they looked too soft and, besides, the kibbutz men would have preferred a single woman, not a married one. Some of the more ardent socialists believed that marriage was an oppressive legal construct. They finally relented when Golda proved herself by climbing up and unclogging a water tower. Golda went to work in an area the local Arabs called the Death Swamp. The latrine, four holes in the ground with no partition, was a quarter-mile walk from the barracks. They were told to plant trees, but the land alternated between marsh and rocks. In the summer work began at 4 a.m. because swarms of tiny flies attacked each afternoon. Workers would slather themselves in Vaseline to cover up, but insects would plug up their eyes, ears, and noses.[25] Golda also worked in the chicken coops and tried to maintain some dignity by wearing a dress and stockings to Friday night dinners. The other women frowned on her attempts to appear less rustic.

SWEATING AND WORKING THE LAND

Let's take a few moments to look at two intertwined themes for Golda, and for us today, work and land. As I discussed in chapter

4, work imparts dignity and it raises one's individual standard of living as well as the community's. But for Golda and the Zionists work did something else: it helped create a national culture and bound them to the soil. An early Zionist, A. D. Gordon, wrote that Jews are a "people without a country, without a national living language, without a culture." Therefore he argued that Jews themselves must roll up their sleeves, sweat hard, and toil in the land, and not "let Ivan, John or Mustafa do the work, while we busy ourselves with producing a culture."[26] Sweat must be central to the culture. In 1934 David Ben-Gurion, who later became Israel's first prime minister, told a Palestinian leader, "We do not want to create a situation like that which exists in South Africa, where the whites are the owners and rulers, and the blacks are the workers. If we do not do all kinds of work, easy and hard, skilled and unskilled, if we become merely landlords, then this will not be our homeland."[27] This line of thinking goes back to John Locke, who begins his treatise on property by quoting King David, and then states that whoever has taken raw nature and "hath mixed his labour with, and joined to it something that is his own . . . thereby makes it his property.[28] For the Zionists, planting, plowing, and harvesting would finally give roots to the long-pitied or despised wandering Jew. The Jewish National Fund extended this quest by launching in 1901 a worldwide, century-long campaign to plant trees and build reservoirs in Israel. Ben-Gurion said, "We must clothe every mountainside with trees, every hill and rocky piece of land which cannot successfully be farmed, the dunes of the coastal plain, the Negev."[29] When a child was born outside Israel, parents and relatives were asked to plant a sapling and a certificate would show an enduring link between the child's name and the tree. In his book *Landscape and Memory*, British historian Simon Schama recalls his childhood memory of filling boxes with sixpence donations, which were commemorated by gluing small green leaves to a paper tree pinned on the wall:

> When the tree was throttled with foliage the whole box was sent off, and a sapling, we were promised, would be dug into the Galilean soil, the name of our class stapled to one of its green twigs. All over north London, paper trees burst into leaf to the sound of jingling sixpence, and the forest of Zion thickened in happy response.[30]

Every nation and every national culture is ultimately linked to soil. President George H. W. Bush embraced an initiative to plant a billion trees, and when Queen Elizabeth II visited the White House in 1991 he invited her to help plant a small linden tree. In 1937, it turned out, the White House had planted two linden trees to honor the coronation of her father, King George VI. During a recent storm, one of those trees had been uprooted. Bush said, "I can think of no better way to show our friendship, nor salute the children of both countries than to plant a new linden tree."[31] I watched the ceremony from the lawn and the event became somewhat infamous because the advance men had forgotten to place a box behind the lectern for the queen to stand on. She was about a foot shorter than the president. So when she began speaking, the audience could see only her purple hat. The press photographers, waiting for their Pulitzer Prize–winning shot, began cursing in terms that you usually do not hear in front of Her Majesty. One more detail on royal protocol. A friend of mine who organized the event, a wonderful, spirited Yankee from New Hampshire named Emily Mead, called up Buckingham Palace to find out whether the queen would be willing to pick up a shovel. "Just a moment," Emily was told. Then the chief protocol officer gave his pronouncement on this important matter: "Yes, Her Majesty will pick up the shovel. Two scoops."

The call of terrain is as primordial as salmon returning to their spawning grounds and it shows up in high culture and low culture. Some of the most climactic and enduring scenes in literature call upon the spiritual strings that bind people to terrain. King Lear howls from the windswept, desolate heath about the birthright he has foolishly given away; Scarlett O'Hara returns to Tara, grabs a withered radish from a clump of earth, and declares, "I'll never be hungry again! No, nor any of my folks . . . As God is my witness." Even Dracula needs some soil from Transylvania if he's going to sleep in his coffin. For the Zionists, it was clear: for two thousand years those in the Diaspora greeted each other, "Next year in Jerusalem." In Hebrew, Arabic, and ancient Syriac the word *Zion* denoted Jerusalem. They would return to that same earth that had been waiting two thousand years, though it had been both trampled and tilled by Romans, Crusaders, Ottomans, and Bedouins.

LAND OF ZION AND CLIFFS OF ALBION

Golda's husband, Morris, knew that English poets had a strong tradition of tying land to folk fables and national culture. The Zionists thought that the British would be more decisively on their side and more passionately feel the millennia-old yearning for an ancient homeland. Let's take a few paragraphs to connect the land, the people, and the literature of the British and the Zionists. In Wordsworth's "Tintern Abbey," a man must reconcile himself to his inescapable memories of an enduring place that has not changed, though he has: "Of five long winters! And again I hear/These waters, rolling from their mountain-springs/With a soft inland murmur." In *Richard II*, we hear of "this sceptered isle, This earth of majesty . . . This other Eden, demi-paradise . . . This precious stone set in a silver sea . . . this realm, this England." It is so stirring that a few years ago British tourism officials used a voice-over of these lines for a television advertisement in the United States. But let's read a little further for something very interesting. Later in John of Gaunt's speech, we hear that those from this land are "Renowned for their deeds as far from home, For Christian service and true chivalry." Remember that after World War I Britain controlled faraway Palestine through the so-called mandate. Echoing Gaunt's words "far from home" British soldiers and civil servants were called to administer a troubled, brawling place. At first the Zionists were pleased and felt a kinship. In 1917 Britain had issued the Balfour Declaration, which "looked with favour" on a Jewish national home (while preserving civil rights for non-Jews). Britons had shown heroism in World War I; and later, during World War II, amid bombs landing in London living rooms, Britain proved itself the bravest, most chivalrous island in history (with the possible exception of Malta during the Great Siege in 1565). Ben-Gurion said, "I am amazed by the . . . inner confidence of this wonderful nation."[32] When Golda begged Americans to support Israel, she dramatically paraphrased Churchill's stirring pledge to "fight on the beaches." She promised that her people "will fight in the Galilee and will fight in the outskirts of Jerusalem until the very end."

The next line in the *Richard II* speech delivers a stunner: "As is the sepulchre in stubborn Jewry." The line is not a blistering insult (in *Exodus* and *Deuteronomy* God calls the Israelites "stiff-necked," so we can't blame Shakespeare for plagiarizing from the best). But here is the irony in Shakespeare's snub: the Zionists admired Britain for its unfailing devotion to its own island, for its bravery, and for its industriousness. Moreover, they trusted the 1917 Balfour Declaration. For these reasons, after World War II ended, Ben-Gurion and Golda were shocked to find that even after millions of Jews were murdered in the Holocaust, the British government stymied straggling escapees from reaching Palestine. Instead, soldiers forced starved survivors into detainment camps or pushed them onto ships like the *Exodus*, which was ordered back to Germany with forty-five hundred souls. The British foreign minister Ernest Bevin was particularly infuriating. During the Holocaust, the Colonial Office contended that Palestine was not large enough to take Europe's Jews. After the war, when the number of Jews had been slashed by 6 million, Bevin still did not think it was the right place and refused President Truman's request to allow even 100,000 refugees into the territory (in 1938 the Dominican Republic had pledged to accept 100,000). Bevin simply did not believe that Jews could constitute a nation, viewing them as just another religion. Bevin's colleague, MP Richard Crossman, challenged him and assured him that "these people are going to fight like a nation." Bevin replied, "Well, then they aren't Jews."[33] But their history, their book, their stories, and their working the land had transformed them into a viable nation.

In fact, throughout the 1920s and 1930s when Golda Meir and her kibbutzniks were digging trenches and trying to plant trees, various European foreign policy experts suggested that the Jews were digging in the wrong place. A new homeland, they suggested, would be better placed in Uganda, the pampas of Argentina, or Manitoba.[34] Meanwhile, in 1934 the Soviets tried to create their own model Jewish homeland beyond the pale of the Pale in a Siberian district called Birobidzhan, not far from China. The pogroms in cities like Kiev and Odessa had been so bloody that thousands of Jews willingly trekked across the entire six-thousand-mile Soviet landscape to get to this remote place, which sounded like a zoo for a truly endangered species. Today, the place still has some menorahs and a statue of the Fiddler on the Roof. One recent visitor compared it to *Jurassic Park.*[35]

During the 1920s and 1930s the Zionists planted, plowed, and heaved the tractors and economy into forward gear. Golda had said that one of her first sights in Palestine was a plow on an Arab farm being pulled by two individuals: one was a woman; her yoke-mate was an ox. Golda did not apologize for ruining the romantic rural image by replacing the sore and fatigued livestock (human and nonhuman) with tractors and combines. Pulling the capital stock from tenth-century to twentieth-century standards made a difference. Real per capita income jumped 160 percent between 1922 and 1935 and the number of telephone lines multiplied fourfold between 1931 and 1933. Between 1921 and 1939 agricultural and manufacturing output multiplied fifteenfold on Jewish-owned lands. There was likely some positive spillover, for Arab-owned properties in Palestine doubled their output. These extraordinary improvements may have induced other Arabs from Egypt and elsewhere to migrate to the newly fertile areas in Palestine.[36] The pioneers and kibbutzniks had no choice but to innovate and conserve natural resources. If a new tool could yield more apricots or almonds and do so without breaking the back of a picker, it was deployed. After the State of Israel was declared in 1948, the speed of innovation grew even more rapid. With scarce freshwater supplies, Israelis tried drip irrigation, keeping humidity in by covering fields with plastic, and creating hybrid plants. At the same time, they sought out European markets for export, especially in the wintertime. Jaffa oranges became a symbol of Israel, and Tel Aviv became the Big Orange, in a nod to New York's moniker, the Big Apple.[37] For the last few years the state of California has suffered through a drought and residents have been told not to water their lawns and to set a timer for their showers. In 2015 a desalination plant opened in Carlsbad, just north of San Diego. The billion-dollar plant is designed to produce 50 million gallons of drinking water each day, enough to fill three Olympic-sized pools in less than an hour.[38] Seventeen other plants are being constructed in the state. An Israeli company called IDE has led the California project, using technology developed in the Israeli desert many years ago.

CREATING A MORE MOBILE NATION

Golda began traveling outside of Palestine to raise funds for this new, yet old nation. In her meetings with American diplomats and citizens she insisted that planting a tree is not simply a matter of botany—it is building a nation and bringing freedom. It might sound counterintuitive, but trees even bring mobility. In a speech in New York in 1935 she reported that young "idealists have to come to dry the swamps of Hadera and plant . . . eucalyptus trees. Now those trees have grown and they make Jewish ships."[39] Remember Golda had sailed on the mutinous SS *Pocahontas*, only to be told that she had to sneak into Palestine by first taking a choppy boat ride to Egypt. To her the sound of a "Jewish ship" launched into the crashing waves of the Mediterranean in Haifa was like the toll of the Liberty Bell to the founding fathers in Philadelphia. Ships, which bring self-reliance and freedom, began as saplings in the desert.

DEFYING CHAUVINISTIC MEN

Of course, not all the desert bloomed, and Golda did not lose her ability to be impressed by barren terrain. In 1946 she visited her daughter at a kibbutz in the Negev. "I thought I was going to die," she said. "For miles around, there was nothing, not a tree, not a blade of grass, not a bird, nothing but sand and glaring sun."[40] Male Zionists could be macho and chauvinistic, but they needed the labor of women, too. If a woman was not sturdy enough to dig up rocks for a vineyard or help pave a road under the searing sun, she would be directed to one of the women's associations to build and maintain tree nurseries.[41] Golda refused to be relegated to the women's section of any task or meeting. One cannot underestimate the psychic and even physical courage it would have taken to continuously barrel through the gender barriers of pioneer builders and politicians. The comedian Jackie Mason joked that the first time he visited Israel he thought the Israeli men looked so tan and macho, he was sure they were Puerto Ricans. Golda became a key adviser to Ben-Gurion, who later called her "the best man in my cabinet." She had no trouble confronting men and, prior to a meeting with her, a British commandant received a warning from his colleague: "Mrs. Meyerson is a very formidable person. Watch out!"[42] When Israel declared independence in 1948, Golda was one of the original twenty-four signers and said that she cried, thinking it was unimaginable that a girl from Pinsk and Milwaukee could be in the middle of something so important. Ben-Gurion asked his cabinet to take on Hebrew names, to further create a bridge between them. His surname had been Green. Golda changed Meyerson to Meir. Then he made a subtle choice in the wording of the Israeli Declaration of Independence. Unlike the US Declaration, the Israeli version does not mention God. The US Declaration begins by honoring "Nature's God" and ends by asking for the protection of "Divine Providence." Wait a moment. After two thousand years of pining for a new Jewish state and tucking prayers into the cracks between the stones of the Wailing Wall, Israel's founding document would not honor God? Ben-Gurion insisted (and Golda agreed) that Israel must be a place even for nonbelievers and devout secularists. In place of a clear reference to "God" or "the Almighty," the founders substituted this phrase: "The Rock of Israel." The phrase "Rock of Ages" is found in both Jewish and Christian hymns (and in a Broadway musical from 2009). In the Declaration, the "Rock of Israel" may refer to the Bible, or to God's promises, or perhaps to the very soil that Ben-Gurion and Golda had tilled, plowed, and harvested.

After the signing, there was no time to celebrate, though, for the Arab states immediately declared war. Ben-Gurion asked Golda to oversee the defense of Jerusalem, acquiring arms and distributing food. She imposed daily rationing, just three ounces of dried fish, lentils, macaroni, and beans. She got by on virtually no sleep. She frequently had to run the gauntlet from Jerusalem to Tel Aviv, as bullets sprayed across the roads. One day while bullets strafed her bus, she covered her eyes. "What are you doing?" a companion asked. "I'm not really afraid to die, you know. Everybody dies. But how will I live if I'm blinded? How will I work?" A few days later her bus was ambushed while careening around a curve just outside Jerusalem. The man next to her died of a bullet wound, in her lap.[43]

NIXON AND THE KINGS OF JORDAN

For all her courage and headstrong attitude, strong, smart men found her appealing. Richard Nixon, despite all his unseemly psychological complexities, admired Golda and showed the rarely seen warm side of his personality. When she served as prime minister and it came to hard-nosed military matters, Nixon overrode Secretary of State Henry Kissinger to fulfill Golda's requests. In the midst of the surprise 1973 Yom Kippur attack, Kissinger dithered as Egyptian forces crippled Israeli air force jets with new Soviet antiaircraft and antitank missiles. Nixon finally ordered: "Look, Henry, we're going to get just as much blame for sending three as if we send thirty or a hundred . . . *so send everything that flies.*"

Even more fascinating than her relations with Nixon were her close ties with the kings of Jordan, Abdullah and his son Hussein. She would secretly meet with them for frank and friendly conversations. Just before Israel declared independence, she snuck to the Jordanian border, put on a black dress and veil, and rode with the king's driver to a safe house in the hills. The king asked, "Why are the Jews in such a hurry to have a state?"

"We've waited two thousand years. That's not my definition of a hurry."[44]

Later during her years as prime minister, she developed a strong personal bond with Abdullah's son, King Hussein. In 1970 he requested that Golda direct the Israeli air force to destroy Syrian tanks massed on Jordan's border. Hussein would sometimes sneak into Israel to see Golda, piloting his own helicopter and landing at a rendezvous point near the Dead Sea. Just days before the Yom Kippur War in 1973 the king flew his Bell heli-

copter to a Mossad safe house to warn her of a possible and immi-
nent attack.[45] Although he sent a brigade to join the Syrian army,
he informed Golda and promised that his soldiers would walk
slowly.[46] She and Hussein both regretted that he did not have
enough sway to hammer out a broad Israeli-Arab peace agreement. Heavy losses in the 1973 war pushed her out of the prime
minister's position. Four years later when Anwar Sadat made his
courageous trip to Israel in 1977 and told a cheering parliament
that "we really and truly welcome you to live among us in peace,"
Golda waited in the receiving line, wishing only that Sadat's visit
had come during her years as prime minister.

A year after Sadat's visit, Golda Meir died at age eighty of
lymphatic cancer. She left behind deserts that bloomed and she
kicked into the dustbin of history the idea that a nation is only
as strong as the stuff in the ground. It is the stuff that people are
made of that matters most.

The year 1948 was a monumental one, a year when two leaders of two vastly different countries ignored handy excuses and
instead took action that would instill new pride and patriotism
in populaces that had been cowering—fearful of bullets, poverty,
hunger, and a deadly geopolitical neighborhood.

CONCLUSION: DO NOT
GO GENTLE

She was eighty years old when the 2004 Indian Ocean tsunami struck the Andaman Islands. A very short woman with dark skin and light hair, she recalled the tribal elders warning her that "the Earth would part, don't run away or move."[1] Instead, as the waves washed over the village, she climbed a tree and saved herself. Her name was Boa and when her neighbors buried her in February 2010 they also buried the language, laws, nursery rhymes, burial rites, and future dreams of her people. She was the last speaker of an ancient tribal language called Bo, and the last direct link to a 65,000-year-old culture. Few of us noticed the death of Bo. I did not send a condolence card, for who would open it?

Boa's elders were wrong. The Earth did not literally split apart but Boa's tribe was swallowed up by other forces, including diseases delivered by European settlers, the Japanese occupiers in World War II, and the lure of civilization to young Andamanese who wandered away from their old relatives. Every nation that exists today, over the course of the next hundred or thousand years, could be buried alongside the lost language of Bo.

There is only one question, then: Do we care to stop the "entropy of nations," the powerful forces that find the weakest seams and begin to tug, unravel, and rip? Each nation must speak for itself and decide whether it can cope with the price of prosperity. As an American, I am most concerned about my own land, of course. In the prior chapters we have seen how falling birthrates, a rise in globalization, a decline of work, and an explosion of debt and bureaucracy have made our national seams more threadbare. I have also argued that these problems have come about, not because of an economic or environmental disaster, but largely because of prosperity. Do not get me wrong. Prosperity is a good thing. We have been right to prefer longer and healthier lives, better medicines, and the choice of fruits, vegetables, flowers, and flatscreens made anywhere around the world. But now we must decide whether to repair the seams or let the forces of prosperity rip them far apart. Betsy Ross, the old legend goes, sewed the American flag. But there is no fabric to hand to a seamstress so that she can sew a country back together again. We have learned in prior chapters how leaders like Alexander, Atatürk, and others battled to hold together or form new nations. It is not hopeless, but it is hard. In his farewell address in 1989, President Ronald Reagan took pride in America's economic renewal but he realized the social task was getting harder. He said there was a "great tradition of warnings in Presidential farewells, and I've got one that's been on my mind for some time." George Washington warned Americans not to "entangle" our peace with faraway foreign forces. Dwight Eisenhower warned of the "military-industrial complex." But Reagan pointed to something more subtle yet more far-reaching and powerful than a B-52 bomber—the tendency of patriotism to fade away over time: "[O]ddly enough it starts with one of the things I'm proudest of in the past 8 years: the resurgence of national pride that I called the new patriotism.

This national feeling is good, but it won't count for much, and it won't last unless it's grounded."[2] Over the course of his two terms in office Reagan's visage seemed to morph into the vintage poster of Uncle Sam (albeit with darker hair). When he died in 2004, his frequent ideological opponent, former French president François Mitterrand, said that Reagan was a piece of America himself. Nonetheless, Reagan recognized that all that is needed for nations to shatter is for patriots to do nothing.

Reagan was not just a patriot. He was also what I term a *patriotist*. There is a difference. A patriot feels love and affection for his country. A patriotist believes that it is a *good thing* to feel love and affection for one's country. In the same way, a child may naturally love his mother but it is another thing to assert, as a philosophical principle, that one should love one's mother. Now, all of this comes with a caveat: we assume, of course, that the specific mother or country deserves such sentiments. A mother that beats her child or a country that acts wickedly does not. One can be a theoretical patriotist but still condemn Cambodians who cheered Pol Pot. Here is the problem for the United States and most of Europe: *at the very same time that the economic forces I discussed early in this book are working to shatter nations, many of their citizens reject the very principle that fellow citizens should feel patriotic.* Some readers may think that I am jumping into the culture wars, often associated with screeching pundits on television. Here is the difference: the conservative ones tend to blame our social fissures on left-wing professors left over from the Vietnam era who infected generations with anti-American hatred. They often cite the name of Bill Ayers and his cloudy relationship with President Obama. I argue, instead, that the fissures stem from the prosperity delivered by market capitalism. (Ironically, my charge carries an element of "dialectical materialism," though I have elsewhere torn apart Marx's works and deplore most of the governments that have attempted to follow them.)[3]

Do "anti-American" professors matter then? Howard Zinn, author of the best-selling *A People's History of the United States*, wrote a July Fourth message asserting that "we must renounce nationalism and all its symbols: its flags, its pledges of allegiances, its anthems. . . . We need to assert our allegiance to the human race. . . . We need to refute the idea that our nation is different from, morally superior to, the other imperial powers of world history."[4] Zinn matters, not so much because he excoriates America and puts its record of deeds side by side with imperialists like Stalin and Pol Pot. Thinkers like Zinn matter because they are also antipatriotists; they impugn attempts to engender feelings of affection for one's country and community. All of this leads to a classroom in San Francisco where students today do not say a pledge of allegiance to the United States, but instead recite the "Pledge of Allegiance to the World."[5] I rather like our planet. But here is the problem: planet Earth does not need patriots to keep it spinning. If a war or plague wipes out every person, the Earth will keep whirling and the sun will still rise in the east. A country is a much more vulnerable thing. If you do not believe me, walk down Dubrovnik's Placa waving either the flag of Ragusa (d. 1808) or that of Yugoslavia (d. 2003). Then go to the railroad station and ask a conductor when the next train leaves for Czechoslovakia (d. 1992) or Bohemia (d. 1918). Or you can try to speak with Boa (d. 2010).

At the end of this chapter, I will try to set forth some simple ways to repair the damage that we have witnessed, on both economic and social policy, and submit a "Patriotist Manifesto."

IT'S JUST LAND, BLOOD, AND GUTS

I was always amused by those James Michener novels that, for example, tell a captivating story about an Alaskan bush pilot in the 1930s but begin by explaining how millions of years ago the continental plates jammed together and clumps of dirt migrated from the 34th parallel to the 64th. I won't go back so far in history. But we can all agree that the North American landmass did not prescribe any specific culture or values to its inhabitants. In other words, Native Americans, Inuits, and European settlers had to create their own culture. Sure, prairies, badlands, and bayous influenced how they found food and what gods they might have worshipped, but the land did not tell them which values they must exalt. They would have to decide whether to embrace or reject such various things as liberty, polygamy, schooling, gambling, traveling, and shaving of legs and armpits. No rock formation instructed Lutheran pioneers to bury their dead alone, yet told Dakota tribesmen to bury their dead in a tree (or scaffolding) with a dead horse beneath, so the steed could carry the body to an afterlife.[6] Of course, evolution played some role in culture by trampling out those individuals and groups who made terrible choices. For example, tribes that might have encouraged rampant sexual anarchy more likely picked up venereal diseases and perished.

Cultural tastes, too, are usually not given by the land, or even by our DNA. Most Caucasians do not care for the smell of fermented kimchi, but Caucasians raised in Korea do. Most fans of Verdi avoid Chinese opera and find it whiny. Most fans of Bob Dylan's whiny voice avoid *Rigoletto*. Rubens and Botticelli thought the ideal woman was very curvy. But if those ideal beauties walked off the paintings and into a Lululemon store today they would be shunned as downright fat and shunted to the warning zone of the BMI measuring stick. Millions of tourists travel to Europe each year to snap photos of towering Gothic cathedrals, but the early Romantics called them "Gothic" as an insult: they seemed ugly, barbarous, and medieval. If preferences in cathedrals and buttocks sizes can switch, why would we think that our emotional attachment to so-called American values is not vulnerable? Cultural values like democracy, freedom, and free markets must be cultivated or else they can be deposed or displaced, or can simply yellow and fade like the linoleum-covered floor of the last soda fountain at the last Woolworth.

MYTHS AND THE PARADOX OF PROGRESS

In the age of cyberspace, outsourcing, insourcing, globalization, and international superstars whose feet barely touch the ground anywhere in order to avoid paying taxes, every country feels as if something is slipping away. In the middle of the twentieth century, like Ahab chasing Moby-Dick, great fiction writers competed to compose the Great American Novel, a term first put forth in 1868. To be an American was a thing. Perhaps the finest and most telling opening sentence in American literature came forth in 1953 in Saul Bellow's *The Adventures of Augie March*: "I am an American, Chicago born—Chicago, that somber city—and go at things as I have taught myself, freestyle, and will make the record in my own way: first to knock, first admitted." Even though Bellow was born in Montreal, he proudly absorbed what he understood as America's brash and gritty values. But by 2004 Norman Mailer stated that the Great American Novel "was no longer writeable."[7] Philip Roth had already escaped the competition by taking the ironic route, entitling his 1973 book *The Great American Novel*. But today, who could possibly create credible characters and make sense of the entropic changes in our country while still holding on to the slippery idea of Americanness? For Mailer, it was not the novel, but the Americanness that had become the too-elusive white whale crashing beyond his grasp.

In 1958, during the era of Mailer, Bellow, and Truman Capote, Leonard Bernstein stood on the stage of Carnegie Hall in front of the New York Philharmonic Orchestra and gave remarkable televised concert-lectures to young people. He began by enticing the children in the audience with Rossini's "William Tell Overture." The kids all shouted, "The Lone Ranger!" The title of his second concert-lecture asked the following question: "What Is American Music?" Bernstein was dashing and intellectually daring and the black-and-white YouTube video has a midcentury *Mad Men* vibe. Bernstein cued up the orchestra and they sampled twentieth-century works that broke free of traditional European concerto constraints and instead integrated jazz, Native American rhythms, Negro spirituals, and sweeping crescendos representing the great western frontier.[8] Then as millions watched on CBS television, he turned over the baton to Aaron Copland, who raised his arms and conducted his "Fanfare for the Common Man." Who would even pose the question today, what is American music? And what fanfare could represent today's common man, who often does not understand the economic forces that turn him from a full-time employee to a consultant and from a vested pensioner to an old-timer dependent on Medicare's shaky finances?

So can we convey American values? We face an additional problem: it all sounds so corny. This brings us to our final paradox: *our economic progress came from defeating fables, myths, and magic and embracing science, yet we need to preserve some myths to maintain our emotional attachment to each other and to the country.* In our practical lives, science is in, magic is out. Most of us, when plagued with the flu, go to a physician, not a tribal medicine man, and farmers rely not on rain dances but on Monsanto. Prometheus stole fire for man and brought the flame down from Mount Olympus, but the Viking range in my kitchen, made in Mississippi, pumps out eighteen thousand BTUs without my offering a sacrifice to the gods. When we get fired from our jobs or earn a promotion, few of us ask whether this is a sign that we are among the "elect," and will be rewarded in the afterlife, as did the early Calvinists. It's a good thing that we have embraced a more rational view of life. For most of human history man lived no better on two legs than he had on four. The rise of science and the Enlightenment catapulted societies into a new world of economic growth and opportunity. People grew taller, lived longer, and found ways to escape impoverished villages. As we discussed earlier, rigid philosophical hierarchies like the Elizabethan Great Chain of Being, which had frightened peasants from breaking free from their lowly station in life, broke apart. When Jean-Jacques Rousseau said, "Man is born free and he is everywhere in chains," he may have been referring to philosophical and religious constraints that bound the ambitions of men and women.

Yet there's always a cost to escaping shackles. The rise of modern science and economies "disenchants" us, to use the term that Max Weber borrowed from the poet-philosopher Friedrich Schiller. In his poem "The Tables Turned," William Wordsworth bemoans that though

> Sweet is the lore which Nature brings
> Our meddling intellect

Mis-shapes the beauteous form of things: —
We murder to dissect.

The unexamined life is not worth living, Socrates taught. But I would argue that the over-examined life is not worth living either. We need some mystery to keep us emotionally healthy. Since we have squeezed myths and magic from the workplace and the economy, people seek them elsewhere. Perhaps that's why in a decade like the 2000s, where nearly every scrap of data and information became available on logical, optimized algorithms over the Internet, the best-selling books featured wizards (*Harry Potter*), vampires (*Twilight*), and a secret code purportedly left behind by Leonardo da Vinci.

Here's another way to see the paradox: every nation needs a bit of magic, but modern civilizations are driven by intellectual exploration to expose the fraud of the magician. William Butler Yeats saw that

> Civilization is hooped together, brought
> Under a rule, under the semblance of peace
> By manifold illusion; but man's life is thought,
> And he, despite his terror, cannot cease
> Ravening through century after century,
> Ravening, raging, and uprooting that he may come
> Into the desolation of reality.[9]

Atatürk faced this paradox. He threw the clerics out of the minarets and toppled the sultan, replacing them with technocrats and scientists. But he knew that the tools of science, test tubes and beakers, could not fill the vacuum and create "Turkishness." Therefore, he took radical steps, including imposing a new alphabet and extolling a questionable anthropology. Few of the Zionists who settled in Palestine spoke Hebrew. Most spoke German, Russian, Yiddish, or English. Many were scientists. Israel's first president, Chaim Weizmann, was a renowned British biochemist. Yet they resurrected an ancient language, full of mysticism, that had been chanted in prayers but not usually spoken on the streets of ghettos and shtetls. The crafty Meiji revolutionaries acted as if they were restoring an all-powerful divine emperor, when they were actually sneaking a confused boy onto the throne. Even Plato lied. Or at least he encouraged good leaders to create bonds through myths that he called "noble lies," sometimes translated as "magnificent myths." In his *Republic*, Plato justified stories that would make citizens more inclined to care for each other. But in the twenty-first century, in the age of snark, when a televised comic parody of the news can draw more viewers than real news reports, would anyone believe a magnificent myth?

THE STORY OF STORIES

Wordsworth described an "inscrutable workmanship that reconciles/discordant elements, makes them cling together/in one society." This is the hard work of institutions, to elicit sentiments of loyalty and patriotism from a disparate collection of people. Propinquity can help, as does continuous exposure. Psychologists tell us that the more we are exposed to someone, the more they tend to like us. This even works for animals and abstract shapes. If you spend each day looking at a photo of a wren sitting in a nest, you'll probably develop an affinity for wrens and nests. Nonetheless, a society cannot depend merely upon the psychological effect of propinquity. There must be more. Binding a nation together does not mean, of course, that each individual must act like a family member to every other person. That would be creepy, even if it were possible. To get along with strangers, we do not have to share some ideal, religious, or metaphysical connection. I frankly do not have the time or courage to inquire into the beliefs of everyone I stop for at a crosswalk or bump into on the New York City subway. No doubt, they have little interest in what is going on in my head. In my book *Rush*, I submit that in a counterintuitive way, a free-market system of competition does a fine job of prodding us to treat strangers well. In a market economy, buyers and sellers frequently meet each other more than once. The Rule of Repeats drives them to grow more honest with each other. Still, mere honesty and propinquity do not make a nation.

Nobody has a fail-safe method to teach virtue or bring disparate people closer to each other. Aristotle thought it was a matter of good habit. Mark Twain thought it was like an acquired taste for poetry, poker, or frog-jumping contests. Unfortunately, a basic method for passing on values such as grit, mobility, confidence, and patriotism in children has been under attack. What is the powerful tool? Telling stories. Now, many of us might think that in the twenty-first century, we've left behind stories, fables, and myths—that once man stepped out of the cave and joined the rat race, he waved farewell to quaint notions of village elders and campfire tales.

Yet we are not so different from primitive societies. Human beings still like to tell and to hear stories. Even our august institutions revolve around instructive tales. What is the Supreme Court but robed elders telling and retelling stories of conflict within our society? Cynical veterans of congressional campaigns speak of campaign "narratives." Aristotle defined *Homo sapiens* as a "featherless biped." I would add that we are a featherless biped who tells stories. Other living things communicate, of course. Bees buzz directions. Dogs bark warnings. But humans have figured out how to begin with a backstory, build to a climax, and end with a denouement.

Since America's birth, schoolteachers have transmitted its values through folklore and American heroes. I recall childhood afternoons running home from elementary school waving hats and banners cut with scissors from multicolored paper and assembled with that thick white paste that so many kids liked to snack on. What holidays did we celebrate with decorations and stories? Columbus Day, Thanksgiving, Washington's Birthday, Valentine's Day, and Memorial Day (and, of course, the last day of school).

Today many adults disdain the very idea of glorifying these holidays and the historical figures they involve. Just before Thanksgiving 2015, a young principal at PS 169 in Brooklyn banned a commemoration, while also abandoning the Pledge of Allegiance. The assistant principal sent a memo supporting the decision and urging the staff to "be sensitive of the diversity of our families."[10] Critics claim that we cannot ignore the harsh "truths" of history. Columbus and the Thanksgiving Pilgrims had warts that cannot be erased from our historical portrait. Following the arrival of Columbus and the Pilgrims, Native Americans found their lands plundered. Columbus, according to some historians, was a vicious, slave-owning, disease-carrying racist. (Of course, other historians claim he was a victim looking to escape the "blood-cleansing" of the Spanish Inquisition.) Although General Washington helped liberate America from the British, he then inspired the United States to trample on others by expanding its territorial reach

Frankly, blaming Columbus, the Pilgrims, and George Washington for all the trouble that followed is like blaming Marco Polo because yuppie restaurants charge thirty bucks for a bowl of linguine.

This cynical view of history is not found solely in the United States and is not a passing fad. The loss of myths is an entropic, shattering force that logically follows from economic development. How so? Why are holidays and national myths undermined? Why is there almost always a search for blemishes on founding fathers and mothers (in the case of Queen Elizabeth I, for example)?

As we learned early in this book, prosperous societies require trade with foreigners and ultimately require immigration. But these do not come easily. At first a society will scorn foreigners. This bias is driven by biology and neuroscience (recall William Hamilton's work on the willingness to sacrifice for family members and for strangers). The bias is also cultural. Aristotle taught Alexander the Great to look at Greeks as "friends and kindred, but to conduct himself toward other peoples as though they were plants or animals." For millennia nations have bonded over their shared dislikes of other peoples, often attributing vile traits to them. A common refrain: foreigners smell bad and were bred from pigs and monkeys or live like pigs and monkeys. Eventually, though, if a country is going to achieve prosperity, it must deal with foreigners as trading partners and as immigrants. At this point, founding national myths and founding heroes appear too old, too homogeneous, and too insular to be shared equally by the new multicultural population. Malcolm X put it memorably: "We didn't land on Plymouth Rock; Plymouth Rock landed on us." (Cole Porter used the same line earlier in his 1934 *Anything Goes*.) In addition, immigrants and foreigners typically accept dirtier jobs than the native-born. Working conditions are usually more dingy and dangerous: "We were told the streets were paved with gold; but we found out they were covered in horse dung, and we would do the paving." Again, the founding myths seem less applicable to newcomers. And if founding myths appear less applicable and less believable, why should they be cherished?

Today the Magna Carta—a nearly sacred text of freedom—is unknown to nearly one-half of the British public.[11] A University of Cardiff professor reported that only about 20 percent of UK university students can name a single prime minister from the 1800s! The names Disraeli and Gladstone mean nothing to most of them. In the United States, fewer than one in four college students can link James Madison to the US Constitution. But do not worry: 99 percent correctly identify *Beavis and Butthead*.

Shared stories and celebrated holidays are among the strongest tools to battle the entropy of nations. That's why John Adams in a letter to his wife, Abigail, wrote that Independence Day "ought to be commemorated, as the Day of Deliverance . . . solemnized with Pomp and Parade." In July 1776 Adams was not a ninny mesmerized by the sparkle of fireworks and the flow of hard apple cider in muggy Philadelphia. In the same letter he warned that the fight for independence would surely cost "toil and blood and treasure." He understood that history had warts, boils, and scars. But it was *because* of war's savagery and the future threat of dissolution that Americans should ennoble Independence Day.

There is one further response to critics who insist that we expose all children to the whole, bitter "truth" about their national forefathers. As developmental psychologist Jean Piaget taught, children require different methods of conveying information at different stages in their lives. A good teacher does not instruct a five-year-old in the same manner as a fourteen-year-old. It's okay to cover up some warts. Much more important, the heroes and holidays traditionally celebrated in elementary school instill the virtues and values that will permit and encourage children to explore truths and respect honest debate as they mature. Here's where I differ from Plato: in the *Republic*, the mighty leaders proclaim noble lies in order to shield commoners from important truths (for example, "We stole the land that we are living on"). I defend patriotic myths and stories to help bind the country, knowing that adults can be aware of elements of fabrication. It is all right to ask citizens to suspend their disbelief from time to time. An example: at a traditional Passover feast commemorating the exodus from Egypt, the assembled read the story of Moses leading slaves to liberation (some may question whether frogs fell from the sky). The book of *Exodus* commands that "you shall tell your son" of the bitter oppression of slavery. But there is more and here is the key: the Talmud insists, "A person is obligated to see himself as if he were leaving Egypt himself."[12] Each year Passover celebrants relive the journey, even though the actual event (which may be disputable) took place thousands of years earlier and none of the attendees at the family feast may have any genetic connection to those who escaped through the Red Sea. It is the *as if* that transforms the mere attendees into participants and that binds them together with thousands of years of history.

Our Thanksgiving story deserves similar reverence. We should be celebrating the feast *as if we ourselves* were among the Pilgrims and the Wampanoags. The original Pilgrims, of course, identified with the Hebrews escaping Egypt. Their wicked pharaoh was King James I of Great Britain. James had vowed to "make these deviants conform" or he would harass them till they fled the land, or worse.[13] Later Benjamin Franklin proposed that the seal of the United States include Moses holding out his arms over the Red Sea, which would slosh over the pharaoh in his open chariot. Thomas Jefferson portrayed the children of Israel in the wilderness, led by a cloud by day and a pillar of fire by night. (On the reverse side of the seal Jefferson suggested Hengist and Horsa, the legendary brothers who settled Britain. I am not disappointed that Jefferson lost his argument for Hengist and Horsa.)

What do traditional holidays actually represent and how do they fit into a revival of a national spirit? Columbus Day does not glorify a Genoan sailor as much as it exalts the virtues of courage, discovery, grit, mobility, and confidence. Halloween does not honor pagans as much as it enchants children while celebrating the discovery of New World crops like pumpkins. Knocking on a door while trick-or-treating teaches that adults will be more generous if children will be more polite. From a psychological point of view, it also guides children to face up to their anxieties (what monster is behind the door?). Thanksgiving teaches the virtues of comity and work, as well as the appreciation for bounty. Washington's Birthday does not enshrine powder-wigged generals so much as it teaches children about freedom and courage. Valentine's Day extols love. And Memorial Day honors sacrifice and inspires children to learn about the past.

These are the true lessons and virtues learned by children carrying pumpkins and wearing buckled hats: freedom, exploration, comity, work, courage, sacrifice, and heritage. Rather than lauding such common lessons and sharing a heritage, misguided adults often tell children to find role models who match their specific ethnic makeup. Blacks should not dream of becoming Albert Einstein. And whites should not strive to emulate Martin Luther King, Jr. This trend splinters communities and clouds our children's dreams. When I was a kid, my hero was not, like me, a blue-eyed boy from the New Jersey shore. My hero was a retired black man from Alabama. His name was Willie Mays. When I received my Little League uniform, I asked my mother to sew the number "24" on the back. My mother was not a terrific sewer and I was not the swiftest center fielder. But I am glad my coach didn't force me to change my number so my complexion matched my hero's.

It is important that a revival in national spirit encompass immigrants, too. A new Polish immigrant, for example, should be able to call George Washington his forefather with just as much conviction as the oldest WASP family in Virginia. A Thanksgiving turkey should look just as tasty whether surrounded by plates of kielbasa, steaming bowls of hoisin beef, or black beans and rice. Immigrants who have braved the seas and the bureaucrats may carry in their DNA an even greater spark for daring and grit. It is a disservice to them if we do not insist that they join in our national story, *as if* they had been here for a very long time.

BEWARE OF THE PRESENT, NOT THE PAST

Is it possible that a country can go too far and begin worshipping the past in a worrisome way? Yes, but citizens should be even more vigilant about reigning monarchs and prime ministers glorifying themselves in the *present*. A long list of despots and demagogues have kindled a cult of personality around themselves while they commandeered troops and used prisons as personal playgrounds in which to torture opponents. Sometimes they even claim divine powers. A painting of Napoleon called *Bonaparte Visits the Plague Stricken in Jaffa* hangs in the Louvre. The painter, Antoine-Jean Gros, portrays the general visiting soldiers in Jaffa who had been struck by the bubonic plague. The men are haggard and frightened, their skin blotchy. Two black men carry a cadaver on a stretcher. Defying the obvious peril, Napoleon stretches out his arm and touches the blister under a man's armpit. What's the problem? First, the image plagiarizes the Gospels and puts Napoleon on equal footing with Jesus. In the Gospels, when a leper staggers up to Jesus and begs his help, Jesus reaches out his hand and touches the man, who is cured. Second, the painting was presented to the public in 1804 between the date Napoleon proclaimed himself emperor and his coronation at Notre Dame. That's too much. Napoleon was not a god or a saint and public worship of an incumbent leader can be lethal. More recently, during the vicious reign of Nicolae Ceaușescu in Romania from 1965 until 1989, he and his wife, Elena, would literally beat the public into thinking that they were nearly divine. Their propagandists convinced the public, for example, that Elena was a world-renowned PhD biochemist who conducted groundbreaking work on polymerization. When she visited the United States in the 1970s, the Illinois Academy of Science offered to grant Elena an honorary degree. But that was not good enough for this fearsome fraud. She threw a fit when Jimmy Carter could not secure for her a degree from a Washington-based university: "Come off it! You can't sell me the idea that Mr. Peanut can give me an Illi-whatsis diploma but not any from Washington. I w-i-l-l n-o-t g-o t-o Illi-whatever it is. I will not!"[14] After the charming Ceaușescus were executed in 1989, an early teacher of Elena dared to reveal her awful school grades, showing that she was a dunce who had flunked out of everything except needlepoint, singing, and gymnastics.[15]

I am less worried about honoring the past than lionizing politicians in the present. I am against naming any buildings or monuments after living leaders. In New Jersey, Brendan Byrne was a bland governor in the 1970s and 1980s. But somehow in 1981, a twenty-thousand-seat sports arena opened up in the Meadowlands to house the New Jersey Nets basketball team and it was called the Brendan Byrne Arena (the name later got changed to Izod Field). I doubt that Mr. Byrne personally paid to build his stadium. I'm not even sure he could dribble a basketball. Such grandeur invites corruption. In the Jersey Shore town of Toms River, an ambitious school superintendant named a new three-thousand-seat arena after himself in 2004 and hosted acts like Maroon 5, Bill Cosby, and Kelly Clarkson.[16] Six years later FBI agents burst into his home to arrest him on bribery charges. The school district quickly threw a tarp over the huge sign that bore his name in front of the arena.

Respect for national myths and holidays can help sew a country back together. I fear that today our fabric is being picked at and pawed like the discount rack at the final Filene's Basement to close down. Our national story and our nation's children deserve better. Somehow, if we care to save the nation, we must honor *e pluribus unum* without getting fatally stuck in the *pluribus*.

Building character and creating community bonds cannot come just from waving Thanksgiving hats in school, of course. In the following section, I propose some new policies to fight the shattering. Though the ideas are focused on the United States, they could be adapted for other countries. My Patriotist Manifesto is written as a universal document and not limited to the United States. The policies would reorient everything from the tax code to the duties of the unemployed to the responsibilities of new immigrants. Some of these proposals might appear trivial in the face of sweeping, entropic forces. But sometimes simple, symbolic gestures can move weighty objects. Consider John F. Kennedy's visit to Berlin in June 1963. When the young president arrived, West Germans felt trapped, encircled by communist power. Soviet leader Nikita Khrushchev called West Berlin a "bone in my throat" and pledged to remove this "splinter from the heart of Europe." Khrushchev threatened to sign a treaty with East Germany that would block Westerners from reaching West Berlin. When Kennedy declared to thousands of Berlin citizens four simple words, *"Ich bin ein Berliner,"* he strengthened their resolve. When President Ronald Reagan came to Berlin in 1987, even his own State Department warned him not to rattle Soviet and East German leaders. But when Reagan bucked his own diplomats and demanded, "Mr. Gorbachev, tear down this Wall!" he unleashed a new wave of hope among free Germans, and among those effectively held hostage by the East German government. Between Kennedy and Reagan a total of ten words, spoken in less than six seconds combined, shifted how Berliners saw themselves and their place in the world.

Here are examples of ideas, some substantive and some symbolic, that can help the United States wrestle with the entropic forces that assault wealthy nations.

FIGHTING THE IMMIGRATION PARADOX AND THE LOSS OF RESPECT FOR US HISTORY

Many peaceful countries require young people to serve in the military or in some other national service role. Finland, which we do not think of as a particularly oppressive place (except for wintry ice), requires six months to a year of military service. Switzerland provides nattily dressed guards for the pope at the Vatican and at home demands that young men serve in the military or in some alternative way, such as assisting old people or rebuilding cultural sites. In 2013, 73 percent of Swiss voters opted against eliminating mandatory service.[17] I do not cite these examples to argue that the United States should institute a military draft or mandatory civilian service. But I would ask this question: if other advanced countries impose six months to an entire year of mandatory service on their own citizens, would it be so terrible to impose some slight inconvenience on immigrants who apply for citizenship, especially an inconvenience that would enhance their knowledge of the country they aspire to join? Here's what I have in mind:

> Require all applicants for citizenship and green cards to have their passports stamped at no fewer than five of the following historical landmarks, museums, and libraries:

> - Paul Revere House (Boston); Independence Hall (Philadelphia); Gettysburg Battlefield; Mount Vernon, Virginia; Monticello, Virginia; the Statue of Liberty; Ellis Island; the Alamo
> - National World War II Museum (New Orleans); National Museum of American History (DC); Museum of Tolerance (Los Angeles); Pearl Harbor Memorial; Memphis Civil Rights Museum
> - The presidential libraries

> I would impose a similar requirement for any US citizen who applies for a student loan through a federal program.[18]

> - Following the model of the Birthright program (a privately funded organization that provides heritage trips for young people to Israel), private US foundations should establish Birthright USA. This program would give deserving teens a chance to visit what I would call the *Freedom Corridor*: Boston–Philadelphia–Washington, DC.

- For those seeking to immigrate to the United States, we should give priority not only to those with STEM skills but also to those who score highly on American history and civics exams.

FIGHTING THE PARADOX OF THEFT, GENERATIONAL THEFT, AND BIRTHRATE DECLINES

- Baby boomers, who will benefit far more from the Social Security program than their grandchildren, should receive an increase in benefits *only if* the overall economy grows and the nation's debt profile improves.
- As life expectancy and health for older people improve, the retirement age should increase for government social programs.
- Young parents should receive a large tax credit, but only for a second and third child, while automatically depositing the funds into a savings account for their children. While we may applaud the birth of a first child, taxpayers need not spend money on an additional incentive to make that happen.

FIGHTING THE MALDISTRIBUTION OF WORK AND BATTLING IMMOBILITY

When pessimists bemoan that governments never improve their policies, consider the landmark welfare reform passed by a Republican Congress and signed by Democratic president Bill Clinton in 1996. Though some of Clinton's own advisers resigned in protest, the measure successfully nudged (or badgered) millions of recipients off the welfare rolls and into the workplace. A Federal Reserve Bank of San Francisco study concluded that "reform has made even the most vulnerable single mother economically more self-sufficient."[19] This is not the place for a full-fledged debate on the bipartisan measure, but the law does suggest that every once in a while policies can get better, not worse.

- Give job seekers mobility credits if they move to another state to take a job, and revamp state unemployment programs to show job seekers potential employment out of county and out of state.
- Give job seekers "bonuses" for accepting jobs prior to their unemployment benefits expiring. A few years ago I presented my proposal on the front page of the Sunday *Washington Post* Outlook section.[20]
- For nonhazardous jobs, eliminate licensing requirements which dramatically raise the cost of learning and practicing a trade.
- Reform the federal disability program so that partially disabled workers continue to work, but in a more suitable job, rather than retiring.
- Give young people incentives to learn the discipline of a job. For example, someone who begins working before age twenty-one should receive extra Social Security bonuses upon his or her retirement.

To cope with the price of prosperity takes brains and brawn. Hard work and careful thought. It also calls for a commitment to shared principles. Foremost among these beliefs: that a nation is worth defending. History warns us that almost every nation eventually grows too tired, too timid, or too splintered to hold together. But it's not an utterly impossible task. The Patriotist Manifesto is both a call and a code to guide people who believe that their nation's very existence brings about more liberty and justice in the world.

The Patriotist Manifesto

A specter is haunting free states, but this shapeless ghost is not fed by disease, bloodshed, or poverty. Instead, it is nourished by the very prosperity of the modern age and the drive for educated men and women to abandon, excuse, or disdain the myths, magic, awe, and enchantment that held nations together. Though human beings may lack the powers to rekindle such ephemeral yet once powerful forces, we should seek to establish principles that may bind us in liberty, justice, and mutual defense. Therefore, we declare that

1   To be patriotic about one's nation—to feel profound affection, to experience joy in its successes and sorrow in its failures—is a good thing, provided that nation defends liberty and justice.

2   A nation's character virtues do not stem from the rocks and soil of its land or the genetic stock of the people, but from their character and the precepts they will fight for.

3   The people have a moral and legal right to protect against attacks, invasions, or overwhelming cultural incursions that would destroy the character of the nation.

4   The doors of the nation must be open for "exit" and for "voice"—to allow citizens to emigrate freely from the country and to voice discontent within its borders.

5   Immigrants have an obligation to understand and embrace the national history of their new home. Native-born citizens should encourage immigrants to feel that they have as much moral right to celebrate national holidays and traditions as those families who trace their ancestors back to the first ships to land or the first wagons to unload.

6   Culture should not be frozen in time but should invite new stories and heroes who enhance the people's appreciation for and attachment to the nation's principles.

7   The nation should establish institutions and voices that speak for future generations on matters of debt and other burdens that they will inherit.

8   While the nation may seek defense alliances and trade with others that do not share its values and principles, it should not share its friendship or its bounties with those who stand opposed.

With these beliefs in our grasp, we may walk toward the future, preserving and renewing a nation so that it will grow, not just more prosperous, but stronger, sturdier, and more free.

A SECOND ACT?

"There were no second acts in American lives," said F. Scott Fitzgerald, who wrote during the roaring 1920s and saw how prosperity can wreck a man's mind or his relationship with his friends and lovers. Some people wrongly interpret Fitzgerald to mean there are no second chances. Instead Fitzgerald was speaking of the second act of a drama. That's where the character's world falls apart. His comforts are shredded, a friend might betray him. It's the half-blind, bloodied boxer who must grab the ropes and climb up off the mat. It's the formerly naïve housewife whose husband cheats and runs off, leaving her to work nights, dark circles under her eyes, to make enough money to keep the kids in school. But these characters cannot do it without confronting their internal demons and figuring how to overcome daunting odds, dastardly villains, slings, arrows, and the tax man. They look back at their past, struggling to find some sliver of wisdom among the glasses of whiskey or fruity punch they guzzled down during the good times. Fitzgerald was not sure that American grit was real. Deep in debt and drowning in his own alcohol, he doubted himself.

Maybe America and Americanness were all a myth. But even so, we had better grasp onto it and use our history and ideals to steer clear of the abyss left by the shattering of nations. Yes, our future depends upon our own strength, but we would be foolish to scoff at the courage of our forefathers and mothers. The past is a ghost, but it is a friend, too. In the finest closing to one of the finest and most troubling books in American literature, the pronoun is *we*. In *The Great Gatsby*, Nick finally observes: "So we beat on, boats against the current, borne back ceaselessly into the past."

Go ahead. Grab an oar.

ACKNOWLEDGMENTS

My family watched patiently and with good humor as I dove deep into economic history. While researching the world leaders profiled in part II, I tried to immerse myself in their lives. I relied on diaries, journals, books, vintage film footage, and the aroma of good coffee. And so while researching, say, Alexander the Great, I would tell the baristas at local coffee joints that my name was Alex. They'd scribble it on the paper cup. Then I was Turk and Pepe. It was tougher to announce my name as Golda, so I muttered something like "Goa," which some recognized as a state in India. It may have been silly, but it kept me energized.

My wife, Debby, and daughters Victoria, Katherine, and Alexia are beautiful and brilliant. They make me laugh, and, thankfully, my daughters have a high tolerance for their father's tendency to embarrass them in front of strangers. My mother, Joan, inspires me with her wit and energy.

I'd also like to thank my faithful and wise agent, Susan Ginsburg, who introduced me to my supersmart and superkind editor Hollis Heimbouch. Thank you to Jin Saito and John Karaagac for incisive comments on chapters covering the Meiji Revolution and Atatürk.

Finally, as a kid, I was lucky to learn from some wonderful

schoolteachers. I still send draft op-ed commentaries to my high school English teacher Martin Meszaros, who knows more about the Lost Generation than anyone attending a Hemingway or Fitzgerald family reunion. David Correll brought excitement to history class and each year turned a mob of hormone-raged adolescents into a community of patriotic high school students. Sally Howe, Vince Heckel, Janet Gelzer, and Jack Milkovitz never gave me an easy A but prodded me to push harder and go further. Two of my favorite elementary school teachers aren't around anymore: a no-nonsense African American lady named Mary Clark, whom I praised in my book *Rush*; and my fifth-grade teacher Raymond Sneden, who revealed to me the mathematics of sports. Each week during the fall, we'd exchange our picks for National Football League games, along with the point spread for bettors. I'm not sure the school superintendent would have approved the gambling lesson, but I guess it paid off: inspired by Mr. Sneden's passion for math, decades later I invented a new way to present numbers to children, the Math Arrow.[1] It makes me smile to think that some kid may find it easier to learn algebra today because Mr. Sneden thought the Green Bay Packers would beat the point spread. In this book we confront a more serious question: Will the United States and other advanced economies defy the odds and survive?

NOTES

PREFACE

1. U.S. Department of State, "Schedule of Fees for Consular Services, Department of State and Overseas Embassies and Consulates—Passport and Citizenship Services Fee Changes," *Federal Register*, September 8, 2015, https://www.federalregister.gov/articles/2015/09/08/2015-22054/schedule-of-fees-for-consular-services-department-of-state-and-overseas-embassies-and#h-26.
2. Though the Stalinist Gulag agency closed in 1960, forced labor camps such as Perm-36 continued in the Soviet Union until the 1980s.
3. John Maynard Keynes, "Economic Possibilities for Our Grandchildren," in *Essays in Persuasion* (New York: W. W. Norton, 1963), pp. 358–73.
4. Joseph A. Schumpeter, *Capitalism, Socialism, and Democracy* (New York: Harper and Row, 1976), p. 61.
5. Karl Marx, *Capital* (Chicago: Charles Kerr, 1906), vol. 1, p. 836.
6. Kalgoorlie Brothel, Register of Heritage Places, Heritage Council of Western Australia, data base no. 2991 (1999), http://inherit.stateheritage.wa.gov.au/Public/Content/PdfLoader.aspx?id=9a73338e-5b7d-489e-9aff-becbcc87909c.

INTRODUCTION: THE PARADOX OF PROSPERITY

1. John Della Volpe, "Survey of Young Americans' Attitudes Toward Politics and Public Service," Harvard University Institute of Politics (December 10, 2015), p. 8, http://www.iop.harvard.edu/sites/default/files_new/pictures/151208_Harvard%20IOP%20Fall%202015%20Report.pdf; Art Swift, "Smaller Majority 'Extremely Proud' to Be an American," *Gallup* July 2, 2015.

2.   Theodore Roosevelt, *The Letters of Theodore Roosevelt* (Cambridge, MA: Harvard University Press, 1951), p. 279.

3.   Neel Ahuja, "Abu Zubaydah and the Caterpillar," *Social Text* 106, no. 29.1 (Spring 2011): 143. The author laments the use of caterpillars in the interrogation of suspected terrorists.

4.   Deborah Haynes and Fiona Hamilton, "Hundreds More UK Muslims Choose Jihad Than Army," *Times* (London), August 22, 2014, http://www.thetimes.co.uk/tto/news/uk/defence/article4183684.ece.

5.   See Cass R. Sunstein, *Republic.com 2.0* (Princeton, NJ: Princeton University Press, 2009).

6.   *The Age of Whatever* is the title of an album of songs about Millennials, https://www.reverbnation.com/victoriabeachwood.

7.   Rustam I. Aminov, "A Brief History of the Antibiotic Era: Lessons Learned and Challenges for the Future," *Frontiers in Microbiology* 1, article 134 (2010).

CHAPTER 1: THE PARADOX OF BORDERS, DIAPERS, AND GOLF COURSES

1.   https://www.youtube.com/watch?v=t2DkiceqmzU.

2.   In October 2015 China announced that it was relaxing its one-child policy and would allow two children per couple.

3.   https://www.avma.org/KB/Resources/Statistics/Pages/Market-research-statistics-US-pet-ownership.aspx.

4.   Mark Lino, "Expenditures on Children by Families, 2013," US Department of Agriculture, Center for Nutrition Policy and Promotion, Miscellaneous Publication no. 1528-2013, p. 7.

5.   Frank Newport and Joy Wilke, "Desire for Children Still Norm in U.S.," *Gallup*, September 25, 2013, http://www.gallup.com/poll/164618/desire-children-norm.aspx.

6.   http://www.newscientist.com/article/mg22530093.700-baby-slump-puts-italy-at-risk-of-dying.html#.VUlGAl5bTwI.

7.   Tomohiro Osaki, "For Many Young Japanese, Marriage—and Sex—Are Low Priorities," *Japan Times*, January 5, 2016, http://www.japantimes.co.jp/news/2016/01/05/national/social-issues/many-young-japanese-marriage-sex-low-priorities/#.VoxYafmLSUk.

8.   Jun Hongo, "Japan's Longevity Champs May Not Win Even Silver Anymore," *Wall Street Journal*, October 17–18, 2015, p. A1.

9.   S. Philip Morgan, "Is Low Fertility a Twenty-First-Century Demographic Crisis?" *Demography* 40, no. 4 (November 2003): 589–603.

10. Bryan Armen Graham, "Abraham Lincoln Was a Skilled Wrestler and World-Class Trash Talker," *Sports Illustrated*, February 12, 2013.

11. "Personal Remittances Received (% GDP)," World Bank, http://data
     .worldbank.org/indicator/BX.TRF.PWKR.DT.GD.ZS.

12. Mead Cain, "Risk and Insurance: Perspectives on Fertility and Agrarian
     Change in India and Bangladesh," *Population and Development Review* 9,
     no. 3 (1981): 435–74.

13. Laura Betzig, "Sex, Succession, and Stratification in the First Six Civiliza-
     tions," in Lee Ellis, ed., *Social Stratification and Socioeconomic Inequality*
     (New York: Praeger, 1993), vol. 1, pp. 37–74. See also Greg Downey, "The
     Man with 1000 Children: The Limit of Male Fertility," *Neuroanthropol-
     ogy* (June 5, 2014), http://blogs.plos.org/neuroanthropology/2014/04/05/
     man-1000-children-limit-male-fertility/.

14. Pedro de Cieza de Leon, *The Incas of Pedro de Cieza de Leon*, ed. Victor
     Wolfgang von Hagen, trans. Harriet de Onis (Norman: University of
     Oklahoma Press, 1959), p. 41.

15. Tatiana Zerjal et al., "The Genetic Legacy of the Mongols," *American Jour-
     nal of Human Genetics* 72, no. 3 (January 2003): 717–21; Mark A. Jobling
     et al., "Y-Chromosome Descent Clusters and Male Differential Reproduc-
     tive Success: Young Lineage Expansions Dominate Asian Pastoral Nomadic
     Populations," *European Journal of Human Genetics* 23 (2015): 1413–22.

16. Laoise T. Moore, Brian McEvoy, Eleanor Cape, Katharine Simms, and Daniel
     G. Bradley, "A Y-Chromosome Signature of Hegemony in Gaelic Ireland,"
     American Journal of Human Genetics 87, no. 2 (February 2006): 334–38.

17. Kermyt Anderson, Hillard Kaplan, and Jane Lancaster, "Paternal Care by
     Genetic Fathers and Stepfathers I: Reports from Albuquerque Men," *Evo-
     lution and Human Behavior* 20 (1999): 405–31; Sandra L. Hofferth and
     Kermyt G. Anderson, "Biological and Stepfather Investment in Children,"
     PSC Research Report no. 01-471 (April 2001): 11–12.

18. Frank Marlow, "Showoffs or Providers? The Parenting Effort of Hadza
     Men," *Evolution and Human Behavior* 20, no. 6 (1999): 391–404; Kermyt
     G. Anderson, Hillard Kaplan, David Lam, and Jane B. Lancaster, "Paternal
     Care by Genetic Fathers and Stepfathers II: Reports by Xhosa High School
     Students," *Evolution and Human Behavior* 20 (1999): 433–51; Kermyt
     G. Anderson, "Relatedness and Investment in Children in South Africa,"
     Human Nature 16 (2005): 1–31.

19. Thomas Malthus, *An Essay on the Principle of Population* (London: Reeves
     and Turner, 1872), p. 92.

20. Becker's pioneering paper was Gary S. Becker, "An Economic Analysis of
     Fertility," in *Demographic and Economic Change in Developed Countries*
     (Princeton, NJ: National Bureau of Economic Research, 1960), pp. 209–31.

21. Joseph A. Schumpeter, *Capitalism, Socialism, and Democracy* (New York:
     Harper and Row, 1942), p. 158.

22.   George Bernard Shaw, *Man and Superman*, act 3. For Shaw on eugenics see George Watson, *Lost Literature of Socialism* (London: Lutterworth, 2010).

23.   See Robert K Fleck and F. Andrew Hanssen, "Rulers Ruled by Women: An Economic Analysis of the Rise and Fall of Women's Rights in Ancient Sparta," September 5, 2007, http://www.law.virginia.edu/pdf/olin/0708/hanssen.pdf.

24.   Aristotle, *Politics*, book 2, http://www.perseus.tufts.edu/hopper/text?doc =Perseus:abo:tlg,0086,035:2:1270a.

25.   Ibid.

26.   Ibid., 1269a37-9. There may have been other forces that limited population, including earthquakes and, according to some, the acceptability of same-sex relations.

27.   Strabo, *Geography*, trans. H. L. Jones, Loeb Classical Library (Cambridge, MA: Harvard University Press, 1927), vol. 4, pp. 121–30.

28.   Polybius, *The Histories of Polybius*, trans. Evelyn S. Shuckburgh (London: Macmillan, 1889), pp. 510–11.

29.   Cheryl Elman, "Fertility Differentials between African American and White Women in the Early Twentieth Century American South," p. 4, http://www.rockarch.org/publications/resrep/elman.pdf. Fertility in the North also fell, but the North experienced even stronger GDP growth for most of the 1800s.

30.   Quoted in Paul Veyne, *A History of Private Life: From Pagan Rome to Byzantium* (Cambridge, MA: Harvard University Press, 1992), pp. 13–14.

31.   Graziella Caselli, Jacques Vallin, and Guillaume J. Wunsch, *Demography: Analysis and Synthesis* (London: Academic Press, 2006), p. 59.

32.   Neil Cummins, "Marital Fertility and Wealth in Transition Era France, 1750–1850," Paris School of Economics, Working Papers n2009-16 (2009).

33.   George Finlay, *Greece under the Romans* (London: Blackwood, 1844), p. 65.

34.   See J. A. Banks, *Prosperity and Parenthood: A Study of Family Planning among the Victorian Middle Classes* (London: Routledge, 1954).

35.   Noah Smith, "Making Babies Making a Comeback," *BloombergView*, January 20, 2015, http://www.bloombergview.com/articles/2015-01-20/ making-babies-makes-a-comeback.

36.   D. B. Dunson, B. Colombo, and D. D. Baird, "Changes with Age in the Level and Duration of Fertility in the Menstrual Cycle," *Human Reproduction* 17 (2002): 1399–1403.

37.   United Nations, Department of Economic and Social Affairs, Population Division (2013), *World Marriage Data 2012* (POP/DB/Marr/Rev2012).

38.   Amalia R. Miller, "The Effects of Motherhood on Career Path," Department of Economics, University of Virginia (September 2009), p. 15, http:// people.virginia.edu/~am5by/fertilitytiming_sept2009.pdf.

39.   Miami Beach's economy also benefited from an influx of yuppies, gays,

and other folks who rediscovered the pleasures of palm trees waving by a turquoise ocean.

40. Susan Eckstein, *The Immigrant Divide: How Cuban Americans Changed the U.S. and Their Homeland* (London: Routledge, 2009), p. 179.

41. *Volunteering in America 2010: National, State, and City Information* (Washington, DC: Corporation for National and Community Service, June 2010), p. 12.

42. Jada A. Graves, "The 20 Fastest-Growing Jobs This Decade," *U.S. News & World Report*, March 6, 2014.

43. Marisa Penaloza, "Immigrants Key to Looming Health Aide Shortage," National Public Radio, October 17, 2012.

44. *The Construction Chart Book: The U.S. Construction Industry and Its Workers* (Silver Spring, MD: Center for Construction Research and Training, 2013), chapter 16, http://www.cpwr.com/sites/default/files/publications/CB%20page%2016.pdf.

45. Michael K. Gusmano, "Undocumented Immigrants in the United States: Demographics and Socioeconomic Status," Undocumented Patients website, Hastings Center, Garrison, NY, February 14, 2012.

46. "Estimates of the Population of the United States by Age, Race, and Sex: July 1, 1968," *Current Population Reports: Population Estimates and Projections* (Washington, DC: U.S. Bureau of the Census), ser. P-25, no. 400, August 13, 1968.

47. Rogelio Saenz, Maria Cristina Morales, and Janie Filoteo, "The Demography of Mexicans in the United States," in *Chicanas and Chicanos in Contemporary Society,* 2nd ed., ed. Roberto M. De Anda (New York: Rowman and Littlefield, 2004), p. 5.

48. Charles Russell and Harry Samuel Lewis, *The Jew in London* (New York: Thomas Crowell, 1901), p. 198.

CHAPTER 2: *MELANCHOLIA MADELEINE* AND THE PARADOX OF TRADE

1. See Mark Pendergrast, *For God, Country, and Coca-Cola* (New York: Basic Books, 2000); Laura A. Hymson, "The Company That Taught the World to Sing," dissertation, University of Michigan (2011); Frank Hefner, "A Better Red: The Transition from Communism to Coca-Cola in Romania," *Quarterly Journal of Austrian Economics* 2, no. 2 (Summer 1999): 43–49.

2. "Ethiopia Hit by Coca-Cola Drought," BBC, March 24, 2009, http://news.bbc.co.uk/2/hi/africa/7960850.stm.

3. Marcel Proust, *Remembrance of Things Past,* vol. 1: *Swann's Way* and *Within a Budding Grove,* trans. C. K. Scott Moncrieff and Terence Kilmartin (New York: Random House, 1982), pp. 50–51.

4.   Friedman's argument was based on an essay by Leonard E. Read, "I, Pencil: My Family Tree," Foundation for Economic Education, Inc. (December 1958).

5.   James Ward, *The Perfection of the Paper Clip* (New York: Touchstone, 2015), p. 96.

6.   W. Michael Cox and Richard Alm, "How Are We Doing?" *The American* (July 3, 2008), http://www.aei.org/publication/how-are-we-doing/.

7.   https://www.aei.org/publication/when-it-comes-to-the-affordability-of-common-household-goods-the-rich-and-the-poor-are-both-getting-richer/.

8.   Tom Jackson, *Chilled: How Refrigeration Changed the World and Might Do So Again* (London: Bloomsbury, 2015).

9.   Felipe Garcia Ribeiro, Guilherme Stein, and Thomas Kang "The Cuban Experiment: Measuring the Role of the 1959 Revolution on Economic Performance Using Synthetic Control," working paper (May 21, 2013), http://economics.ca/2013/papers/SG0030-1.pdf.

10.   David Dollar and Aart Kraay, "Trade, Growth and Poverty," World Bank Policy Research Working Paper, no. 2615, June 2001, p. 2.

11.   See my speech "From Paper Umbrellas to Prosperity," broadcast on the Korean Broadcasting System, August 24, 2015, https://www.youtube.com/watch?v=h1deP3sDkk4.

12.   Of course, the tourist flow was interrupted during 1991–92, when Dubrovnik was bombed in battles between Croatia and Yugoslav/Serbian forces; it had earlier been disrupted during World War II, when the Nazis established a puppet state.

13.   Stevan Dedijer, "Ragusa Intelligence and Security (1301–1806)—A Model for the Twenty-First Century?" *International Journal of Intelligence and Counter Intelligence* 15, no. 1 (2002): 106.

14.   Lovro Kuncevic, "On Ragusan *Libertas* in the Late Middle Ages," *Dubrovik Annals* 14 (2010): 64–65.

15.   Dedijer, "Ragusa Intelligence," p. 106. The five-thousand-ducat bribe would be roughly equivalent to $650,000 today, depending on the precise date and the price of gold.

16.   Nenad Vekaric, "The Population of the Dubrovnik Republic in the Fifteenth, Sixteenth and Seventeenth Centuries," *Dubrovnik Annals* 2 (1998): 23–26.

17.   See Oleh Havrylyshyn and Nora Srzentc, "The Economy of Ragusa: 1300–1800, the Tiger of Mediaeval Mediterranean," Eighteenth Dubrovnik Economic Conference, June 2012, http://www.hnb.hr/dub-konf/18-konferencija/havrylyshyn-srzentic.pdf.

18.   Luigi Villari, *The Republic of Ragusa* (London: J. M. Dent, 1904), p. 398.

19.   Nachum Gross, "Economic Growth and the Consumption of Coal in Austria and Hungary 1831–1913," *Journal of Economic History* 31, no. 4 (1971), 901–2.

20. Nachum Theodor Gross, *Industrialization in Austria in the Nineteenth Century* (Berkeley: University of California Press, 1966), p. 45.

21. Even taking into account a Vienna stock market collapse in 1873.

22. "Austrian Riots: Disorder Continues and Many Arrests Are Made," *Los Angeles Herald*, December 14, 1897, p. 1.

23. Mark Twain, "Stirring Times in Austria," in *Literary Essays*, vol. XXII (New York: Harper and Brothers, 1899), pp. 215–20.

24. Quoted in Paula Sutter Fichtner, *The Habsburg Empire: From Dynasticism to Multinationalism* (Malabar, FL: Krieger, 1997), p. 168.

25. See the story of Sony in my *New Ideas from Dead CEOs* (New York: Harper-Collins, 2007), p. 169.

26. Scott Thurm, "U.S. Firms Add Jobs, but Mostly Overseas," *Wall Street Journal*, April 27, 2012.

27. Catherine L. Mann, "Globalization in IT Services and White Collar Jobs: The Next Wave of Productivity Growth," IEE Policy Brief PB03-11, Institute of International Economics, December 2003. For divergent analyses, see Jagdish Bhagwati, Arvind Panagariya, and T. N. Srinivasan, "The Muddle over Outsourcing," *Journal of Economic Perspectives* 18, no. 3 (2004): 93–114; and Paul A. Samuelson, "Where Ricardo and Mill Rebut and Confirm Arguments of Mainstream Economists Supporting Globalization," *Journal of Economic Perspectives* 18, no. 3 (2004): 135–46.

28. Les Christie, "Millennials Are Staying Put at Mom and Dad's Place," CNN, September 17, 2014, http://money.cnn.com/2014/09/17/real_estate/ millennials-still-home/index.html?iid=HP_LN; Jed Kolko, "Basement-Dwelling Millennials Are for Real," Trulia, July 8, 2014, http://www.trulia.com/blog/ trends/basement-dwelling-millennials/.

29. Laurie Burkitt and Julie Jargon, "China Woes Put Dent in Yum Brand," *Wall Street Journal*, January 8, 2013.

30. "KFC Sues Chinese Firms over Eight-Legged Chicken Rumours," BBC, June 1, 2015, http://news.bbc.co.uk/2/hi/africa/7960850.stm.

31. Julie Jargon, "Yum Brands to Split Off China Business," *Wall Street Journal*, October 20, 2015, http://www.wsj.com/articles/yum-brands-to-spin -off-china-business-1445338830.

32. "Big Unions Stiff Pledge to Pledge Allegiance," *Corporate Crime Reporter*, August 6, 2012, http://www.corporatecrimereporter.com/news/200/unions nader08062012/.

CHAPTER 3: THE PROBLEM WITH OTHER PEOPLE'S MONEY

1. See my "Biblical Laws and the Economic Growth of Ancient Israel," *Journal of Law and Religion* 6, no. 2 (1988): 389–427.

2. http://biblehub.com/hebrew/5391.htm.

3. Some modern interpretations, starting with Edmund Kean and Henry Irving in the nineteenth century and extending to Al Pacino in the twenty-first century, present Shylock more sympathetically. Though Shakespeare wrote Shylock as a very complex character, it is hard to argue that Shylock was heroic or noble in his bearing or ambitions. Though his skin was lighter than Othello's, his heart was darker.

4. Rafael Efrast, "The Evolution of Bankruptcy Stigma," *Theoretical Inquiries in Law* 7 (2006): 373.

5. http://consumerfed.org/_wp/wp-content/uploads/2010/08/California_Subprime_2006.pdf.

6. Peter Y. Hong, "California Home Prices Fall to 2002 Levels," *Los Angeles Times*, February 20, 2009, http://articles.latimes.com/2009/feb/20/business/fi-homesales20; http://www.pcasd.com/the_san_diego_housing_bubble.

7. Clea Benson, "Fannie-Freddie Regulator's 3% Down Loans Draw Jeers," *Bloomberg News*, November 14, 2014.

8. Unless the parent leaves assets that can be liquidated.

9. http://founders.archives.gov/documents/Hamilton/01-01-02-0645.

10. http://founders.archives.gov/documents/Hamilton/01-02-02-1167.

11. William D. Hamilton, "The Genetical Evolution of Social Behavior," *Journal of Theoretical Biology* 7, no. 1 (1964): 1–52.

12. Jill M. Mateo, "Kin-Recognition Abilities and Nepotism as a Function of Sociality," *Proceedings of the Royal Society of London B* 269 (April 7, 2002): 721–27.

13. John Maynard Keynes, *The General Theory of Employment, Interest and Money*, in *The Collected Writings of John Maynard Keynes*, vol. 7 (Cambridge: Cambridge University Press, 1973), p. 111.

14. The Keynesian model, as taught by Samuelson, included the Balanced Budget Multiplier, which implies that fiscal spending is more powerful and ultimately more efficient than tax cuts.

15. See Franco Modigliani, "Life Cycle, Individual Thrift, and the Wealth of Nations," *American Economic Review* 76, no. 3 (June 1986): 297–313.

16. Please note that during the Russia crisis of 1998–99, the debt-to-GDP ratio hit 99 percent.

17. http://www.tradingeconomics.com/russia/government-debt-to-gdp.

18. Laurence J. Kotlikoff, "America's Fiscal Insolvency and Its Generational Consequences," Testimony to the U.S. Senate Budget Committee, February 25, 2015; Giovanni Callegari and Laurence J. Kotlikoff, "Estimating the 2013 U.S. Fiscal Gap" (August 2013), http://d3n8a8pro7vhmx.cloudfront.net/tckb/pages/284/attachments/original/1378836788/EstimatingThe

_U.S._2013_Fiscal_Gap_-_The_Can_Kicks_Back.pdf?1378836788.

19. http://www.treasurydirect.gov/NP/debt/current.

20. These examples are drawn from my "Washington Should Lock In Low Rates," *Wall Street Journal*, June 19, 2012; and Todd G. Buchholz and James Carter, "Our Children Will Thank Us for Locking In Today's Rates," *Investor's Business Daily*, July 30, 2013.

21. A. J. Tatem, D. J. Rogers, and S. I. Hay, "Global Transport Networks and Infectious Disease Spread," *Advances in Parasitology* 62 (2006): 294.

22. Stephanie A. Shwiff et al., "Potential Economic Damage from Introduction of Brown Tree Snakes, Boiga irregularis (Reptilia: Colubridae), to the Islands of Hawaii," *Pacific Science* 64, no. 1 (2010): 6; https://www.aphis .usda.gov/wildlife_damage/nwrc/publications/10pubs/shwiff101.pdf; http://www.npr.org/sections/thetwo-way/2013/12/03/248386912/dead -mice-update-tiny-assassins-dropped-on-guam-again.

CHAPTER 4: THE PROBLEM WITH WORK

1. http://www.bls.gov/lau/ststdsadata.txt.

2. Shigeru Fujita, "On the Causes of Declines in the Labor Force Participation Rate," Federal Reserve Bank of Philadelphia, February 6, 2014, http:// philadelphiafed.org/research-and-data/publications/research-rap/2013/on -the-causes-of-declines-in-the-labor-force-participation-rate.pdf; David Aaronson, Jonathan Davis, and Luojia Hu, "Explaining the Decline in the U.S. Labor Participation Rate," *Chicago Fed Letter*, no. 296 (March 2012).

3. "Job Openings and Labor Turnover Survey Release," Bureau of Labor Statistics, June 9, 2015.

4. Cited in Peter Whoriskey, "U.S. Manufacturing Sees Shortage of Skilled Factory Workers," *Washington Post*, February 19, 2012.

5. Ian Hathaway and Robert E. Litan, "Declining Business Dynamism in the United States: A Look at States and Metros," *Economic Studies at Brookings*, May 2014, 1–5.

6. Thomas J. Weiss, "U.S. Labor Force Estimates and Economic Growth: 1800–1860," in *American Economic Growth and Standards of Living before the Civil War*, ed. Robert E. Gallman and John Joseph Wallis, National Bureau of Economic Research (Chicago: University of Chicago Press, 1992), p. 45, http://www.nber.org/chapters/c8007.pdf.

7. Today, the labor participation rate remains higher for immigrants (66 percent) than for the native-born population (63 percent). This makes sense, since immigrants are typically less affluent and are more likely to need the work. But note that their participation rate is nowhere near the 90 percent of past eras. One-third of immigrant adults do not work.

8. See Michael Bliss and William Osler, *A Life in Medicine* (New York: Oxford University Press, 1999).

9. Eleanor Roosevelt, A Speech before the Monday Evening Club, DC Branch of the American Association for Social Security, and the Council of Social Agencies, February 8, 1934, http://www.gwu.edu/~erpapers/documents/articles/oldagepensions.cfm.

10. While some families were tethered to their towns because they could not sell their homes, mobility has declined even for renters.

11. Raj Chetty, Nathaniel Hendren, and Lawrence Katz, "The Effects of Exposure to Better Neighborhoods on Children: New Evidence from the Moving to Opportunity Experiment," National Bureau of Economic Research, August 2015, p. 18, http://www.equality-of-opportunity.org/images/mto_paper.pdf.

12. See Andrew Sum, Robert Taggart, and Ishwar Khatiwada, "The Path Dependence of Teen Employment in the U.S.: Implications for Youth Workforce Development Policy," Center for Labor Market Studies, Northeastern University, Boston, 2007; Andrew Sum, Neeta Fogg, and Garth Mangum, "Confronting the Youth Demographic Challenge: The Labor Market Prospects of At-Risk Youth," Sar Levitan Center for Social Policy Studies, Baltimore, 2000.

13. National Math + Science Initiative, 2014.

14. Dulgunn Batbold and Ronald A. Wirtz, "Disability and Work: Challenge of Incentives," *FedGazette*, Federal Reserve Bank of Minneapolis, January 29, 2015.

15. "Tyson and UFCW Mark Two Decades of Workplace Safety Progress," Reuters, November 24, 2009.

16. Chana Joffe-Walt, "Unfit for Work: The Startling Rise of Disability in America," NPR Planet Money (March 22, 2013), apps.npr.org/unfit-for-work.

17. Fujita, "On the Causes of Declines," p. 7.

18. Batbold and Wirtz, "Disability and Work."

19. Todd G. Buchholz, "Instead of Unemployment Benefits, Offer a Signing Bonus," *Washington Post*, June 10, 2011.

20. Susann Rohwedder and Robert J. Willis, "Mental Retirement," *Journal of Economic Perspectives* 24, no. 1 (Winter 2010): 137.

21. Arthur Brooks, *Gross National Happiness* (New York: Basic Books, 2008), p. 167.

22. See the photos at http://agso.uni-graz.at/marienthal/e/pictures/15_marienthal_study.htm.

23. Marie Jahoda, Paul F. Lazarsfeld, Hans Zeisel, and Christian Fleck, *Marienthal*, 4th ed. (New Brunswick, NJ: Transaction Publishers, 2002).

24. Paul Neurath, "Sixty Years since Marienthal," *Canadian Journal of Sociology* 20, no. 1 (Winter 1995): 100.

25. Here we define cheating as not reporting supplemental work to the government.

26. Neurath, "Sixty Years since Marienthal," p. 13.

27. See Christian Stogbauer, "The Radicalization of the German Electorate," *European Review of Economic History* 5, no. 2 (2001): 251–80.

28. See Mancur Olson, *The Rise and Decline of Nations* (New Haven, CT: Yale University Press, 1982), and, for a modern take on Washington, DC, see Jonathan Rauch's fine *Government's End: Why Washington Stopped Working* (Washington, DC: Public Affairs, 1999). Gunnar Trumbull of Harvard argues that Olson may be wrong and that general citizens' groups like the AARP and Sierra Club can trounce business groups in the court of public opinion. I am not convinced but see Trumbull's *Strength in Numbers* (Cambridge, MA: Harvard University Press, 2012).

29. Elizabeth E. Bailey, "Air Transport Deregulation," American Economic Association, 2008, https://www.aeaweb.org/annual_mtg_papers/2008/2008_264.pdf.

30. Morris M. Kleiner and Alan Krueger, "Analyzing the Extent and Influence of Occupational Licensing on the Labor Market," *Journal of Labor Economics* 31, no. 2 (April 2013): S183.

31. See my *Bringing the Jobs Home* (New York: Penguin, 2004), chapter 5, "Barriers to Entry"; and Diana Furchtgott-Roth and Jared Meyer, *Disinherited* (New York: Encounter, 2015), chapter 5.

32. Alison Cathles, David E. Harrington, and Kathy Krynski, "The Gender Gap in Funeral Directors: Burying Women with Ready-to-Embalm Laws," *British Journal of Industrial Relations* 48, no. 4 (2010): 688–705.

33. Tom Rademacher, "Don't Try This at Home," *Ann Arbor News*, February 9, 1997, p. A-11.

34. Sidney L. Carroll and Robert J. Gaston, "Occupational Restrictions and the Quality of Service Received: Some Evidence," *Southern Economic Journal* 47, no. 4 (April 1981): 959–76.

35. See http://www.sproglit.com/math-arrow.

36. Perhaps Uber should pay some funds to offset the collapse in the value of taxi medallions/licenses that were mandated by local governments.

CHAPTER 5: PATRIOTISM, IMMIGRATION, AND GRIT IN THE ERA OF THE SELFIE

1. https://richardwiseman.files.wordpress.com/2011/09/ll-final-report.pdf.

2.   Lesley Chamberlain, *Nietzsche in Turin: An Intimate Biography* (New York: St. Martin's Press, 1996), pp. 208–16.

3.   Anna S. Lau, Joey Fung, Shu-wen Wang, and Sun-Mee Kang, "Explaining Elevated Social Anxiety among Asian Americans: Emotional Attachment and a Cultural Double Bind," *Cultural Diversity and Ethnic Minority Psychology* 15 (2008): 77–85; Eli Lieber, Heidi Fung, and Patrick Wing Leung, "Chinese Childrearing Beliefs: Key Dimensions and Contributions to the Development of Culture Appropriate Assessment," *Asian Journal of Social Psychology* 9 (2006): 140–47.

4.   Martin D. Lampert, Kate L. Isaacson, and Jim Lyttle, "Cross-Cultural Variation in Gelotophobia within the United States," *Psychological Testing and Assessment Modeling* 52 (2010): 212.

5.   Nora Ephron, *When Harry Met Sally* (New York: Alfred A. Knopf, 2002), p. 22.

6.   See Steve Farmer, Richard Sprout, and Michael Witzel, "The Collapse of the Indus-Script Thesis: The Myth of a Literate Harappan Civilization," *Electronic Journal of Vedic Studies* 11, no. 2 (2004): 19–57; and by the same authors, "A Refutation of the Claimed Refutation of the Nonlinguistic Nature of Indus Symbols: Invented Data Sets in the Statistical Paper of Rao et al.," *Science* (2009), at www.safarmer.com/Refutations3/pdf.

7.   Physics teachers may disagree with the metaphor of centrifugal force and point out that it is technically not a force but a sensation created by inertia and the lack of centripetal force. Still, I'm happy with the metaphor.

8.   See *Ephesians* 6:10–17.

9.   http://www.churchleaders.com/pastors/pastor-articles/139575-7-startling -facts-an-up-close-look-at-church-attendance-in-america.html.

10.   Robert Manchin, "Religion in Europe: Trust Not Filling the Pews," *Gallup Religion and Social Trends*, September 21, 2004.

11.   Charles W. Perdue, John F. Dovidio, Michael B. Gurtman, and Richard B. Tyler, "Us and Them: Social Categorization and the Process of Intergroup Bias," *Journal of Personality and Social Psychology* 59, no. 3 (September 1990): 475–86, http://dx.doi.org/10.1037/0022-3514.59.3.475.

12.   Letter from John Adams to Abigail Adams, July 3, 1776, "Had a Declaration," Adams Family Papers, Massachusetts Historical Society.

13.   www.leonardbernstein.com/mass_notes.htm.

14.   Robert Cialdini and K. Ascani, "Basking in Reflected Glory: Three (Football) Field Studies," *Journal of Personality and Social Psychology* 34 (1976): 366–75.

15.   Abigail Adams to Elizabeth Smith Shaw, letter from London, November 21, 1786, http://www.masshist.org/publications/apde2/view?id=ADMS -04-07-02-0149.

16.   Nathaniel Hawthorne, *Passages from the French and Italian Note-Books*

of Nathaniel Hawthorne (Boston: Houghton, Osgood, 1879), p. 35. https://books.google.com/books?id=GkIpAQAAIAAJ&pg=RA1 -PA35&lpg=RA1-PA35&dq=hawthorne+passages+genuine+painting+scu lpture&source=bl&ots=agLSlv0S-N&sig=AUkjr5alV-YSB7oYerLlFoofZ 6M&hl=en&sa=X&ei=AEycVaboGNa6ogTxnIrQDw&ved=0CCkQ6A EwAg#v=onepage&q&f=false.

17. Monologue from *Stripes* written by Len Blum, Harold Ramis, and Daniel Goldberg (1981).

18. Nassau William Senior, *Political Economy*, 2nd ed. (London: Griffin, 1850), p. 12.

19. See Robert Frank, *Choosing the Right Pond: Human Behavior and the Quest for Status* (New York: Oxford University Press, 1985).

20. Jean M. Twenge, W. Keith Campbell, and Brittany Gentile, "Increases in Individualistic Words and Phrases in American Books, 1960–2008," *PLoS One* 7, no. 7 (2012): e40181.

21. Emma Barnett, "Women 'Deliberately Post Ugly Photos of Friends Online,'" *Telegraph*, July 2, 2012.

22. See Jean M. Twenge and W. Keith Campbell, *The Narcissism Epidemic: Living in the Age of Entitlement* (New York: Free Press, 2009).

23. Jimmy Stamp, "American Myths: Benjamin Franklin's Turkey and the Presidential Seal," *Smithsonian Magazine*, January 25, 2013.

24. Angela L. Duckworth, Christopher Peterson, Michael D. Matthews, and Dennis R. Kelly, "Grit: Perseverance and Passion for Long-Term Goals," *Journal of Personality and Social Psychology* 92, no. 6 (2007): 1087–1101.

25. Victoria J. Buchholz, "Locus of Control and Political Orientation: A Relationship," dissertation, University of Cambridge, May 2013.

26. Carolyn Dimitri, Anne Effland, and Neilson Conklin, "The 20th Century Transformation of U.S. Agiculture and Farm Policy," US Department of Agriculture, Economic Information Bulletin no. 3 (June 2005): 2.

27. Joe Nocera, "Real Reason for Ousting H.P.'s Chief," *New York Times*, August 13, 2010.

28. Mary C. Waters and Marisa Gerstein Pineau, eds., *The Integration of Immigrants into American Society* (Washington, DC: National Academy of Sciences, Engineering, and Medicine, 2015), chapter 4, pp. 4–5 and fig. 4-2.

29. Benjamin Franklin, *Observations Concerning the Increase of Mankind, Peopling of Countries* (Boston: S. Kneeland, 1755), p. 224.

30. Neil Simon, *Brighton Beach Memoirs* (New York: Samuel French, 1984), pp. 7, 9 (ellipses in text).

31. David Laskin, "Ethnic Minorities at War (USA)," *International Encyclopedia of the First World War*, http://encyclopedia.1914-1918-online.net/arti cle/ethnic_minorities_at_war_usa.

32. Amy Lutz, "Who Joins the Military? A Look at Race, Class, and Immigration Status," *Journal of Political and Military Sociology* 36, no. 2 (2008): 169.

33. Jeanne Batalova, "Immigrants in the U.S. Armed Forces," *Migration Policy Institute* (May 15, 2008).

34. Herman Melville, *Redburn: His First Voyage* (1st ed., 1842), chapter 33.

35. In 1782 a French immigrant named J. Hector St. John de Crèvecoeur wrote that in American "individuals of all nations are melted into a new race." Ralph Waldo Emerson later described a "fusing process" that transforms immigrants like "chips of brass thrown into the melting pot." See Crèvecoeur's Letter 3, "What Is an American," in J. Hector St. John de Crèvecoeur, *Letters from an American Farmer and Other Essays*, ed. D. Moore (Cambridge, MA: Harvard University Press, 2013); Ralph Waldo Emerson, *Journals* (Boston: Houghton Mifflin, 1911), vol. 7, p. 116; Luther Luedtke, "Ralph Waldo Emerson Envisions the 'Smelting Pot,'" *MELUS* 6, no. 2 (Summer 1979): 3–14.

36. LeAna B. Gloor, "From the Melting Pot to the Salad Bowl Metaphor: Why Coercive Assimilation Lacks the Flavors Americans Crave," http://hilo.hawaii.edu/academics/hohonu/documents/vol04x06fromthemeltingpot.pdf.

37. Donald Fisk, "American Labor in the 20th Century," *Compensation and Working Conditions* (Washington, DC: US Bureau of Labor Statistics, Fall 2001), http://www.bls.gov/opub/mlr/cwc/american-labor-in-the-20th-century.pdf.

38. See my *New Ideas from Dead CEOs* (New York: HarperCollins, 2007), chapter 5.

39. Jens Manuel Krogstad and Michael Keegan, "From Germany to Mexico: How America's Source of Immigrants Has Changed over a Century," *FactTank: News in the Numbers*, Pew Research Center (May 27, 2014).

40. Quoted in Liza Q. Bundesen, "Biography of Alejandro Portes," *Proceedings of the National Academy of Sciences of the United States of America* 101, no. 33 (August 17, 2004): 11917–19.

41. Mark Hugo Lopez, "What Univision's Milestone Says about U.S. Demographics," *FactTank: News in the Numbers*, Pew Research Center (July 29, 2013).

42. Susannah Fox and Lee Rainie, *The Web at 25 in the U.S.*, "Part 1: How the Internet Has Woven Itself into American Life," Pew Research Center (February 27, 2014): 9–19.

43. Philip C. Dolce and Rubil Morales-Vazquez, "Teaching the Importance of Place in the World of Virtual Reality," *Thought and Action* (Summer 2003), p. 42.

44. Deborah Sontag and Celia A. Dugger, "The New Immigrant Tide: A Shuttle between Worlds," *New York Times*, July 19, 1998.

45. Although UKIP has only four seats in Parliament, the Conservative Party frequently seems on the defensive.
46. Bobby Duffy and Tom Frere-Smith, "Perception and Reality: 10 Things We Should Know about Attitudes to Immigration in the UK," Ipsos MORI (January 2014); "American Values Survey," Pew Research Center: US Politics and Policy, question 40n (2012).
47. Damien Cave, "A Generation Gap over Immigration," *New York Times,* May 17, 2010.
48. Robert D. Putnam, ""E Pluribus Unum: Diversity and Community," *Scandinavian Political Studies* 30, no. 2 (2007): 150.

PART II (OPENING)

1. Mark Twain, *A Connecticut Yankee in King Arthur's Court* (New York: Harper and Brothers, 1889), p. 352.
2. Kiron K. Skinner, "An Alternative Conception of Mutual Cooperation," in *Turning Points in Ending the Cold War,* ed. Kiron K. Skinner (Stanford, CA: Hoover Press, 2007), p. 110. The expert was Richard V. Allen, who had worked with Henry Kissinger in the Nixon White House and later became Reagan's national security adviser.

CHAPTER 6: ALEXANDER AND THE GREAT EMPIRE

1. http://www.studentsoftheworld.info/penpals/stats.php3?Pays=GRE; http://www.factmonster.com/spot/babynames1.html#2007.
2. Some scholars think that Dante may be referring to a different Alexander. For a diversity of views see George Cary, *The Medieval Alexander,* ed. D. J. A. Ross (Cambridge, UK: Cambridge University Press, 2009).
3. Phillip Freeman, *Alexander the Great* (New York: Simon and Schuster, 2011), p. 2.
4. Plutarch, *Lives,* vol. 7, *Demosthenes and Cicero, Alexander and Caesar,* trans. Bernadotte Perrin, Loeb Classical Library (Cambridge, MA; Harvard University Press, 1919), p. 233.
5. See Steven Colvin, *Dialect in Aristophanes and the Politics of Language in Ancient Greek* (Oxford: Oxford University Press, 1999).
6. Peter Green, *Alexander of Macedon* (Berkeley: University of California Press, 1991), p. 58.
7. Daniel Ogden, "Alexander's Sex Life," in *Alexander the Great,* ed. W. Heckel and L. A. Tritle (New York: Wiley-Blackwell, 2009), p. 209; and Athenaeus, 435a.
8. Plutarch, *Lives,* vol. 7, chapter. 21, section 4, p. 286.

9. Ibid., chapter 22, section 4, p. 289.
10. Ibid., chapter 6, section 5, p. 239.
11. Diodorus Siculus, *The Library of History*, trans. C. Bradford Welles, Loeb Classical Library (Cambridge, MA: Harvard University Press, 1963), vol. 8, book 16, p. 92.
12. Ibid., 16.94.
13. Peter John Rhodes, *Greek Historical Inscriptions, 359–323 B.C.* (London: London Association of Classical Teachers, 1971), p. 23.
14. The Goldwyn quotation, which appeared in an early biography, is probably misattributed. See quoteinvestigator.com/2014/01/06/verbal-contract/.
15. Justin, *Epitome of the Philippic History Pompeius Trogus*, trans. J. C. Yardley (Oxford: Clarendon Ancient History Series, 1997), p. 329.
16. David Phillips, *Athenian Political Oratory* (London: Routledge, 2004), p. 114.
17. See the student-faculty petition supporting the ban at https://docs.google .com/forms/d/1t1ZhPZN2ohzgARuXwQUCwbB3YXNPgXGZQMI 8heUYZnQ/viewform.
18. Arrian, *The Campaigns of Alexander*, ed. J. R. Hamilton, trans. Aubrey de Sélincourt (New York: Penguin, 1976), p. 323.
19. See Shaye J. D. Cohen, "Alexander the Great and Jaddus the High Priest According to Josephus," *AJS Review* 7/8 (1982–83): 41–68.
20. www.iraqcoalition.org/regulations/#Orders.
21. Quoted in Robert Draper, *Dead Certain* (New York: Free Press, 2007), p. 207.
22. Paul D. Shinkman, "You Can Literally Count the Number of U.S.-Trained Syrians Fighting ISIS on One Hand," *U.S. News & World Report*, September 16, 2015, http://www.usnews.com/news/articles/2015/09/16/general -only-4-or-5-us-trained-syrian-fighters-operating-against-isis; Michael D. Shear, Helene Cooper, and Eric Schmitt, "Obama Administration Ends Effort to Train Syrians to Combat ISIS," *New York Times*, October 9, 2015, http://www.nytimes.com/2015/10/10/world/middleeast/pentagon -program-islamic-state-syria.html?_r=0.
23. Arrian, *The Campaigns of Alexander*, p. 88.
24. In some versions, told by Artistobulus, Alexander removes a pin rather than slicing the knot.
25. Dante Alighieri, *Inferno* 4.131.
26. Some commentators suggest that Dante intended to identify the ruler Alexander of Pherae, not Alexander the Great.

CHAPTER 7: THE ORIENT EXPRESS HEADS WEST

1. See Deniz Y. Talug and Begum Eken, "Islamic Art: Restrictions and Figural

Representations," *Global Journal on Humanties and Social Sciences* 1 (2015): 565–70, http://www.world-education-center.org/index.php/pntsbs.

2. Peter N. Stearns, Michael Adas, Stuart Schwartz, and Marc J. Gilbert, *World Civilizations* (New York: Pearson Longman, 2005).

3. Ibn Abi Shaybah, *al-Musannaf* (Beirut: Dar Qurtuba, 2006), Hadith 38339, *Mishkat al-Masabih.*

4. The definition of Macedonia was fluid and controversial. See Alexander Maxwell, "Slavic Macedonian Nationalism: From 'Regional' to 'Ethnic,'" in *Region, Regional Identity, and Regionalism in Southeastern Europe*, part 1, ed. Klaus Roth and Ulf Brunnbauer, *Journal for Southeastern European Anthropology* 11 (2007): 133–34.

5. Many of the *Dönmes* descended from Jews who had proclaimed Sabbetai Sevi the Messiah in the 1600s. They added elements of Jewish mysticism to their practice of Islam.

6. Halil Inalcik, Suraiya Faroqhi, and Donald Quataert, *An Economic and Social History of the Ottoman Empire* (Cambridge, UK: Cambridge University Press, 1994), vol. 2, p. 831; Angelo Georgakis, "Ottoman Salonika and Greek Nationalism before 1908," Académie des Sciences Bulgaire, Institut d'Études Balkaniques, no. 1 (2005): 114.

7. http://www.globalsecurity.org/military/world/europe/orient-express.htm.

8. Charles King, *Midnight at the Pera Palace: The Birth of Modern Istanbul* (New York: W. W. Norton, 2014), p. 25.

9. Lucy M. J. Garnett, *The Women of Turkey and Their Folk-Lore* (London: David Nutt, 1891), p. 19.

10. Ibid., p. 42.

11. Andrew Mango, *Ataturk* (New York: Overlook Press, 1999), p. 33.

12. Christopher de Bellaigue, "Turkey's Hidden Past," *New York Review of Books*, March 8, 2001, footnote 1, http://www.nybooks.com/articles/2001/03/08/turkeys-hidden-past/.

13. Quoted in A. L. MacFie, *The Eastern Question* (New York: Routledge, 1996), p. 5.

14. D. Quatert, "Dilemma of Development: The Agricultural Bank and Agricultural Reform in Ottoman Turkey: 1888–1908," *International Journal of Middle East Studies* 6 (1975): 210.

15. Inalcik et al., *Economic and Social History*, p. 831.

16. See my "Biblical Law and the Economic Growth of Ancient Israel," *Journal of Law and Religion* 6, no. 2 (January 1988): 389–427.

17. Ebru Boyar and Kate Fleet, *A Social History of Ottoman Istanbul* (Cambridge: Cambridge University Press, 2010), p. 331. Fikret's poem, published in 1901, is called *Sis* ("Fog").

18. Quoted in Mango, *Ataturk*, p. 17.

19. Ibid., p. 68.
20. Note that the official website leaps from section 3: Civil War to section 4: World War II, http://amhistory.si.edu/militaryhistory/resources/educa tion.asp.
21. Quotes in Sean McMeekin, *The Berlin-Baghdad Express: The Ottoman Empire and Germany's Bid for World Power* (Cambridge, MA: Harvard University Press, 2010), pp. 85–86.
22. Mango, *Ataturk*, p. 104.
23. Ibid., p. 146.
24. www.awm.gov.au/encyclopedia/ataturk/.
25. While the words reflect Ataturk's sentiments, the line about Johnnies and Mehmets may have come later, http://www.theguardian.com/news/2015/apr/20/ataturks-johnnies-and-mehmets-words-about-the-anzacs-are-shrouded-in-doubt.
26. Tom Bridges, *Alarms and Excursions: Reminiscences of a Soldier* (London: Longmans, Green, 1938), p. 258.
27. Quoted in Graham Freudenberg, *Churchill and Australia* (Sydney: Macmillan, 2008), p. 157.
28. Alexander C. Diener, *Borderlines and Borderlands: Political Oddities at the Edge of the Nation-State* (Lanham, MD: Rowman and Littlefield, 2010), p. 189.
29. James Baar, *A Line in the Sand* (New York: Simon and Schuster, 2011), p. 56.
30. https://www.youtube.com/watch?v=qyA-A3mYV6A.
31. King, *Midnight at the Pera Palace*, pp. 54–56.
32. Ernest Hemingway, *Dateline: Toronto* (New York: Scribner, 2002), pp. 281–82.
33. Nur Bilge Criss, *Istanbul under Allied Occupation 1918–1923* (Leiden, Netherlands: Koninklijke Brill, 1999), p. 48.
34. *Turkish Studies in the History and Philosophy of Science*, ed. Gurol Irzik and Guven Guzeldere (New York: Springer, 2005), p. 307.
35. Grace Ellison, *Turkey Today* (London: Hutchinson, 1928), p. 24.
36. Yael Navaro Yashin, *Faces of the State: Secularism and Public Life in Turkey* (Princeton, NJ: Princeton University Press, 2002), p. 188.
37. Mango, *Ataturk*, p. 150.
38. J. E. R. McDonough, "The Treatment of Syphilis in 1915," in *Practitioner's Encyclopaedia of Medical Treatment* (Oxford: Oxford Medical Publications, 1915), http://www.vlib.us/medical/syphilis.htm.
39. Dan Bilefsky, "Pieces of the Quran, Perhaps as Old as the Faith," *New York Times*, July 23, 2015, p. A1.
40. Ayse Kudat, "Ataturk's Impact on the Status of Turkish Women," speech at Georgetown University, 1991, p. 4.

41. Patrick Kinross, *Ataturk: The Rebirth of a Nation* (London: Weidenfeld and Nicolson, 1964), pp. 342–43.

42. http://www.hurriyetdailynews.com/default.aspx?pageid=438&n=zubeyde -hanim----mother-of-a-rebel-hero-1997-08-26.

43. Ian Traynor and Constanze Letsche, "Brussels Urges Turkish PM Erdogan to Redraft Law Purging Police and Judiciary," *Guardian*, January 22, 2014.

44. http://memory.loc.gov/service/pnp/ggbain/35700/35770v.jpg.

45. Mango, *Ataturk*, p. 434.

46. King, *Midnight at the Pera Palace*, pp. 150–51, quoting from Marc David Wyers, *"Wicked" Istanbul: The Regulation of Prostitution in the Early Turkish Republic* (Piscataway, NJ: Gorgias, 2013).

47. Arnold Reisman, *Turkey's Modernization: Refugees from Nazism and Atatürk's Vision* (Washington, DC: New Academia, 2006), p. 88. Hindemith did sometimes win praise from Nazis and had a complicated relationship with the regime, from which he escaped with his Jewish wife in 1938. See Michael H. Kater, *Composers of the Nazi Era* (Oxford: Oxford University Press, 2002), pp. 31–56.

48. Andreas Kazamias, *Education and the Quest for Modernity in Turkey* (Chicago: University of Chicago Press, 1967), p. 175.

49. See Rebecca Bryant, "The Soul Danced into the Body," *American Ethnologist* 32, no. 2 (2005): 222–38.

50. https://www.youtube.com/watch?v=DctWBdv2HfE.

51. Sylvia Kedourie, ed., *Seventy-Five Years of the Turkish Republic* (London: Frank Kass, 2000); Andrew Mango, "Ataturk and the Kurds," *Middle Eastern Studies* 35 (1999), p. 11.

52. Quoted in Kinross, *Ataturk*, p. 428.

53. Mango, *Ataturk*, p. 434.

CHAPTER 8: CAN EAST MEET WEST?

1. David J. Lu, *Inside Corporate Japan: The Art of Fumble-Free Management* (Tokyo: Charles E. Tuttle, 1987).

2. For a skeptical view see Yohtaro Takano and Eiko Osaka, "An Unsupported Common View: Comparing Japan and the U.S. on Individualism/Collectivism," *Asian Journal of Social Psychology* 2, issue 3 (December 1999): 311–41. For a more supportive view on group dynamics, see Takahiko Masuda, Phoebe C. Ellsworth, Janxin Leu, et al., "Placing the Face in Context: Cultural Differences in the Perception of Facial Emotion," *Journal of Personality and Social Psychology* 94, no. 3 (2008): 365–81.

3. The scene described has been reenacted in movies and written about in numerous books, both nonfiction and historical fiction.

4. "Who Is Sakamoto Ryoma?" *Wilson Quarterly* (Summer 2007), reporting on Nippon Television Network, "History's Most Influential People, Hero Edition," April 1, 2007, www.japanprobe.vom/?p=1471.

5. Rice yield was measured in a unit called a *koku* (5.11 bushels).

6. See Hugh H. Smythe, "The Eta: A Marginal Japanese Caste," *American Journal of Sociology* 58, no. 2 (September 1952): 194.

7. Takano Tsunemichi quoted in David John Lu, *Sources of Japanese History* (New York: McGraw-Hill, 1973), vol. 2, pp. 4–5. Lu's two-volume set provides an outstanding selection of translated historical documents from officials, eminent scholars, and laypeople including students and housewives.

8. Ibid., pp. 4–5.

9. Ibid.

10. Charles David Sheldon, *The Rise of the Merchant Class in Tokugawa Japan 1600–1858* (Locust Valley, NY: J. J. Augustin, 1958), pp. 119–22.

11. Gregory M. Bornmann and Carl M. Bornmann, "Tokugawa Law: How It Contributed to the Economic Success of Japan," KIBI International University, 2002, p. 192, http://www.academia.edu/339800/Tokugawa_law_How_it_contributed_to_the_economic_success_of_Japan.

12. Herbert Passin, *Society and Education in Japan* (New York: Teachers College, 1960), p. 43–49.

13. See *The Complete Journal of Townsend Harris*, ed. M. E. Cosenza (New York: Doubleday, 1930), p. 227.

14. Lu, *Sources of Japanese History*, vol. 2, p. 10.

15. The interpreter's journal can be found as Henry Heusken, *Japan Journal 1855–1861*, ed. and trans. Jeanette C. van der Corput and Robert A. Wilson (New Brunswick, NJ: Rutgers University Press, 1964).

16. Jun Hongo, "Sakamoto, the Man and the Myth," *Japan Times*, April 27, 2010, http://www.japantimes.co.jp/news/2010/04/27/reference/sakamoto-the-man-and-the-myth/#.Vbu09F5bTwI.

17. Estimates range from thirty-five hundred to seven thousand deaths. In the French Revolution, over sixteen thousand died by the guillotine alone, not to mention other methods of execution and deaths in battle.

18. Donald Keene, *Emperor of Japan: Meiji and His World 1852–1912* (New York: Columbia University Press, 2002), p. 31.

19. The doctor wrote a book about his experiences: Toku Baelz, *Awakening Japan: Diary of a German Doctor*, trans. Eden and Cedar Paul (New York: Viking, 1932).

20. Lu, *Sources of Japanese History*, vol. 1, p. 51.

21. *The Iwakura Mission in America and Europe*, ed. Ian Nish (Surrey, UK: Curzon Press, 1998), p. 104.

22. Ibid., p. 21.

23. Andrew Cobbing, "Life in Victorian London through the Eyes of Kune Kunitake, Chronicler of the Iwakura Mission," London School of Economics and Political Science, discussion paper no. IS/98/349 (March 1998), p. 7.

24. Olive Checkland, "The Iwakura Mission, Industries and Exports," London School of Economics and Political Science, discussion paper no. IS/98/349 (March 1998), p. 25.

25. John Breen, "Public Statement and Private Thoughts: The Iwakura Embassy in London and the Religious Question," London School of Economics and Political Science, discussion paper no. IS/98/349 (March 1998), p. 35.

26. Quoted in Robert S. Wells, *Voices from the Bottom of the South China Sea: The Untold Story of America's Largest Chinese Emigrant Disaster* (Jacksonville, FL: Fortis, 2014).

27. Nishikawa Shunsaku, "Fukuzawa Yukichi," *Prospects: The Quarterly Review of Comparative Education* 23, no. 3/4 (1993): 504.

28. Lu, *Sources of Japanese History*, vol. 1, p. 75.

29. John M. Rogers, "Divine Destruction: The Shinpuren Rebellion of 1876," in *New Directions in the Study of Meiji Japan*, ed. Helen Hardacre and Adam L. Kern (New York: Brill, 1997), p. 417.

30. Lu, *Sources of Japanese History*, vol. 1, p. 41.

31. Ibid., p. 45.

32. Mark Ravina, *The Last Samurai: The Life and Battles of Saigo Takamori* (New York: Wiley, 2003). Some commentators suggest that he died of a bullet wound rather than suicide.

33. See Kazushi Ohkawa and Henry Rosovsy, "The Role of Agriculture in Modern Japanese Economic Development," *Economic Development and Cultural Change* 9, no. 1 (1960): 43–67.

34. Eugene K. Choi, "Reconsidering the Innovations in the Meiji Cotton Spinners' Growth Strategy for Global Competition," *Business and Economics* 8 (2010): 1, http://www.thebhc.org/sites/default/files/choi.pdf; Richard T. Chang, *Historians and Meiji Statesmen* (Gainesville: University of Florida Press, 1970), p. 185.

35. Gary R. Saxonhouse, "A Tale of Japanese Technological Diffusion in the Meiji Period," *Journal of Economic History* 34 (1974): 150.

36. *Meiji Japan: Political, Economic and Social History: 1868–1912*, ed. Peter Kornicki (New York: Taylor and Francis, 1998), p. 132.

37. Serguey Braguinsky and David A. Hounshell, "History and Nanoeconomics in Strategy: Lessons from the Meiji-Era Japanese Cotton-Spinning Industry," *Strategic Management Journal* (August 2015), p. 29, http://www.andrew.cmu.edu/user/sbrag/SMJ_final.pdf.

38. James C. Abegglen and Hiroshi Mannari, "Leaders of Modern Japan:

Social Origins and Mobility," *Economic Development and Cultural Change* 9 (October 1960): 109–34.

39.   Natsume Soseki, *Kokoro* (CreateSpace, 1916), trans. Edwin McClellan (Chicago: Henry Regnery, 1957).

40.   Giacomo Puccini, *Madama Butterfly* (1904; trans. R. H. Elkin), was based on a play by David Belasco, which was based on a short story, *Madame Butterfly* (1898) by John Luther Long, which was influenced by an 1887 novel by Pierre Loti, *Madame Chrysanthème*.

CHAPTER 9: TWO AUDACIOUS LEADERS AND NO EXCUSES

1.   *World History Encyclopedia* (New York: Barnes and Noble, 2003), p. 241.

2.   "Costa Rican Chief Foils Jet Hijackers," UPI, December 12, 1971, https://news.google.com/newspapers?id=kD4aAAAAIBAJ&sjid=4SgEAAAAIBAJ&pg=4943,1885967&hl=en.

3.   https://slice.mit.edu/2010/08/16/mit-in-costa-rica/.

4.   Mike Faulk, "Henrietta Boggs, the First Lady of the Revolution," *Tico Times*, October 5, 2007, http://www.ticotimes.net/2007/10/05/henrietta-boggs-first-lady-of-the-revolution.

5.   The US naval captain whose ship sank the U-boat was demoted because his superiors did not believe his report. In 2014 evidence of the sinking vindicated the captain. See Brian Clark Howard, "72 Years Later, Snubbed Captain Credited with Downing German U-Boat," *National Geographic*, December 19, 2014.

6.   uboat.net/allies/merchants/ships/1881.html.

7.   Zach Dyer, "The Story of Costa Rica's Forgotten World War II Internment Camp," *Tico Times*, December 15, 2014.

8.   "Iniciada Ayer en Esta Capital la Construcción de un Campo de Concentración," *La Tribuna*, December 11, 1941, p. 4.

9.   Quotation is from Faulk, "Henrietta Boggs." Her memoirs are Henrietta Boggs, *Married to a Legend: Don Pepe* (Raleigh, NC: Lulu, 2011).

10.   Charles D. Ameringer, *The Caribbean Legion* (State College: Penn State University Press, 2010), p. 64.

11.   Calderón did order some progressive reforms limiting, for example, workers' hours.

12.   Richard E. Clinton, "The United States and the Caribbean Legion: Democracy, Dictatorship, and the Origins of the Cold War in Latin America, 1945–1950," dissertation, Ohio State University, 2011.

13.   "Costa Rica Capital Looted," *New York Times*, July 29, 1947, p. 10.

14.   Philip Freneau, "Occasioned by General Washington's Arrival in Philadelphia, on His Way to His Residence in Virginia," December 1783, https://

www.poets.org/poetsorg/poem/occasioned-general-washingtons-arrival
-philadelphia-his-way-his-residence-virginia.

15. Gideon Burrows, *Kalashnikov AK47* (Oxford: New Internationalist, 2006), p. 25.

16. Geoff Harris, "Military Expenditure and Social Development in Costa Rica: A Model for Small Countries?" *Pacifica Review* 8, no. 1 (1996): 97.

17. Elinor Burkett, *Golda* (New York: HarperCollins, 2009), p. 262.

18. Kenneth L. Sokoloff and Stanley L. Engerman, "History Lessons: Institutions, Factor Endowments, and Paths of Development in the New World," *Journal of Economic Perspectives* 14, no. 3 (2000): 218.

19. Voltaire, *Candide* (1759), chapter 23.

20. Mark Twain, *The Innocents Abroad* (Hartford, CT: American Publishing Company, 1908), vol. 2, pp. 391–92.

21. Golda Meir, "My Life," 1972 interview about a Labor Day parade.

22. Ibid.

23. "Accuses Ship Crew of Sabotage at Sea: Captain of Pocahontas Reports to Consul at Naples, Who Starts Inquiry," *New York Times*, July 10, 1921.

24. Burkett, *Golda*, p. 47.

25. Ibid., p. 49.

26. Gordon's ideas led to some job discrimination against Arab migrants, who offered to work for less money than the Jewish immigrants. See Gershon Shafir, *Land, Labor and the Origins of the Israeli-Palestinian Conflict, 1882–1914* (Berkeley: University of California Press, 1996).

27. Shabtai Teveth, *Ben-Gurion and the Palestinian Arabs: From Peace to War* (London: Oxford University Press, 1985), p. 140.

28. John Locke, *Two Treatises of Government and a Letter Concerning Toleration* (1690), chapter 5, sec. 27.

29. Quoted in Irus Braverman, "Planting the Promised Landscape: Zionism, Nature, and Resistance in Israel/Palestine," *Natural Resources Journal* 49 (2009): 317.

30. Simon Schama, *Landscape and Memory* (New York: Vintage, 1996), p. 5.

31. *Public Papers of the Presidents of the United States: George H. W. Bush* (Washington, DC: U.S. Government Printing Office), May 14, 1991, bk. 1, p. 509.

32. Anna Shapira, *Ben-Gurion* (New Haven, CT: Yale University press, 2014), p. 117.

33. Victoria Honeymoon, "Britain, Palestine, and the Creation of Israel: How Britain Failed to Protect Its Protectorate," University of Leeds, Polis Working Paper no. 1, (2011–12), http://www.polis.leeds.ac.uk/assets/files/research/working-papers/britain-palestine-and-the-creation-of-Israel.pdf. Also see http://www2.warwick.ac.uk/services/library/mrc/explorefurther/digital/crossman/urss/israel/.

34.   A copy of the 1903 British offer to allocate a parcel in East Africa can be found at https://www.jewishvirtuallibrary.org/jsource/images/uganda .jpg.

35.   David M. Herszenhorn, "Despite Predictions, Jewish Homeland in Siberia Retains Its Appeal," *New York Times*, October 3, 2012.

36.   Robert Szereszewski, *Essays on the Structure of the Jewish Economy in Palestine and Israel* (Jerusalem: Maurice Falk Institute, 1968), p. 56, table 9; Jacob Meltzer, *The Divided Economy of Mandatory Palestine* (Cambridge, UK: Cambridge University Press, 1998), pp. 228–31; Sa'id B. Himadeh, *Economic Organization of Palestine* (Beirut: American University of Beirut Press, 1939), p. 565; Gudrun Kramer, *History of Palestine* (Princeton, NJ: Princeton University Press, 2008), p. 267; U. O. Schmelz, "Population Characteristics of Jerusalem and Hebron Regions According to Ottoman Census of 1905," in *Ottoman Palestine: 1800–1914*, ed. Gad G. Gilbar (Leiden, Netherlands: E. J. Brill, 1990), pp. 32–41.

37.   Today Jaffa oranges are the object of a pro-Palestinian boycott.

38.   Erik Anderson, "Eyes Look to Carlsbad's Desalination Plant," KPBS, July 27, 2015.

39.   Michael Brown, *The Israeli-American Connection: Its Roots in the Yishuv, 1914–1945* (Detroit: Wayne State University Press, 1996), p. 188.

40.   Burkett, *Golda*, p. 121.

41.   Nili Liphschitz and Gideon Biger, *Green Dress for a Country: Afforestation in Eretz-Israel—The First 100 Years 1850–1950* (Jerusalem: Ariel Publishing House, 2000), p. 91.

42.   Burkett, *Golda*, p. 130.

43.   Ibid., p. 133.

44.   Ibid., p. 142.

45.   Uri Bar-Joseph, "Israel's 1973 Intelligence Failure," in P. R. Kumaraswamy, ed., *Revisiting the Yom Kippur War* (New York: Cass, 2000), p. 14.

46.   Ofer Aderet, "Jordan and Israel Cooperated during the Yom Kippur War, Documents Reveal," *Haaretz*, December 12, 2013, http://www.haaretz .com/news/diplomacy-defense/.premium-1.546843?v=92E14C2CEA296 DE01DE78C7F4FC81259.

CONCLUSION: DO NOT GO GENTLE

1.   Jonathan Watts, "Ancient Tribal Language Becomes Extinct as Last Speaker Dies," *Guardian*, February 4, 2010, http://www.theguardian.com/ world/2010/feb/04/ancient-language-extinct-speaker-dies.

2.   Ronald Reagan, "Farewell Address to the Nation," January 11, 1989, http:// www.reagan.utexas.edu/archives/speeches/1989/011189i.htm.

3. See my *New Ideas from Dead Economists* (New York: Penguin, 2007), chapter 6, "The Angry Oracle Called Karl Marx."

4. Howard Zinn, "Howard Zinn's July 4 Wisdom: Put Away Your Flags," *Progressive*, July 4, 2006, http://www.progressive.org/news/2014/07/187763/howard-zinn's-july-4-wisdom-put-away-your-flags.

5. Jill Tucker, "Many Schools Skip Pledge of Allegiance," *San Francisco Chronicle*, March 23, 2013.

6. http://www.nanations.com/burialcustoms/scaffold_burial.htm.

7. http://www.poynter.org/archived/20881/norman-mailer-on-the-media-and-the-message/.

8. https://www.youtube.com/watch?v=pgj7_DmgDqs.

9. W. B. Yeats, "Meru," in *The Collected Poems of W. B. Yeats*, ed. Richard J. Finneran (New York: Collier, 1996), p. 320.

10. "Holiday Icon Banned at NYC Elementary School: Report," CBS News, December 15, 2015, http://www.cbsnews.com/news/santa-christmas-thanksgiving-pledge-of-allegiance-banned-at-nyc-elementary-school-report/.

11. "Magna Carta What?" *Daily Telegraph*, March 13, 2008.

12. *Talmud Pesachim*, 116b.

13. Martin Marty, *Pilgrims in Their Own Land* (New York: Penguin, 1985), p. 59.

14. Ion Mihai Pacepa, *Red Horizons* (Washington, DC: Regnery, 1990), p. 189.

15. Edward Behr, *Kiss the Hand You Cannot Bite* (New York: Villard, 1991), p. 67.

16. The superintendent had been my sister's fifth-grade teacher. Now he sits in federal prison.

17. See official tally at http://www.parlament.ch/d/wahlen-abstimmungen/volksabstimmungen/volksabstimmungen-2013/abstimmung-2013-09-22/seiten/default.aspx.

18. At the time of this writing, the cross-country student fare on a Greyhound bus from Los Angeles to Washington, DC, is $120.

19. Mary Daly and Joyce Kwok, "Did Welfare Reform Work for Everyone: A Look at Young Single Mothers," *Federal Reserve Bank of San Francisco Economic Letter*, August 3, 2009.

20. Todd G. Buchholz, "Instead of Unemployment Benefits, Offer a 'Signing Bonus,'" *Washington Post*, June 10, 2011, https://www.washingtonpost.com/opinions/instead-of-unemployment-benefits-offer-a-signing-bonus/2011/06/08/AG46vHPH_story.html.

ACKNOWLEDGMENTS

1. See https://en.wikipedia.org/wiki/Math_Arrow and http://www.sproglit.com/math-arrow.

INDEX

ABOUT THE AUTHOR

TODD G. BUCHHOLZ is a former White House director of economic policy and was awarded the annual teaching prize by Harvard's Department of Economics. He has served as a Fellow at Cambridge University and a managing director of the Tiger hedge fund. He has written for the *New York Times*, the *Wall Street Journal*, and *Forbes*. He is the author of *New Ideas from Dead Economists* and *New Ideas from Dead CEOs*, among other books.